BOMBS, BULLETS, AND POLITICIANS

HUMAN DIMENSIONS IN FOREIGN POLICY, MILITARY STUDIES, AND SECURITY STUDIES

Series editors: Stéphanie A.H. Bélanger, Pierre Jolicoeur, and Stéfanie von Hlatky

Books published in the Human Dimensions in Foreign Policy, Military Studies, and Security Studies series offer fresh perspectives on foreign affairs and global governance. Titles in the series illuminate critical issues of global security in the twenty-first century and emphasize the human dimensions of war such as the health and well-being of soldiers, the factors that influence operational effectiveness, the civil-military relations and decisions on the use of force, as well as the ethical, moral, and legal ramifications of ongoing conflicts and wars. Foreign policy is also analyzed both in terms of its impact of human rights and the role the public plays in shaping policy directions.

With a strong focus on definitions of security, the series encourages discussion of contemporary security challenges and welcomes works that focus on issues including human security, violent conflict, terrorism, military cooperation, and foreign and defence policy. This series is published in collaboration with Queen's University and the Royal Military College of Canada with the Centre for International and Defence Policy, the Canadian Institute for Military and Veteran Health Research, and the Centre for Security, Armed Forces, and Society.

Bombs, Bullets, and Politicians

France's Response to Terrorism

CHRISTOPHE CHOWANIETZ

McGill-Queen's University Press
Montreal & Kingston • London • Chicago

ISBN 978-0-7735-4795-7 (cloth)
ISBN 978-0-7735-4837-4 (ePDF)
ISBN 978-0-7735-4838-1 (ePUB)

Legal deposit fourth quarter 2016
Bibliothèque nationale du Québec

Printed in Canada on acid-free paper that is 100% ancient forest free (100% post-consumer recycled), processed chlorine free

This book has been published with the help of a grant from the Canadian Federation for the Humanities and Social Sciences, through the Awards to Scholarly Publications Program, using funds provided by the Social Sciences and Humanities Research Council of Canada.

McGill-Queen's University Press acknowledges the support of the Canada Council for the Arts for our publishing program. We also acknowledge the financial support of the Government of Canada through the Canada Book Fund for our publishing activities.

Library and Archives Canada Cataloguing in Publication

Chowanietz, Christophe, 1972–, author
   Bombs, bullets, and politicians : France's response to terrorism / Christophe Chowanietz.

(Human dimensions in foreign policy, military studies, and security studies)
Includes bibliographical references and index.
Issued in print and electronic formats.
ISBN 978-0-7735-4795-7 (cloth). – ISBN 978-0-7735-4837-4 (pdf). – ISBN 978-0-7735-4838-1 (epub)

   1. Terrorism – Political aspects – France. 2. Terrorism – History. I. Title.
II. Series: Human dimensions in foreign policy, military studies, and security studies

HV6433.F73C56 2016   363.3250944   C2016-904271-5
                                                 C2016-904272-3

This book was set by True to Type in 11/14 Sabon

To my parents, and to Kian and Lana

Contents

Acknowledgments

This book would have been markedly different and of a lesser quality without the support of key individuals. My sincerest thanks and gratitude to André Blais and Marie-Joelle Zahar; their enthusiasm and precious advice facilitated this study immensely. I am also grateful for the encouragement I have received over the years from colleagues and students at John Abbott College.

I am particularly grateful to Jacqueline Mason, my editor at McGill-Queen's University Press. This book would simply not have seen the light of day without her. I am also thankful to Carol Harrison, my very efficient copy editor, and Ryan Van Huijstee, managing editor at MQUP.

Finally, my thanks to Lisa Pinheiro whose support at key moments early in the research process helped me put this study on the right track, and to Dahlia Namian for her encouragement and for setting the example.

This book has been published with the help of a grant from the Federation for the Humanities and Social Sciences, through the Awards to Scholarly Publications Program, using funds provided by the Social Sciences and Humanities Research Council of Canada.

BOMBS, BULLETS, AND POLITICIANS

Introduction

What is called union in a political body is a very equivocal thing. The
true kind is a union of harmony, whereby all the parts, however opposed
they may appear, cooperate for the general good of society – as disso-
nances in music cooperate in producing overall concord. In a state where
we seem to see nothing but commotion there can be union – that is, a
harmony resulting in happiness, which alone is true peace. It is as with
the parts of the universe, eternally linked together by the action of some
and the reaction of others.

> Montesquieu, *Considérations sur les causes de la grandeur des Romains
> et de leur decadence*

On 12 September 2001, after the worst terrorist crisis in US history,
Republican and Democratic members of Congress stood side by
side on the steps of the Capitol, pledging their support to President
George W. Bush in a rare display of unity. In the days that followed
the tragic events of 9/11, Bush's public approval ratings rose from
51 per cent to an unprecedented 86 per cent.[1] Both Congress and
the nation rallied around the flag in a way unseen in the United
States since the attack on Pearl Harbor some sixty years before. Over
the ensuing two weeks, the mainstream political elite in Washington
acquiesced to every major decision taken by the Republican administration. For all intents and purposes, partisan politics in Congress had ceased, and in case anyone on Capitol Hill was tempted to
publicly question the course of action adopted at 1600 Pennsylvania
Avenue, Attorney General John Ashcroft reminded the legislators
that "the American people do not have the luxury of unlimited time
in erecting the necessary defenses to future terrorist acts."[2]

During this silent autumn, the US government was able to launch a major military operation abroad and severely restrict the rights of its citizens at home – all in the name of the "war on terror," all with minimal interference by the Senate and the House of Representatives. Meanwhile, mainstream media remained by and large uncritical of the Republican administration, and the general population, draped in the Star-Spangled Banner, entered in a frenzy of patriotism. To be fair, the rally was not complete, at least not in the literal sense. It never is. By 24 September 2001, the hearings on the Patriot Act held by the Judiciary Committees of the House and Senate provided a stage for dissent. Representative Robert Barr, a Republican from Georgia, questioned the wisdom of rushing the debate on the act and asked whether the government was seeking "to take advantage of what is obviously an emergency situation to obtain authorities that it has been unable to obtain previously."[3] Yet a month later just 1 senator out of 100 and 66 representatives out of 423 voted against the passage of the Patriot Act.[4] Only after the White House entered a diplomatic stalemate with some of its traditional allies abroad did major figures within the Democratic Party, such as Senators Tom Daschle and John Kerry, openly question the government's strategy in the war on terror. Meanwhile, the cloud of dust surrounding lower Manhattan barely dissipated; known "dissidents" and radical minds such as Gore Vidal and Noam Chomsky explained the whys and hows of the tragedy that had befallen the "land of the free" and pointed fingers at the political elite in Washington, DC.[5] The blame game had started. Whether to unite the country or to criticize the government, the elites – mainstream and radical – were playing politics with terrorism.

The events of 9/11 had not only profoundly changed the hierarchy of issues within the political debate, as national security became once again the paramount issue, but they also redefined the prevailing cleavages in US politics, dividing the hawks from the doves, the patriots from the internationalists, the strong from the weak, us from them. For those running the executive branch of the government, the choice was clear: rally around the flag or be lambasted as an enemy of the state. Rallying became a sign of support for the president/commander-in-chief, and an acknowledgment that the patriotic imperative required "good citizens" to remain uncritical of his decisions. As national security topped the agenda, the political elite was expected to abandon, at least temporarily, party politics for the greater good of the country. Security was all that mattered, and many perceived the political debate as just a hindrance for the swift passage of antiterrorism bills. Bipartisanship and co-operation across the aisle were the order of the day.

Fifteen years later, much of the US political debate still revolves around 9/11. Pressing concerns like the state of the economy have fought their way back to the top of the political agenda, but the Boston marathon bombings, the rise of ISIS, the National Security Agency's (NSA) eavesdropping, and even Hillary Clinton's use of her private email account for official communications while Secretary of State have made sure that national security will remain a hotly debated issue in the coming years. Republicans and Democrats use resolute and patriotic rhetoric. The 2016 presidential primaries remind us that in the post–9/11 United States, one can never be too close to Old Glory. In that respect, the effect of 9/11 promises to be long lasting.

Of course, not all terrorist events are synonymous with "all hell breaking loose"; not all of them have a profound and lasting impact both domestically and internationally. In fact, many terrorist acts – often nothing more than blown-up mailboxes – do not register on the media radar or initiate any kind of reaction from the political elite and public opinion. The multiple attacks of 11 September 2001 in the United States; 11 March 2004 in Spain; 7 July 2005 in England; 7–9 January, 13 November 2015, and 14 July 2016 in France are in that respect exceptional, at least in the Western world. Yet all acts of terror, regardless of whether they claim any victims or destroy any property, represent a direct and at times a serious challenge to the political system, particularly within open societies. The intention of the perpetrators rather than the act itself – and its consequences – is what matters. To paraphrase a Corsican nationalist: terrorism is the military occupation of the political space.[6] Indeed, what is terrorism in representative democracies if not an attempt to bypass the long and arduous process of debate and compromise by coercing through deeds rather than convincing through discourse, by menacing rather than by appealing? As such, terrorism is in essence a repudiation of party politics, a denial of a key democratic institution.

The definition of terrorism is, of course, a complex subject matter that will be addressed at some length in this book, but one should bear in mind that terrorism is not primarily about killing or maiming, although the combination of drama-seeking media corporations ("if it bleeds it leads") and a brand of genocidal terrorism bent on carnage might mislead the casual news follower as to the intentions of terrorist groups. Terrorism is and always was about gaining political ascendancy. The most effective strategy to gain the upper hand in their struggle against the legitimate holders of political power is for terrorists to drive a wedge between the government and public opinion by pressing the former to react in a manner which the latter might consider disproportionate. This Machiavellian strategy – divide and conquer – is particularly challenging for open societies whose raison d'être (i.e., upholding civil liberties) seems at odds with the raison d'état that prevails in times of national emergency, such as a terrorist attack.

Following the rallying cry "Je suis Charlie!" heard across France and abroad in the aftermath of the *Charlie Hebdo* shootings on 7 January 2015 came sinister variants like "Je ne suis pas Charlie!" and "Je suis Kouachi."[7] Just like in the United States in the wake of 9/11, the attack brought together a large swath of French society and its political elite. Never since the liberation of France in the summer of 1944 had so many marched in the streets of Paris and other cities across the country. And never since the signing of the armistice in 1918 had the members of the French National Assembly spontaneously sung "La Marseillaise." The brothers Saïd and Chérif Kouachi and their partner in crime, Amedy Coulibaly, failed to divide French society. Or did they? The French government, much like the US government after 9/11, rushed to pass a series of antiterror laws. The expedient debate and the limits on civil liberties have left far more insidious scares. The fragile nature of the rally-around-the-flag phenomenon was obvious in the days following the 13 November attacks, as numerous members of Parliament broke ranks to rail against either the perceived negligence of the socialist government or its perceived right-wing turn and tougher antiterror policies – all that amid an international outpouring of support for France.

Bombs, Bullets, and Politicians studies the behaviour of political parties and elites in exceptional periods; that is, when the national community is threatened or attacked. Many scholars have examined the effects of military or diplomatic crises on elites, as well as on media and public opinion. Most of these works suggest that rallies around the flag following wars and major diplomatic crises are the rule. But what about terrorism? What are its effects on party politics and the behaviour of political elites? Despite mounting evidence that terrorism influences the behaviour of political elites in government and in opposition, this question has yet to be answered in a systematic and comparative way. This book attempts to fill an important gap in the literature by analyzing the reactions of political parties to terrorism in five countries – France, Germany, Spain, the United Kingdom, and the United States – and determine whether political elites rally around the government and why. In the process, I intend to make sense of party politics in times of terror and hope to contribute to a better understanding of how terrorism affects Western societies.

1

Terrorism

Politics by Other Means

When the Patriot Act was passed, smoke was still coming out of the rubble of the Pentagon and the twin towers. We rushed in order to provide some comfort to the people of the United States. It was a huge mistake.

Butch Otter, Republican Representative from Idaho, 17 August 2003

INTRODUCTION

If war is a continuation of politics by other means, as Carl von Clausewitz believed, then terrorism, as Bruce Hoffman explains, is "fundamentally and inherently political" (Hoffman 2006, 2). From its onset in Mesopotamia more than 4,000 years ago, terrorism has been used to achieve political objectives – whether those of empires, states, or groups – affecting in the process the lives of many and in some cases altering the course of history. And yet, terrorism as a distinct field of study is relatively young, having emerged in the early 1970s. Since then the phenomenon has been dissected and explored from many different angles, but its effects on party politics until recently have been largely ignored. A worrying gap in the literature to say the least, especially when one considers that terrorism in democracies is in effect an attempt to alter the political decisions taken by parties and their elites, that is, a negation of party politics.

AN ANCIENT PHENOMENON

Human violence is ageless; it is a permanent feature of human behaviour. That violence has been prevalent over the last few thousands of years is obvious to historians and anthropologists. And despite the civilizing process announced by German sociologist Norbert Elias (1939) more than seventy years ago and reaffirmed most recently by Steven Pinker (2011), it is fair to say that *Homo sapiens* have not yet ushered in an era of blissful harmony. To be sure, occurrences of wars, genocides and homicides seem to be declining, at least for those fortunate enough to live in some of the more advanced democracies (Pinker 2011).

Yet terrorism is an altogether different form of violence. It is different from genocide and different from the primeval and permanent terror that characterizes the lives of our early ancestors. It is different from other types of violence, such as that associated with the organized crime, which deliberately seek to terrorize in order to achieve their goals. Though terrorism is often portrayed as a criminal activity, it is in essence political. It is about power and can therefore only occur in hierarchical societies. While it is not strictly speaking the "weapon of the poor," terrorism remains a relatively cheap way for non-state actors to matter in a political system structured, though certainly not always controlled, by the state. Case in point: as of 2014, the United States has spent $4.4 trillion as part of the war on terror in Afghanistan, Iraq, and elsewhere in the world,[1] a war that began in reaction to an attack mounted by a small group of jihadists for a million US dollars.[2]

Terrorism first emerged around 2300 BCE in one of the first-known hierarchical communities: the Akkadian Empire. There the governing elites instrumentalized terror to subdue their subjects. As Gérard Chaliand and Arnaud Blin point out in *The History of Terrorism*, "In the despotic societies that make up the major portion of history's fabric, it [terrorism] has served as the tool of enslavement and guarantor of mass obedience" (2007, vii). What Thomas Thornton (1964) aptly called "enforcement terrorism" was first and foremost a means of governance for despots and autocrats. Yet in a more recent period, enforcement terrorism has also been used by liberals and

democrats. For instance, what Michael Walzer termed "war terrorism," that is the "effort [by democrats and autocrats alike] to kill civilians in such large numbers that their government is forced to
surrender" (such as the bombings of Hiroshima, Nagasaki, Coventry,
and Dresden during World War II), has been the single most murderous terror campaign of the twentieth century (2002, 5).

Notwithstanding transnational state-sponsored terrorism, which
some governments still rely on, enforcement terrorism has receded
dramatically over the past fifty years, owing to the democratization
process under way in many parts of the world.[3] Yet, one should not
forget that over the course of history state terrorism has claimed
countless number of lives, far more than non-state terrorism ever
has.[4] The "Reign of Terror" in its most brutal version has often
blurred the distinction between state terrorism and outright genocide.[5] The atrocious repression carried out by President Bashar al-
Assad's army against large parts of the Syrian population since the
start of the uprising in 2011 is a sad reminder that before becoming
a strategy used by substate groups in their struggle for political ascendancy, terrorism was a means to govern and subjugate people. A
lesson that has not been lost on the leaders of the would-be Islamic
State of Iraq and Syria.

The first documented acts of terrorism by non-state entities, or
group terrorism as it is often called, took place in the Roman
province of Palestine in the fifth century CE. However, not until the
late nineteenth century did group terrorism really challenge the political establishment in the form initially of an "anarchist wave,"
emerging in Tsarist Russia before spreading to the rest of Europe
(Rapoport 2004). Carlo Pisacane wrote at the time that "ideas result
from deeds, not the latter from the former," hence the expression
"propaganda by the deed" coined by Peter Kropotkin. The belief
among anarchists, such as Albert Parsons, was that dynamite "made
all men equal and therefore free" (Townshend 2002, 25). Violence
was meant to draw attention to their cause and educate the people
so that ultimately they would support the revolution. Narodnaya
Volya ("People's Will"), the best known of these Russian groups, targeted exclusively symbols of the state and representatives of the tsar,
and was careful not to shed innocent blood. But as this phenomenon spread to Western Europe, the Balkans, and Asia, this discrimi-

nate approach soon faded away. By the 1880s the Skirmishers in Ireland had already killed and injured innocents (Hoffman 2006). A few years later Émile Henry, one of the most notorious anarchists turned terrorist of his time, declared during his trial, "There are no innocents!" Terrorism had entered a new era.

The anarchist wave all but disappeared at the beginning of the twentieth century and was soon replaced by an "anticolonial wave," which lasted from the 1920s to the 1960s. Terrorism was used by national liberation movements as a strategy to wear down the colonizing forces, and became throughout this period an important aspect of low-intensity conflicts throughout Africa and Asia. Though these wars of liberation were fought primarily outside urban areas, terrorism represented a mean to bring the conflict into the cities controlled by the adversary (Chaliand and Blin 2007, 236). As a liberation strategy, terrorism was successful in Palestine during the British mandate, Cyprus, and Algeria.

By the early 1970s, a social-revolutionary brand of terrorism aimed at overturning the capitalist order appeared with groups such as the Rote Armee Fraktion (RAF) in Germany or Brigate Rosse (BR) in Italy attempting – just like late-nineteenth-century anarchists – to awaken the people through violence by targeting politicians and prominent businessmen, usually through assassination or kidnapping. The situation was particularly tense in Italy where literally hundreds of these radical groups wrought havoc to the country – a situation made even worse by the terrorist activities of right-wing groups. The "years of lead," as they came to be known, culminated in the kidnapping and subsequent murder of former prime minister Aldo Moro in 1978, and the killing by right-wing terrorists of eighty-four people in an explosion at the Bologna railway station in 1980.[6] Meanwhile, groups such as the RAF (a.k.a. the Baader-Meinhof gang) and Bewegung Zwei Juni (B2J) in Germany, the Weather Underground in the United States, and Action Directe (AD) in France were conducting similar operations although often on a smaller scale than their Italian counterparts. The Weather Underground, for instance, decided early on to target infrastructures and avoid casualties.

Social-revolutionary terrorism all but died out at the end of the 1980s, but the "nationalist-separatist wave" spearheaded by groups such as the Palestinian al Fatah, the Provisional Irish Republican Army (PIRA or IRA), and the Basque Euskadi ta Askatasuna (ETA), which had emerged in the late 1960s and early 1970s, proved far more resilient. In fact, PIRA and its splinter groups could trace their ancestry to the Irish Revolutionary Brotherhood active in the 1850s. Most of these groups were able to sustain their activities thanks to relatively large support within parts of the population at home and the diaspora abroad. Demonstrating that terrorism is a continuation of politics, many of these groups carried out their activities in tandem with legal political representatives of the cause. In Ulster's case, Sinn Féin represented the moderate advocates of the Irish republican cause, proving a crucial factor in ending years of terror.

The "religious wave," which many see starting with the 1979 Islamic Revolution in Iran, is often identified as the latest manifestation of modern terrorism. Yet this version is older than the previous waves. Terrorist acts perpetrated in the name of a religion have been recorded as far back as antiquity (e.g., the Zealots). In fact, none of the three monotheist religion is blameless. Today, the religious wave refers primarily to jihadists or radical Islamic terrorists, yet covers other types of religious fundamentalism as well: Christian (particularly anti-abortionists), Jewish, Sikh, et cetera. What differentiates this wave of terrorism from previous ones has to do with the self-imposed limits (or lack thereof) that determine the magnitude of operations. Jerrold Post (2005, 620) remarks that unlike social-revolutionary and national-separatist terrorists, many jihadists are "not constrained by Western reaction" and are thus ready to cause heavy casualties. Current terror campaigns by ISIS, Boko Haram, al Shabaab and various al Qaeda–affiliated groups against Muslim and non-Muslim populations alike suggest that these terrorists are not constrained by any reactions, Western or not.

Yet religion is often just a pretext hiding a political objective.[7] Terrorism, regardless of the claims issued by its perpetrators, is always about political power. The multiple attacks in New York (2001), Madrid (2004), London (2005), Boston (2013), and Paris (2015) were not the result of a clash of civilization but rather an attempt by some to export the power struggles taking place within Islam outside the confines of the *umma*. By striking on 9/11 at the heart of America's economic and military power, al Qaeda was trying to get rid of the reigning House of Saud in Saudi Arabia (David and Gagnon 2007, 14).

Although more than a century old, group terrorism came of age in the early 1970s, when according to Brian Jenkins, a long-time observer of the terrorist phenomenon,

> Jet air travel gave terrorists worldwide mobility. The development of radio, television, and communication satellites gave them almost instantaneous access to a global audience. The increasing availability of weapons and explosives made it easy to arm, while the vulnerabilities inherent in our modern-technology-dependent society, from electrical pylons to Boeing 747s, provided ample targets. (2001a, 321)

In other words, group terrorism remains an instrument of coercion to achieve political goals but its methods have evolved. The availability of more lethal weapons coupled with a logic reminiscent of early anarchists such as Émile Henry has increased substantially the death toll. Whereas terrorists used to rely on the attack of state symbols to publicize their cause and rally their supporters, they are now more murderous, even at times genocidal. Sean MacBride and Michael Collins – both historical figures of the IRA – took pride in preserving the lives of innocents and civilians (Leiser 1977, 39–40). And when an explosion killed twenty-eight people in Omagh, Ulster, in 1998, the Real IRA issued a public apology claiming it had warned the authorities of the attack.[8] Likewise, ETA was keen to distance itself from the 11 March 2004 attacks in Madrid that claimed the lives of 191 people by quickly issuing a statement denying its implication.

Terrorism is not all blood and threat of more blood. To successfully spread their political message, terrorist groups need to sway part of the public opinion in their favour, and they will issue warnings to the authorities and inform them of their next target in an effort to "control" the damage caused by their attack.[9] The Weather Underground, after initially contemplating murderous attacks, took pride in avoiding human casualties.[10] The relative restraint of such groups seems lost on al Qaeda and ISIS for which carnage seems to be the avowed operational objective. Brian Jenkins offers a chilling perspective on terrorism at the start of the twenty-first century:

[The] new breed of terrorists [is] less constrained by the fear of alienating perceived constituents or angering the public. Some of the notions that I once offered about self-imposed constraints on terrorist behaviour appear to be eroding as terrorists move away from political agendas and into realms where they are convinced that they have the mandate of God. Large-scale, indiscriminate violence is the reality of today's terrorism. (2001a, 324)

A PHENOMENON ON THE RISE?

Is terrorism on the rise in the Western world? Are there more victims of terrorist attacks today than there were ten or twenty years ago? In other words, how acute is the problem? The answer is complex. Recent statistics on terrorism are confusing and at times even contradictory. Much like defining terrorism (discussed later in the chapter), interpreting the evolution of terrorism has become politicized, particularly in an age when a global war on terror is still being waged, some fifteen years after it started. Experts using the same datasets and analyzing the same figures on global terror draw different conclusions. This controversy results from a disagreement on what should and should not be considered a terrorist act and thus be included in datasets recording this type of event. As such, the definition of terrorism and the interpretation of statistics on this phenomenon are closely linked.

For instance, figures released by the Global Terrorism Database indicate that the number of terrorist attacks worldwide has increased tremendously over the last forty years, particularly after 2001 and even more so after 2011. The US Department of State reports that in 2013, 9,707 terrorist attacks occurred in the world. The same report indicates that 18,000 people were killed in terrorist attacks in 2013, a mind-boggling 60 per cent increase over the previous year. The culprits are the known villains of our time: ISIS, Boko Haram, al Qaeda, and the Taliban. They are also involved in civil and guerrilla warfare, making it difficult to differentiate the victims of intrastate conflict from the victims of terrorism. The human suffering and the atrocities are real; the way we label them is complex. In fact, the massive increase over the last five years corresponds with the start of the Syrian civil war, which has spread to Iraq. Crucially, 80 per cent of the fatalities since 2013 have occurred in Iraq, Afghanistan, Pakistan, Nigeria, and Syria. North America and most of Europe have been spared. In fact, since 2000 only 5 per cent of terrorist-related fatalities have occurred among members of the Organisation for Economic Co-operation and Development (OECD).[11]

A few years ago researchers at the Vancouver-based Human Security Project contested the interpretation of similar figures, attributing the increase in fatalities to the massive increase of civilian casualties following the US-led military invasion of Iraq in 2003.[12] Examining statistics for the period 1998–2006, the researchers found that once we exclude Iraq from the dataset, the worldwide trend of fatalities had, in fact, decreased by 40 per cent since 2001.

Human Security Project researchers argue that "describing the intentional killing of civilians in civil wars as 'terrorism' is both unusual and somewhat controversial."[13] In their view, the majority of civilians killed in Iraq since 2003 are better described as victims of insurgencies and the war. As such, they are comparable to other victims of civil wars in the recent past, such as the Democratic Republic of Congo, Bosnia, and Guatemala. In those countries, as in Iraq, the murder of civilians was "intentional, politically motivated, and perpetrated by non-state groups," yet it was rarely if ever described as terrorist at the time.[14] The same could be said of the 470,000 civilians killed in Syria since 2011.[15]

The overlap between acts of terrorism and large-scale political violence such as civil wars makes it difficult to assess the current situation and decide whether or not terrorism is indeed progressing. There is certainly a case for arguing that figures on Syria and Iraq tend to distort the picture on global terrorism, and that if we treat the killings occurring there as instances of war crimes or even genocide, then we might be able to conclude that terrorism worldwide is receding rather than increasing.

Figures published by Europol show that terrorist attacks in the European Union (EU) increased from 174 in 2011 to 219 in 2012 before receding to 152 in 2013 and again increasing to 201 in 2014.[16] The majority of attacks occurring in the EU were, according to Europol, perpetrated by separatist groups operating in France and Spain. Europol reported since 2011 an increase in the number of arrests for "religiously inspired terrorism" – from 110 in 2009 to 216 in 2013 and 395 in 2014.[17]

A limitation on the availability of data makes it difficult to determine trends in terrorist activities over longer periods of time. According to the RAND Corporation, international terrorism grew throughout the 1970s and 1980s (from 100 attacks in 1968 to roughly 450 twenty years later), declined during the 1990s before rising again at the start of the new millennium (David and Gagnon 2007, 5). Likewise, the number of victims caused by international terrorism peaked several times during the 1980s and 1990s before declining. Subsequently, the high death toll caused by the multiple attacks of 9/11 has distorted the trend.

Terrorism remains a relatively limited threat. John Mueller pointed out in 2006 that "the total number of people killed since 9/11 by Al-Qaeda or 'Al-Qaeda-like' operatives outside of Afghanistan and Iraq is not much higher than the number of people who drown in bathtubs in the United States in a single year, and that the lifetime chance of an American being killed by international terrorism is about one in 80,000 – about the same chance of being killed by a comet or a meteor" (Mueller 2006). What is also clear is that the risk of a chemical, biological, radiological, or nuclear (CBRN) terrorist attack has been blown out of proportion and is, in fact, very small (Mueller 2007; 2008). John Mueller (2008) estimates the odds of terrorists actually setting off a nuclear bomb at a mind-boggling 1 in 3.5 billion.

Whether global terrorism is rising is still unclear and depends on how inclusive our definition of terrorism is. What is clear, however, is that the terrorist threat has not been contained let alone eliminated, and remains a thorn in the side of many countries.

A CONCEPTUAL QUAGMIRE

Terrorism is a common occurrence, if not in our immediate surroundings, then at least in our "imagined community." The phenomenon is inescapable. Not one day goes by without news of carnage somewhere in the world. Fifteen years after 9/11, the images of the two Manhattan skyscrapers crumbling down to the ground still haunt our collective memory. They have penetrated our consciousness, reminding us of our mortality and of the vulnerability of our open societies. Who has not once felt unease while boarding a commercial airplane? And yet we find it hard to describe this phenomenon, let alone define it. Despite massive media coverage and countless books on the topic, we are still no closer to agreeing on what terrorism is; even experts and scholars in the field have yet to find a consensus. How can we then hope to eradicate an ill-defined and often misunderstood phenomenon? Over the last fourteen years, the United States has spent more than \$4 trillion waging war on terror – an amount that would allow NASA to plan and develop forty manned missions to Mars.[18]

A BLURRED MEANING

Jonathan Barker remarks that "the walk on the ugly side [of politics] is fraught with emotion" (2002, 9) and it is tempting to join him in arguing that our failure to agree on a set of words to describe a phenomenon as common as terrorism is attributable to emotions. The debate has certainly generated more heat than light. What is required then is a dispassionate analysis. Unfortunately, pundits, journalists, politicians, and scholars are unable or unwilling to think about terrorism in a clearheaded and genuinely impartial way. Yet emotions are just part of the story. Ultimately, our failure to agree on a common ground lies in the fact that terrorism is time and culture bound, and more importantly, political.

Terrorism is a subjective concept like many others in social sciences. Its meaning changes across time, across land, and across cultures. As the old adage goes, "One person's terrorist is another person's freedom fighter."[19] One could add, with the necessary precautions, that some of today's terrorists are the heirs to yesterday's freedom fighters. There are certainly a number of troubling similarities between certain existing groups of terrorists and activists of yesteryear, which history books reverently and often deservedly describe as resistant. The vantage point is crucial. Mine is that of Western mainstream political elites, not because of my personal views on the matter, but because of the subject matter of this research.

Everything about terrorism is political, even its definition. It is a pejorative term easily manipulated to discredit a political opponent.

The problem is as much defining terrorism as agreeing on who fits the description of a terrorist. The first modern terrorists (i.e., Narodnaya Volya in Russia) accepted being labelled as terrorists. The term carried with it a certain prestige, that of selfless have-nots fighting the "good" fight against the haves. Nowadays, few would readily accept this damning label and would rather be called insurgents or rebels. The T-word, as Brigitte Nacos (2007) calls it, is a loaded one. Richard Rubenstein (1987, 17–18) pointedly remarks that to "call an act of political violence terrorist is not merely to describe it but to judge it ... nobody wants to be called a terrorist; terrorism is what the other side is up to." As a result perpetrators of violence have had to look for more appropriate synonyms. The Ku Klux Klan, for instance, described its actions as "resistance to reconstruction" or "vigilantism" (Kronenwetter 2004, vii).

Recent developments have rendered the task of defining terrorism even more difficult. Bruce Hoffman (2006, 1) points out that "virtually any especially abhorrent act of violence perceived as directed against society – whether it involves the activities of antigovernment dissidents or governments themselves, organized crime syndicates, common criminals, rioting mobs, people engaged in militant protest, individual psychotics, or lone extortionists – is often labeled terrorism." This confusion has been fuelled, particularly in the post-9/11 period, by a Manichean rhetoric of victims versus terrorists. In this battle for the moral high ground the other one, belligerent or mere ideological opponent, is often labelled a terrorist. In the process, the distinction between militant, combatant, activist, resistant, or insurgent has been lost. It does not come as a surprise then when Walter Laqueur (2004, 232), one of the foremost experts in the study of terrorism, remarks that "after thirty years of hard labor there is still no generally agreed definition of terrorism."[20]

A PLETHORA OF DEFINITIONS

In its simplest expression "terrorism is a form of violent strategy used to alter the freedom of choice of others" (Paust 1977, 79). Michael Walzer sees in these acts the "deliberate killing of innocent people, at random, in order to spread fear through a whole population and force the hand of its political leaders" (2002, 79). Likewise, Raymond

Aron underlines the psychological dimension of terrorism, which he defines as an instrument of pressure designed to bend the will of an adversary by inflicting psychological damages that far surpass its purely physical results (in Chaliand and Blin 2007, 17). These are just a few examples in an ever-increasing list of definitions.

From this intellectual maelstrom, two definitions stand out, both the result of compilations of existing definitions. The first one, put forth by Alex Schmid and Albert Jongman (1988), is the outcome of a questionnaire filled by more than one hundred scholars and in which respondents were asked to define what they understand by terrorism. Out of the twenty conceptual elements identified throughout these definitions, the authors chose the sixteen that came up most frequently in the answers. The condensed definition that they obtained is the following:

> Terrorism is an anxiety-inspiring method of repeated violent action, employed by (semi-) clandestine individual, group, or state actors, for idiosyncratic, criminal, or political reasons, whereby – in contrast to assassination – the direct targets of violence are not the main targets. The immediate human victims of violence are generally chosen randomly (targets of opportunity) or selectively (representative or symbolic targets) from a target population, and serve as message generators. Threat – and violence – based communication processes between terrorist (organization), (imperilled) victims, and main target (audiences), turning it into a target of terror, a target of demands, or a target of attention, depending on whether intimidation, coercion, or propaganda is primarily sought. (Schmid and Jongman 1988, 28)

This conceptual mosaic is not flawless. For instance, why should terrorism be characterized by "repeated violent action"? What about isolated acts of violence? Are they any less terrorist? Moreover, are we to understand that assassination is never a terrorist act?

The second definition is also the result of a compilation. The logic used is similar to that of Schmid and Jongman, but rather than analyzing answers to a questionnaire, Leonard Weinberg, Ami Pedhazur, and Sivan Hirsch-Hoefler (2004) examine seventy-three definitions of terrorism found in fifty-five articles published by three academic journals – *Terrorism, Terrorism and Political Violence* and *Studies in Conflict and Terrorism* – and produce a definition based on the elements of convergence between their text analysis, and the analysis of the Schmid-Jongman questionnaire. The result is far more concise: "Terrorism is a politically motivated tactic involving the threat or use of force or violence in which the pursuit of publicity plays a significant role" (Weinberg, Pedhazur, and Hirsch-Hoefler 2004, 782). This consensual definition leaves aside any reference to the psychological aspect of terrorism as well as the difference between combatants and non-combatants. To be fair, the authors themselves acknowledge the limits of such a definition, and use the exercise primarily as a way of underlining the risks inherent in seeking too large a consensus.[21]

Other scholars argue that what makes an act of political violence terrorist are its targets. Traditionally, terrorists have targeted symbols of the state (including its "flesh-and-bone" representatives), of the economic system, or of religious and ethnic groups. Yet, since the end of the nineteenth century civilians and innocent bystanders have been increasingly in the crosshairs. Boaz Ganor (1998), for example, defines terrorism as "the intentional use of, or threat to use violence against civilians or against civilian targets, in order to attain political aims."

Lately many definitions have referred to non-combatants rather than just civilians, the idea being to include militaries as potential victims. Michael Walzer (2006) suggests that only acts intentionally directed against non-combatants are terrorist. By that rationale, soldiers and government representatives are combatants. Following this line of reasoning, Walzer is telling us that had it not been for the presence of non-combatants aboard the plane that crashed into the Pentagon on 9/11, this attack – but obviously not the other ones that happened on that day – would not have been terrorist. The question concerning the status of soldiers or civil servants, although legitimate, creates more problems. Indeed, should one consider the assassination by ETA of a municipal councillor in a small Spanish town as a terrorist act or as an act of war against the Spanish government? What of the assassination of a retired soldier or a soldier on leave? And what of an explosion in a public place to indiscriminately kill passersby? Such an attack could or could not be terrorist depending on who happens to be there at the time of the blast.

In fact, what really matters to terrorists is often not the direct target but the target audience. In his anarchist newspaper *Freiheit*, Johann Most, a late-nineteenth-century anarchist, reveals a logic that has not aged since. The terrorist, he argues, must capture the public's imagination through the use of outrageous violence (see Garrison 2004). Targeting a few in order to claim the attention of many is the ageless terrorist motto. The role of the media is crucial and some scholars have underlined the symbiotic relationship between terrorism and the media. Schmid and de Graaf (1982, 4) for instance suggest that "an act of terrorism is in reality an act of communication." Put differently, terrorism relies on spreading fear, and the media as fear merchants are incremental in that process. In a fiercely competitive news market, blood and drama will attract attention (Nacos 2007, 38). Media allow terrorism "to be everywhere but physically nowhere," remarks Ranstorp (2007, 2), and Nacos (2000, 175) adds that "without massive news coverage the terrorist act would resemble the proverbial tree falling in the forest: if no one learned of an incident, it would be as if it had not occurred." The terrorists' primary objective is not to kill but to get their message through. If the message does not get through, then the act loses its purpose.[22]

The argument that terrorism is a media construct gains currency when one sees how more blood and threats of more blood are rewarded by increased attention. For instance, Nacos (2007, 189) observed that in the United States increases in terror alerts were reported in lead stories, unlike rollbacks, which were often ignored. As Sloan reminds us, the old adage "if it bleeds, it leads" applies more than ever in the electronic age (2005, 141). Television has allowed terrorists to go much further than Sun Tzu's motto "Kill one person and frighten a thousand" by literally killing thousands and frightening millions.

Media outlets act as a "force multiplier" (Sloan 2005, 136), ultimately deciding whether or not an incident or an act of violence deserves to be labelled as terrorist or even reported. In effect, then, as Philip Jenkins (2003, ix) remarks, terrorism is "socially constructed … the concept is shaped by social and political processes, by bureaucratic needs and media structures."

These days many incidents pass as terrorist, yet we can only speak of terrorism when a specific political intent is involved. This is never clear. Jenkins (2003, 6–7) gives the example of Egypt Air flight 990 that crashed near Nantucket, Massachusetts, in 1999 killing all 217 passengers and crew onboard. Shortly before the crash as the plane was diving, the co-pilot Gameel al-Batouti repeated in Arabic, "I put my trust in God." Was he simply repeating this phrase in a moment of extreme stress as he was trying to solve the technical problem at hand? In which case the crash was accidental. Was he committing suicide as a result of depression? In which case the crash was criminal. Or was he, as some people have argued, carrying out a plan to intentionally crash the plane for political reasons (some high-level Egyptian officials were onboard)? In which case the incident was terrorist in nature.[23] The media covered all three possibilities over the course of the investigation. In the end, the crash was deemed an accident.

THE VANTAGE POINT

Wanton act for some, act of heroic resistance for others, the perception of terrorism varies inevitably from one social and historical context to another. Its semantic ambiguity is thus inescapable. Its perpetrator is at the same time martyr and criminal, saviour and murderer. The quest for a widely accepted definition is near impossible.

The vantage point is crucial. The semantic ambiguity of the word *terrorism* does not affect this study too much because what is of interest is the reaction of Western mainstream parties and elites to acts of political violence that they themselves perceive as unequivocally terrorist.[24] Most of the definitions discussed share this Western vantage point. By and large they define terrorism as a politically motivated criminal strategy used by subnational groups to intimidate governments and populations, and limit their freedom of choice by physically striking a few in order to scare many. The existing differences are often subtle, such as the one that distinguishes between non-combatants and civilians; yet the search for a universal and timeless definition is futile. More importantly, even if one were to stumble on a universal definition, there would still be disagreement as to whom or which group should be labelled terrorist. After all, much of the debate hinges on what is viewed as a legitimate recourse to violence, the tendency being to view illegitimate use of violence as terrorist.

Inevitably conceptual considerations must accommodate operational considerations. The definition chosen for this project is the one used by the Terrorism Knowledge Base (TKB) – the dataset used to create the database introduced in this book:

> Terrorism is violence, or the threat of violence, calculated to create an atmosphere of fear and alarm. These acts are designed to coerce others into actions they would not otherwise undertake, or refrain from actions they desired to take. All terrorist acts are crimes. Many would also be violation of the rules of war if a state of war existed. This violence or threat of violence is generally directed against civilian targets. The motives of all terrorists are political, and terrorist actions are generally carried out in a way that will achieve maximum publicity. Unlike other criminal acts, terrorists often claim credit for their acts. Finally, terrorist acts are intended to produce effects beyond the immediate physical damage of the cause, having long-term psychological repercussions on a particular target audience. The fear created by terrorists may be intended to cause people to exaggerate the strengths of the terrorist and the importance of the cause, to provoke governmental overreaction, to discourage dissent, or simply to intimidate and thereby enforce compliance with their demands. (Schmid 2011, 308)

Beyond operational considerations, the TKB definition is suitable from a conceptual point of view. It incorporates most of the characteristics of terrorism discussed previously: it is a political act, which aims at coercing and spreading fear by achieving maximum publicity. Unlike many other definitions, this one underlines the fact that terrorism might provoke "governmental overreaction" and "discourage dissent." Crucially, the TKB definition leaves room for interpretation. In many instances, acts of political violence are not necessarily as clear-cut as one would hope. The TKB definition allows for borderline cases, such as those taking place during a war, to be reviewed separately.

CONCLUSION

Terrorism is a political act as potent today as it was 4,000 years ago when tyrants used it as an instrument of coercion. Relied upon by states and substate actors alike, terrorism has brought down empires, triggered wars, and led to millions of deaths. Its impact on our societies is inescapable, and so is its impact on politics. For what is terrorism in electoral democracies but a negation of the peaceful practice of democracy. Terrorist groups are the exact opposite of what political parties stand for. They seek to bypass the processes of representative democracy by coercing rather than by convincing. And yet our understanding of the impact of terrorism on the domestic political game has not improved markedly since the pioneering days of terrorism studies in the early 1970s.

To be sure, the attacks of 11 September 2001 in the United States and 11 March 2004 in Spain have transformed terrorism studies by bringing into the discipline much needed input from scholars working in other fields. Yet, whereas there is an information overload on certain aspects of terrorism, there is too little on other aspects. It is striking that so much is published on counterterrorism, yet so little is written on the effects of terrorism on political parties and their elites; yet, those political elites are in charge of responding to terror and devise counterterrorist legislations. Understanding how terrorism affects their behaviour as politicians, legislators and decision makers is therefore crucial. My own modest effort is an attempt at analyzing whether terrorism (domestic and international) changes the way party politics operates, and in particular whether it brings government and opposition elites closer, the implication being that a rapprochement between these two sets of actors can have an impact on the response to terror, and in particular on counterterrorist legislation, but also on electoral outcomes.

2

The Context of Party Politics

I have confidence in Lyndon Johnson ... We must give this man our full cooperation and our prayers and work with him; and let's see the kind of president he will be ... President Johnson certainly has the training; he has the instincts; he has the ability. I think we must now, as a nation, unite behind him and help him all we can, and go the usual course of helping a president, of being critical when it is needed and helpful when that's needed.

Barry Goldwater, candidate for the Republican presidential primaries, 24 November 1963

INTRODUCTION

With America's War of Independence barely over and its democratic project still in its infancy, a bemused Thomas Jefferson remarked that if he "could not go to heaven but with a party, [he] would not go there at all" (in Katz and Crotty 2006, 9). His unflattering view of a hallmark of representative democracy was common among the Founding Fathers; indeed, George Washington, John Adams, and James Madison were quite vocal in their criticisms. They echoed a long-held belief among political thinkers and practitioners of all ages, not least those of the French Revolution, that parties would spread division and chaos to the nations (Sartori 1976, 9–12). The derogatory meaning of the word *party* was entrenched in its Latin root *partire*, "to divide," a meaning which evolved into a more forbearing and even promising sense; that is, "partaking" or the French *partage* (Sartori 1976, 4).

That parties were initially despised was because they were a political novelty, conceptually barely distinguishable from the older form of political organization known as factions. Factions were often thought to be the epitome of selfish interests adverse to that of the community (Sartori 1976, 12). Sartori reminds us that the Latin word *factio* came to describe "a political group bent on a disruptive and harmful *facere*, on 'dire doings'" (1976, 4). Not until the late eighteenth century did this misrepresentation of parties give way to a more enlightened understanding. Edmund Burke was, by most accounts, the first one to make a difference between *faction* and *party*. He defined the former as an enterprise for the advancement of the personal interests of a few and the latter as "a body of men united, for promoting by their joint endeavours the national interest, upon some particular principle in which they are all agreed" (in Katz and Crotty 2006, 6).

Burke's praise did little to attenuate suspicions that parties were factions in disguise unlikely to serve the interest of the state, particularly during critical times. Even a celebrated "democrat" like Abraham Lincoln concluded that partisanship is divisive and disloyal in wartime (Smith 2006, 5), an opinion shared by a *New York Times* editorial published shortly before the start of the Civil War, claiming "[t]he party has failed us. Party organization is dead" (Smith 2006, 9).

The fortunes of parties and their role within the democratic game changed favourably with the re-examination of what representative democracy should be about. As Jacob Leib Talmon reminds us, "what is today considered as an essential concomitant of democracy, namely, diversity of views and interests, was far from being regarded as essential by the eighteenth-century fathers of democracy. Their original postulates were unity and unanimity" (1952, 44). Through a slow and arduous process, as the fear of disunity and diversity subsided, parties became accepted and regarded as different from factions, and were finally understood as "parts *of* the whole" rather than "parts *against* the whole" (Sartori 1976, 13–14).

Today diversity is embraced, and parties provide diversity, but the debate on the role of parties and elites in our democracies is far from over. Sartori remarks that "what is central to the pluralistic *Weltanschauung* is neither consensus nor conflict but dissent and praise of dissent" (1976, 16). Indeed, we have come to expect our parties and their elites to oppose and criticize one another. Debating grand schemes and bickering about minutiae are essential albeit, sometimes, exasperating aspects of party politics. This is the normal state of affairs, the default mode for our elites. It is a feature of what we might call *ordinary* politics, a concept which we will discuss again. As a result, co-operation across the aisle, bipartisanship and any other forms of non-partisan approach to politics represent in most advanced democracies the exception rather than the rule. At the same time, we expect our parties and their representatives to exercise restraint in their criticisms, and even temporarily end their rivalry when national interests are at stake, when parties enter the realm of *extraordinary* politics. Pluralism then cannot be taken for granted. Inherent in our modern representative democracies is this tension between the need for diversity and the necessity under certain circumstances to unite in order to preserve the collective interests of the greater community.

My objective is to shed light on the behaviour of political parties and their elites during extraordinary or critical times; or, more precisely, to understand how these elites react to terrorist events. Do they choose to carry on opposing and criticizing one another as they do in quieter times, or do they favour co-operation instead? Answering this question implies that we distinguish party politics during *ordinary times* (the absence of major foreign policy or security crises) from party politics during *extraordinary times* (the presence of a major crisis).

There are, of course, different types of crises, reflecting different levels of gravity. A crisis represents a "phase of disorder in the seemingly normal development of a system," a transition "during which the normal ways of operating no longer work" (Boin, 't Hart, Stern, and Sundelius 2005, 2). This aspect is crucial: "in a crisis the modus operandi of a political system or community differs markedly from the functioning in normal time" (Boin et al. 2005, 16). In this chapter, I focus on human-caused crises such as wars, diplomatic disputes, and terrorism; however, crises can result from natural disasters compounded by humans (earthquakes, tsunamis, hurricanes, wildfires, epidemics, economic and financial breakdowns, etc.). Not all of these crises affect our societies and communities as profoundly and

durably as the 9/11 terrorist attacks, but all of them challenge political elites and particularly public office holders. In ordinary times,
elected officials maintain business as usual, but in extraordinary periods they must become crisis managers. As such, these elites and
the political parties they represent become accountable for their actions and reactions during the crisis. Some will not come out of
these crises unscathed, as opposition elites rarely miss an opportunity to play the blame game.

This chapter is divided into two sections. The first discusses the
role of parties and their elites in representative democracy. The
second examines party behaviour during ordinary and extraordinary times.

PARTY POLITICS

Parties have not always been viewed positively. What yesterday
caused these misgivings (their tendency to divide rather than to
unite) is today hailed as a hallmark of representative democracy. In
fact, as early as 1888 James Bryce remarked that "no-one has shown
how representative government could be worked without them
[parties]. They bring order out of chaos to a multitude of voters" (in
White 2006, 7). E.E. Schattschneider (1942, 1) in *Party Government*
considered "modern democracy" to be "unthinkable save in terms
of the parties," and more recently John Aldrich (1995, 3) deemed
democracy to be "unworkable save in terms of parties." Likewise Sartori (1976), Crotty (2001), and Lai and Melkonian-Hoover (2005)
have claimed that parties and a competitive party system are essential to democracy and democratization as they provide a crucial link
between people and government. Parties are, to use Giovanni Sartori's words, "the central intermediate structures between society
and government," a bond, unlike factions, between a people and its
decision makers (1976, ix).

The idea that parties fulfill an essential role in the democratic
process by providing a link between society and government is generally not questioned. Yet, many have talked about the demise of
parties, from David Broder's *The Party's Over* (1972) to Martin Wattenberg's *The Decline of American Political Parties* (1990) and *Parties
without Partisans* (2002) edited by Russell Dalton and Martin Wat-

tenberg, and more recently *Ruling the Void* (2013) by Peter Mair. Of particular concern is the weakening of partisanship within the electorate (Aldrich and Niemi 1990; Milner 2002). Aldrich (1995, 17) notes that these days "elections are more candidate centred and less party centered." Another argument points to the decline of parties as mediating institutions as they are increasingly bypassed by technologically savvy citizens who prefer to exchange ideas via the Internet than in political meetings (Davis 1999; 2005). A more general argument links partisan decline to the increasing number of policy demands placed on democracies that far surpasses their capacity to address these issues (Crozier, Huntington, and Watanuki 1975; Huntington 1981).

Decline, resurgence or just transformation, the debate on the fate of parties is not over. Russell Dalton and Martin Wattenberg (2002) suggest that it all depends on whether we refer to parties in the electorate, as organizations, or in government – three analytical levels originally suggested by V.O. Key (1964). Their view is that parties in the electorate seem to be weakening, whereas parties in government have by and large kept their role, and parties as organizations are adapting to the new environment.[1]

Although the role of parties as information providers and mediating institutions might not be as exclusive as it once was, parties remain essential for the actual working of representative democracy. Aside from informing voters and shaping the political debate, parties fulfill the basic electoral role of presenting candidates for public offices. They then perform the equally important task of organizing the government and providing the state apparatus with an elite of political practitioners. A party is, thus, a multipurpose organization. It is, to use Robert Huckshorn's concise definition, "An autonomous group of citizens having the purpose of making nominations and contesting elections in hope of gaining control over governmental power through the capture of public offices and the organization of the government" (1984, 10).

Implicit in this definition is the role of the opposition party whose task it is to dissent and "present a political alternative that acts to limit the present government and offers a potential for change at the next election" (Dalton and Wattenberg 2002, 8–10).

More importantly, a party is a "social organism" (Eldersveld in Crotty, Freeman, and Gatlin 1966, 42). It is, as Aldrich noted, "the creature of the politicians, the ambitious office seeker and officeholder" (1995, 4). "Their [the parties'] basis," he adds, "lies in the actions of ambitious politicians that created and maintain them" (1995, 19). As such, parties represent institutional conduits through which power, this quintessential political goal, is harnessed by the elite (see Schlesinger 1991).

Politics is often about hard choices made by politicians and party leaders who need to balance a host of often diverging interests. In view of the subject matter of this book, this raises two important questions: What drives the political elite? And is the behaviour of political elites context sensitive? The next section examines the determinants of political behaviour under two different sets of conditions: ordinary and extraordinary.

POLITICS IN ORDINARY AND
EXTRAORDINARY TIMES

The school of rational choice influences most scholarly works published on party politics. These works posit a world where business as usual means performing in elections by either maximizing the number of votes or the number of governmental portfolios, or simply the influence on policy-making. The assumption is that political parties and elites, just like voters or any other actors in domestic politics, function and behave in a largely pacified environment, free of major military conflicts, diplomatic crises or other security-related issues. In essence then, what is being studied is politics during ordinary times as opposed to politics during extraordinary or unsettled times. This is hardly surprising since most studies concerning political behaviour have been conducted in the post–World War II era in Western countries and regions finally free from the tragedy of war, which until then had featured so prominently throughout their histories. In comparison, the literature on political behaviour in extraordinary times (broadly defined here as times when the nation is under threat) is sparse. Wedged between two subfields of political science – electoral behaviour and international relations – it has never been a research priority for students of the former. Yet there is something intuitively wrong about studying a set of domestic political actors with no regard for the international context in which they evolve, unless the context is perceived as stable. For their part, international relations scholars have been far less hesitant to look into the interplay between international affairs and domestic politics (see Müller and Risse-Kappen 1993; Keohane and Milner 1996; Gaubatz 1999). The realist and neo-realist schools of thought have downplayed the importance of this interplay, leaving the intricacies of party politics in an oubliette or black box, and treating the state as a unitary actor. However, many scholars in the past forty years have pursued a different approach and have opened the proverbial black box. For example, Graham Allison (1969) in his groundbreaking article "Conceptual Models and the Cuban Missile Crisis," introduced his bureaucratic politics model whereby he developed a theory on the impact of bureaucracy on foreign policy decision making, arguing that government behaviour is the result of bargaining games.[2] Later on, Peter Gourevitch (1978) coined the expression "second image reversed" – in reference to Kenneth Waltz' notion (1959) – to describe how pressures on the international stage influence domestic politics and how in turn domestic factors influence international relations. More recently, Robert Putnam (1988) in "Diplomacy and Domestic Politics: The Logic of Two-Level Games" demonstrated rather convincingly how governments engaged in international negotiations must play simultaneous games at the domestic level and international level.[3] Examples of studies on the interplay between domestic politics, or one set of domestic factors, and international affairs abound particularly in works on international political economy. Many have also written on the behaviour of democracies on the international scene, with some stressing that they are inherently pacific and others demonstrating that they are as likely to go to war as autocracies, if not more (see Brown, Lynn-Jones, and Miller 1996 on the democratic peace; Gaubatz 1999 on the impact of elections; Reiter and Stam 2002 on why democracies win war). These and countless other examples underscore the need for more studies like Allison's and Putnam's that incorporate subnational actors or institutions into the study of issues such as foreign policy or security crises. This approach can shed light as much on international affairs as on domestic politics.[4]

THE CLOSED GATES OF JANUS:
PARTY POLITICS IN PEACE-TIME CONDITIONS

Closing the doors to the Temple of Janus meant that the Roman republic was at peace, which by all accounts was seldom the case. Even then, the end of military activities and the return of the legions rarely meant the end of political violence. Party strife was often settled through violent means, and armed force became the modus operandi of many prominent politicians, such as Pompey and Caesar (Taylor 1949, 21). In effect, the Roman political elite behaved during peaceful and ordinary times much like they did during extraordinary and unsettled times. They fought each other – sometimes literally to the death – and remained often unable to unite for the greater good of the city. In other words, the context did not seem to affect their behaviour all that much. Alternatively one could also argue that the context did not change much, as wars and military interventions were more or less a constant feature for Rome's overstretched empire, and thus did not warrant a change of behaviour.

Leaving aside the atypical case of ancient Rome, let us turn to contemporary politics and ask ourselves, have the gates to the Temple of Janus ever really been closed in the recent past? It is doubtful. The world might not be at war now but war is still very much part of this world. In fact, it would be difficult to pinpoint when, after World War II, Western democracies were not embroiled in some international military or diplomatic crisis. From 1946 to 2001, there were 225 armed conflicts of which 34 were still active in 28 countries at the beginning of 2001 (Gleditsch, Wallensteen, Eriksson, Sollenberg, and Strand 2002). Since 2001, the number of interstate and intrastate conflicts remains about 30. The Cold War generated diplomatic crises and military conflicts throughout the world, particularly in Latin America, Southeast Asia, Africa, and continental Europe, which became the mainstay of international affairs from the late 1940s to the early 1990s. During this period, Europe's attempt to extricate itself from its overseas possessions was anything but peaceful. These events influenced the domestic politics of countless Western democracies. They shaped the nature of the political debate, as with McCarthyism and the Vietnam War in the United States. They altered the political landscape and constitutional structure, as in France with the decolonization process – particularly in Indochina and Algeria – and the polarization of French politics between pro-Soviets and anti-Soviets that brought about the demise of the Fourth Republic and the advent of the Fifth. The post–Cold War era has been as war-torn, with 115 armed conflicts between 1989 and 2001 (Gleditsch et al. 2002, 616), not to mention countless other foreign policy– or security policy–related events.

The second half of the twentieth century was, by all accounts, crisis-ridden and one could conclude that this is the standard situation; that this is the context of ordinary politics. Extraordinary politics would then come to characterize periods of peaceful conditions. While this may be true for some countries, this view does not hold for most advanced democracies. First, the turmoil that has come to characterize much of the international affairs over the past seventy years is not constant. Brinkmanship is followed by détente and major military crises are a seldom occurrence. In fact, the number of military conflicts has started to decrease since the end of the Cold War (Gleditsch et al. 2002, 616). Second, and closely related to the first point, not all foreign policy– or national security–related crises are of the same magnitude. It is worth noting that Western democracies have seldom been engaged in interstate wars – defined commonly as armed conflicts causing at least 1,000 battle-deaths.[5] Over the last seventy years, Western powers have been engaged in three such military conflicts.[6] As for diplomatic crises, they have not all had the implications of the 1962 Cuban Missile Crisis, and have generally been limited in time, although recent years have kept many Western diplomats alert. Finally, none of the wars involving Western powers took place on their national territory. In fact, most conflicts have occurred in Africa and Asia (Gleditsch et al. 2002, 616). Save perhaps for the all-encompassing Cold War, only a few Western countries have actually been directly involved in these crises.[7]

My aim is not to belittle the military conflicts and diplomatic crises that have troubled our world; rather, I want to underline that their impact was limited and that Western democratic states, on which the present study focuses, have been spared. For these particular countries, foreign policy and national security policy crises are rare and exceptional. They are in a word *extraordinary* occurrences. This being said, there is a rather large grey area especially for diplomatic crises. How then do we distinguish an ordinary context from an extraordinary one? More importantly, how do we define ordinary and extraordinary?

A crucial measure of whether a context is extraordinary is whether the crisis at hand threatens, or is perceived to threaten the country's interest, its people, its territory, or indeed its very survival. An ordinary context, for the purpose of this study, describes a situation where the political elite does not feel sufficiently threatened by foreign or security policy events to alter its day-to-day political behaviour. Obviously, in many instances, the elites will disagree on whether a situation is threatening but there are times when the danger to the nation is unmistakably clear and present. Rosenthal, Charles, and 't Hart consider that we speak of a crisis when policymakers experience "a serious threat to the basic structures or the fundamental values and norms of a social system, which under time pressure and highly uncertain circumstances necessitates making critical decisions" (1989, 10). Most Western democracies face theoretical security threats, such as a nuclear strike, but none of them seem to present clear and present dangers. The action of Russian forces in eastern Ukraine is an exception. ·

What then is ordinary political behaviour in a representative democracy? How does politics, particularly party politics, operate during ordinary times? An essential aspect of politics during ordinary times is its predictability, particularly in terms of the electoral process. Although elections might not always be held on fixed dates, electoral laws ensure their frequency, typically every four to five years for parliamentary elections. The political activity of parties and elites, particularly those of the mainstream, rests on this predictability.

Anthony Downs suggested in his groundbreaking book, *An Economic Theory of Democracy* (1957), that parties are first and foremost interested in winning elections; that this is their raison d'être. This assumption and its implications sparked an entire literature devoted to determining the objectives of political parties and their elites. Paramount in this literature is the view that parties are rational and predictable actors. It posits a world where humans make rational choices to maximize utility. Over the past sixty years, three models of competitive political party behaviour have tried to establish this assertion: the vote-seeking model, the office-seeking model, and the policy-seeking model.

The vote-seeking model put forth by Downs (1957) argues that parties want to maximize the number of votes. Although it might capture the main purpose of mainstream political parties, critics have pointed out that it falls short of describing the intention of smaller parties or fringe parties that are more likely trying to appeal to particular voters than trying to maximize the number of votes (Riker 1962; Robertson 1976). The office-seeking model developed by Riker (1962) addresses some of these concerns and suggests that parties are in fact seeking to maximize their control of political offices and government portfolios. Yet, offices can be prized for their intrinsic value and for their instrumental, electoral, or policy value (Strøm and Müller 1999, 6). Moreover, the office-seeking model fails to take into account parties that either refuse to enter into coalition governments and thus obtain portfolios or those who enter coalitions but eventually resign and relinquish the portfolios they were seeking in the first place (Strøm 1990). The policy-seeking model provides a partial solution by claiming that the objective of parties is to have maximum control over public policy. However, parties are likely to pursue as much office as policy, the former being a precondition for the latter (Axelrod 1970; Lijphart 1984; Budge and Laver 1986). In the end, it remains difficult to distinguish these various electoral objectives and one is left to conclude, as Strøm and Müller do, that "pure vote seekers, office seekers, or policy seekers are unlikely to exist" (1999, 12).

The three models outlined above assume an electoral rationale. They are, as Kaare Strøm reminds us, "less models of party behaviour than of electoral competition and coalition formation" (1990, 570). This, in itself, is not necessarily problematic since ordinary politics is centred on elections. What is more troubling is that these models tend to look at parties as unitary actors insulated from both the institutional and the international context. Yet the behaviour of parties depends to a large extent on the institutional features and the electoral system. If coalition formation is expected, then the number of seats will be crucial as it will determine the leverage and bargaining power the party has. In addition, rational choice models often tend to forget that parties are complex entities and that the influence of adherents and partisans cannot be discounted altogether. In other words, the unconstrained and "dictatorial" leader does not exist (Strøm 1990, 574). Party leaders are expected to remain fairly consistent in their policy choices (Downs 1957, 103–9) and party activists and members are likely to limit their leaders' choice by reminding them of the party line, especially in the case of labour-intensive party organizations (Strøm 1990, 578).

Institutional variables have started to be factored into models of rational behaviour toward the end of the 1970s (Hall and Taylor 1996).[8] Rational choice institutionalism, much like historical institutionalism, contends that institutions structure political behaviour (see Weingast 2002). Yet whereas historical institutionalists are first and foremost interested in understanding the context of politics through an inductive approach, rational choice institutionalists aim at deductively uncovering "the Laws of political behaviour and action" (Steinmo 2001). As Fiorina eloquently puts it "for most PTI scholars [Positive Theory of Institutions, i.e., rational choice] breadth trumps depth; understanding 90 percent of the variance in one case is not as significant an achievement as understanding 10 percent of each of nine cases" (Fiorina 1995, 110–11). In addition, rational choice institutionalists view institutions as essentially stable throughout time and very unlikely to be modified consciously by the rational actors (Steinmo 2001). In other words, rational choice institutionalists are unable to explain changes in the set of institutional rules, such as the ones provoked by political transitions. As Steinmo remarked, "[T]his is unfortunate, because we know that human history is replete with change. A theory whose goal is to predict, but which cannot explain change has some difficulties" (2001, 573).[9] The rational choice institutionalists' most important contribution is best summarized by Peter Hall and Rosemary Taylor:

They [rational choice institutionalists] postulate, first, that an actor's behaviour is likely to be driven, not by impersonal historical forces, but by a strategic calculus and, second, that this calculus will be deeply affected by the actor's expectations about how others are likely to behave as well. Institutions structure such interactions, by affecting the range and sequence of alternatives on the choice-agenda or by providing information and enforcement mechanisms that reduce uncertainty about the corresponding behaviour of others. (1996, 945)

However, despite this effort to bring the institutional variable into the equation, scholars working on the determinants of elite behaviour do not consider contextual matters pertaining to the international situation, although many useful studies have been undertaken over the years.[10] This gap in the literature is evident in the case of terrorism. As discussed, the failure to assess the impact of terrorism on party behaviour is troubling when one considers that terrorism is a negation of party politics.

Ordinary politics applies to a peaceful context; that is, a situation when the country is not under threat and political elites seek to maximize their gains at the next election whether in terms of votes, portfolios, or policy influence. However, what happens when the context changes due to foreign policy– or national security–related issues? Can the political earthquakes shake the foundations on which party politics stand? One would expect a certain behavioural flexibility. Dramatic contextual changes, such as a declaration of war, should lead political elites to reassess their priorities and focus more on the national interest than on partisan interests.

OPENING THE GATES OF JANUS' TEMPLE: PARTY POLITICS IN UNSETTLED TIMES

Strøm and Müller (1999, 5) write that "the scholarly literature that examines political parties is enormous, and yet our systematic knowledge of party objectives and behaviour is still quite modest." They point out in passing that the domestic and international context may affect party behaviour through what they call "exogenous situational factors," which include scandals, death of political figures, and social or economic events such as riots, economic recessions, events associated with powerful collective memories and so on (Strøm and Müller 1999, 25–6). Alas, they choose not to elaborate.

Richard Katz and William Crotty, in the aptly titled *Handbook of Party Politics* (2006), which invites contributions from leading experts, do not even allocate a paragraph to party behaviour in times of foreign policy or national security crises. They do mention, however, that parties have had to adapt to changes brought about by the globalization of trade, finance and markets, the creation of regional political alignments such as the European Union, the electronic media, et cetera (Katz and Crotty 2006, 1). Incomprehensibly, international crises are not mentioned as events worthy of attention. The only international development that seems relevant to them, though not specifically for the behaviour of parties, is the so-called third wave of democratization, which increased the number of parties and party systems over the last fifteen years (Katz and Crotty 2006, 2). Perhaps extraordinary times are assumed to "suspend" politics in which case one is left to wonder where the authors draw the line between extraordinary and ordinary times.

The overall impression left by a survey of the literature on party politics is that foreign policy and national security contexts are not sufficiently taken into consideration. The assumption must be that traditional models of party behaviour are sufficient to account for the actions of parties during extraordinary times. Since these are models of electoral behaviour, one must conclude that maximizing votes, offices, or policy influence is the prime objective no matter what, even when "all hell breaks loose" on the international or national scene. A troubling assumption, to say the least.

To be sure, a number of important studies have dealt with party and electoral behaviour during foreign policy and military crises. For instance, Kurt Gaubatz in *Elections and War: The Electoral Incentive in the Democratic Politics of War and Peace* (1999) and Kristopher Ramsay in "Politics at the Water's Edge: Crisis Bargaining and Electoral Competition" (2004) consider the impact of diplomatic crises and war on the electoral strategy of parties. Both authors point to the crucial role played by the opposition, which must balance at once its electoral strategy with the national interest. Kenneth Schultz's "Domestic Opposition and Signalling in International Crises" (1998) points to exactly the same dilemma. Schultz observes that opposition parties can reinforce the government's credibility by siding with it against an external foe, while at the same time forcing the government to be irreproachable on the international scene, and avoid using a foreign policy crisis for partisan reasons in what is commonly referred to as "wagging the dog." At the same time one could argue that during exceptional times the opposition has less room for manoeuvre than the government. Opposing the government during a severe crisis or accusing it of playing politics with the crisis at hand can lead to counter-accusations of disloyalty. Siding with the government and recognizing the primacy of the national interest over the partisan or electoral interest might be the safest course of action for the opposition.

Of course elections are always part of the equation, and to some extent the behaviour of political elites remains influenced by the electoral timetable, even in the worst of times. World War II certainly did not prevent most free and democratic belligerents – Australia, Canada, New Zealand, and the United States – from organizing "khaki elections," although Britain represents an interesting exception.[11] Up to a certain point, foreign policy crises can be construed as just one more set of issues that parties can choose to bring into the political debate, much like they decide to debate about the unemployment rate or tax reform. The assumption, however, is that the gravity of the context brought about by the crisis will dictate what kind of behaviour is preferable.

To illustrate this assumption and shed light on the behaviour of elites during extraordinary times, I look at three historical cases during which the US political elite had to deal both with a looming election and a severe foreign policy crisis: the 1940 US presidential campaign, which unfolded during the initial stages of World War II; the 1948 US presidential campaign, which coincided with the Berlin Blockade, the first major crisis of the Cold War; and the 1962 campaign for the mid-term congressional elections, the tail end of which overlapped with the Cuban Missile Crisis. These high-stakes events had immediate implications for the American political elite, representing a turning point for the United States and much of the so-called free world. More importantly, these crises unfolded during election campaigns, forcing opposition parties to choose between their narrow electoral interest and the broader national interest. Because of the severity of the selected crises, these are cases where the foreign policy emergency at hand was *most likely* to have an impact on the behaviour of the political elite.

One of the most noticeable differences between these crises concerns the chronology of events and the point during the electoral campaign at which each crisis peaked. In the case of the 1940 election, the world, or at least the better part of the northern hemisphere, might have been at war but the United States was still not a belligerent, although its stakes in the conflict were anything but trivial. The Japanese attack of Pearl Harbor took place more than a year after the presidential election, and the United States until then had been relatively shielded from the events unfolding in Europe. In the case of the 1948 election, the climax of the Berlin Blockade took place during one of the most crucial moments of the campaign: the Republican convention. Finally, in the case of the Cuban Missile Crisis, the "Thirteen Days" crisis unfolded late in the campaign and ended a mere nine days before election day.

ROOSEVELT AND THE ISOLATIONISTS

By the time the 1940 presidential campaign got underway, most of the Western world was already at war. Even though the United States tried to remain neutral, the Democratic president Franklin D. Roosevelt, who was seeking an unprecedented third mandate, told Congress in January 1940 that "the time is long past when any political party or any particular group can curry or capture public favor by labeling itself the peace party" (Divine 1974, 5). More than anyone, Roosevelt understood that the events unfolding in Europe would determine the outcome of the election. As Robert Divine remarks, "[A]ny dramatic turn in the conflict was likely to rally the nation behind his leadership, while a continued stalemate would help the Republicans, who focused on domestic discontent" (1974, 5).

Throughout 1940, Roosevelt and Wendell Willkie, the main contender for the Republican nomination, openly debated whether or not the United States should enter the conflict. Roosevelt favoured a more interventionist role contrary to public opinion that clearly leaned toward the isolationists like Willkie (Gaubatz 1999, 70–8).[12]

Willkie, unlike other Republicans such as Thomas Dewey, believed it was imperative that the United States did not directly or indirectly become involved in the war, yet he did not go as far as presidential hopeful Robert Taft who believed that US involvement would be more dangerous for democracy at home than a Nazi victory in Europe (Divine 1974, 15–16). In other words, Willkie was an *isolationist* but not an *insulationist*. After the start of the German blitzkrieg in May 1940, he called for "anything short of war" to help France and England, and later on declared that these two countries were "our first line of defense against Hitler" (Divine 1974, 19). Willkie's rhetoric struck a chord with an American public opinion reluctant to get involved militarily in Europe but still keen on providing assistance to beleaguered France and Britain. His standing in the polls made him a clear favourite for the Republican nomination. In order to clinch it, Willkie had to appear less interventionist than Roosevelt and reassure the isolationists in his party. He did just that in the week before the convention, reminding his audiences throughout the country that he would not send soldiers to Europe (Divine 1974, 20). From then on, although sharing many of Roosevelt's interventionist ideas, Willkie presented himself as the isolationist candidate.

The movement against intervention was growing. The percentage of people opposed to a war against Germany grew from 83 per cent before the invasion of Poland in September 1939 to 94 per cent after (Gaubatz 1999, 72). In addition, the interventionist versus antiwar divide cut across partisan lines. Roosevelt's resolve was particularly tested by western and midwestern isolationists, many of whom were Republicans ready to vote for the Democratic incumbent and his New Deal program provided he backtracked on his decision to intervene on the international scene (Gaubatz 1999, 70).

The political elite was not warming to Roosevelt's interventionist plan either. Already in 1935, the Senate passed the first of the Neutrality Acts with seventy-nine votes in favour and two against (Gaubatz 1999, 71). Eventually both Congress and the public became less isolationist, lifting the prohibition on arms sales, but a clear majority remained opposed to sending the army and the navy anywhere close to the frontline.[13] In fact, Burton Wheeler and other

Democratic isolationists threatened to create a third party unless Roosevelt declared himself opposed to intervention (Gaubatz 1999, 73). Even after the May 1940 blitzkrieg during which the Nazi war machine overpowered its European adversaries, Roosevelt was still unable to push forward his plans for intervention. Instead, he had to content himself with a plan to beef up the national defence with $1 billion in emergency defence appropriations, a move that drew massive support from both interventionists and isolationists in Congress (Divine 1974, 9).

Following the German invasion of Europe, *Time* magazine boldly declared that "the Republican Party was the first US casualty in World War II" (Divine 1974, 10). Yet polls indicated that even though a clear majority would vote for Roosevelt, an even larger majority was opposed to intervention unless the country was attacked (Divine 1974, 11). Eventually, unable to secure the backing of the elite and of public opinion, and unwilling to risk breaking up his New Deal coalition, Roosevelt decided to adopt the isolationist position so as not to hurt his chances of winning the November election. Gaubatz (1999, 74) remarks that "as the election drew nearer through October 1940, there were escalations in antiwar rhetoric by both candidates" with Roosevelt declaring in a public speech, "I have said this before, but I shall say it again and again and again: Your boys are not going to be sent into any foreign wars." Electoral considerations had finally convinced Roosevelt to publicly turn around.

Despite the growing tension in Europe, the United States was not under threat. The context was still peaceful. With no clear and present danger, foreign policy could be debated just like any other issue. Willkie projected himself as more isolationist than he really was, thereby forcing Roosevelt to put on hold his interventionist agenda until after the election. Clearly Willkie and the Republicans did not feel the urge to rally around their president and allow him to choose his preferred course of action. However, had Roosevelt and Willkie been on the campaign trail in the aftermath of the attack on Pearl Harbor a year later, the question of America's entry into war would likely not have been disputed. By 7 December 1941, this "day of infamy," the Washington political elite rallied around its president like an army behind its commander-in-chief.

DEWEY AND THE BERLIN CRISIS

For the Republicans, the 1948 US presidential campaign was the first since Herbert Hoover's in 1928 for which their candidate, in this case Thomas Dewey, was the clear favourite to win the election. Having won the 1946 mid-term elections, members of the Grand Old Party were convinced that the White House was within their grasp. For his part Harry Truman, the incumbent, still had to convince the Democrats that he, rather than Ike Eisenhower, should be their candidate. To make matters worse, in the spring of 1948, his approval rating in the Gallup poll reached an all-time low with 32 per cent (Divine 1974, 188).

The campaign was fought primarily over foreign policy, which according to polls was the number one problem facing the country (Ramsay 2004, 19). A slight majority of Americans also believed that the Republicans were the best choice to conduct their foreign policy (Ramsay 2004, 19). As a consequence, Dewey repeatedly attacked Truman's record on the international front regarding the fate of Eastern Europe (Ramsay 2004, 18). Dewey lambasted the Truman administration for having "delivered" 200 million Europeans into Stalin's hands (Divine 1974, 189). Polls also indicated that almost three-quarters of respondents felt that the United States was "too soft" with the Soviets (Divine 1974, 200).

On 23 June 1948, the day Dewey received the Republican nomination, the USSR closed the corridor linking West Germany and Berlin, creating the first great crisis of the Cold War and what *Newsweek* called "the greatest diplomatic crisis in American history."[14] The Soviets' bold move was a reaction to Western plans of creating an independent West German entity. At the Potsdam conference in 1945, the Soviet Union and the Western powers agreed on the division of Germany and Berlin into four zones of occupation, which would remain part of the same political entity. When the United States and its Western allies realized that the deal reached with the Soviets was unworkable, they decided to merge their zones and create a West German entity. The Berlin Blockade was an attempt by the Soviets to prevent their former allies to proceed with their plan.

Despite leading in the polls, Dewey faced a difficult choice: carry on the attacks against Truman's perceived mismanagement of foreign policy issues, or rally around Truman "the president" during a severe crisis.[15] For his part Truman declared that "foreign policy should be the policy of the whole Nation and not the policy of one party or the other .... Partisanship should stop as the water's edge" (Divine 1974, 219). Congress lost little time in giving Truman the support he needed and both Democrats and Republicans approved the airlift announced on 30 June. Charles Eaton, the Republican chairman of the House Foreign Affairs Committee, underlined the necessity for the United States to remain in Berlin: "If the United States should withdraw, it would remove any confidence in us as world leaders. It would be more of a fateful calamity to mankind than Munich was. It would be a signal to the world that we intend to turn over everything to the dictatorship of Russia" (Lodge and Shlaim 1979, 75).

In the end, Dewey decided that recognizing the legal ambiguity of Berlin's status brought about by the mismanagement of the White House would only play into Stalin's hands and legitimize his claims, and instead decided that the Berlin Blockade would not be made into an electoral issue (Ramsay 2004, 19). With the fate of his country's foreign policy in the balance, Dewey declared, "The present duty of Americans is not to be divided by past lapses but to unite to surmount present danger ... We shall not allow domestic partisan irritations to divert us from indispensable unity" (Divine 1974, 225).

Truman went on to win the election. Dewey, for the sake of his country, had indeed "snatched defeat from the jaws of victory" (Ramsay 2004, 21). Despite an electoral victory in sight, American national interest proved in the end too much to brush aside. "The fear of war," as noted by Robert Divine, "rallied the people around Truman's leadership" (1974, 226).[16]

JOHN F. KENNEDY
AND THE CUBAN MISSILE CRISIS

Perhaps more than the two crises described above, the events of October 1962 were seen as severely jeopardizing the national interest of the United States – and potentially countless other countries –

and threatening the survival of millions in what Timothy McKeown describes as "our closest brush with thermonuclear war" (2000, 70). Graham Allison sombrely remarks:

> For thirteen days of October 1962, there was a higher probability that more human lives would end suddenly than ever before in history. Had the worst occurred, the death of 100 million Americans, over 100 million Russians, and millions of Europeans as well would make previous natural calamities and inhumanities appear insignificant. Given the probability of disaster – which President Kennedy estimated as "between 1 out of 3 and even" – our escape seems awesome. (1969, 689)

Ever since Fidel Castro seized power in January 1959, Cuba was a pressing concern for the US administration and a sore point for Kennedy who had greenlighted the CIA fiasco at the Bay of Pigs in April 1961. Yet during the fall of 1962, Kennedy had other issues on his mind. Congressional elections were looming and although the Democrats controlled both the Senate (65–35) and the House of Representatives (263–174), a working majority was often missing because House committees were controlled by conservatives from the South, and in the Senate southern Democrats often opposed Kennedy. As pointed out by Paterson and Brophy "the president and his aides eagerly looked to the forthcoming elections to produce a more sympathetic Congress" (1986, 88). Yet mid-term elections up to that point had almost always been unfavourable to the incumbent's party. Republicans were thus expecting to gain seats in both assemblies and perhaps even become the majority party in the House. However, throughout the first ten months of 1962 the Democratic Party retained a lead in the Gallup polls on voters' preferences; the Democrats enjoyed a twenty-point margin on the Republicans in January 1962 but only an eleven-point margin in early November (Paterson and Brophy 1986, 92). Democrats were also perceived as more capable than Republicans to handle national problems (Paterson and Brophy 1986, 93). Yet Kennedy's record regarding Cuba remained problematic, with a Louis Harris poll showing a majority of interviewees disapproving the president's actions (Paterson and Brophy 1986, 93). Not surprisingly, the Republicans tried to make Cuba the main issue of the congressional campaign, whereas the Democrats were trying to focus the debate on Medicare. The Republican opposition, it should be pointed out, was critical of the Kennedy administration's handling of Cuba even before the October Crisis. Essentially, Republicans were arguing that the missiles installed by the Soviets on the island had an offensive purpose, whereas Kennedy described them as defensive or short-range and thus unable to reach the United States (Paterson and Brophy 1986, 95). In any event, the Republican opposition in Congress argued that the United States could not stay inactive and had to resort to either a blockade or an invasion of Cuba (Paterson and Brophy 1986, 95). In an attempt to appease the hawks, Kennedy declared at a press conference held on 13 September that he would do whatever needed to be done to protect the security of the country (Paterson and Brophy 1986, 96). Even though the president did not adopt their strategy, the Republicans had succeeded in promoting Cuba as one of the top issues of the campaign.

The crisis reached a climax on 16 October when the president was informed that photographs taken by a US spy plane two days before revealed the presence of offensive surface-to-surface missiles on the Caribbean island. With elections a mere three weeks away, President Kennedy had to take into account the forceful alternatives put forth by the hawkish Republicans and the preferences of public opinion, which according to polls favoured doing something while avoiding the use of force (McKeown 2000, 72). The week that followed can best be described as a long brainstorming session involving members of the Executive Committee of the National Security Council, better known as ExCom. In light of the massive amount of material available, such as primary documents, Paterson and Brophy conclude that "politics was very seldom discussed and did not determine the choice of the naval blockade" (1986, 100).[17] The most ardent critic of Kennedy on Cuba, Senator Kenneth Keating, was not invited to offer his ideas. During that fateful week, Kennedy carried on campaigning across the country, revealing nothing about the extent of the crisis to the public, proof enough for Paterson and Brophy that Kennedy did not play politics with Cuba. Most of the political elite was not aware of the reconnaissance photographs and of the extent of the crisis. As a result, criticism, especially from Republican politicians, continued.

The situation changed dramatically after the full extent of the crisis was revealed to the world on 22 October during a television address. Kennedy announced a "strict quarantine on all offensive military equipment under shipment to Cuba" and gave Soviet First Secretary Nikita Khrushchev an ultimatum, asking him to "halt and eliminate this clandestine, reckless, and provocative threat to world peace" (Allison 1969, 704). Republicans by and large sided with Kennedy, and Keating himself declared that the president had "taken Cuba out of politics" (Paterson and Brophy 1986, 106). Throughout the remainder of the crisis the Kennedy administration worked at creating a bipartisan consensus by bringing top Republicans in foreign policy meetings. As McKeown points out, "[G]iven the pronounced public support for the blockade compared to more violent options, the blockade was the ideal response in terms of gratifying public opinion" (2000, 74). At the same time, this option was strong enough to appease the hawks and other warmongers roaming on Capitol Hill. Even the media rallied around the flag following the announcement of the embargo (Kern, Levering, and Levering 1983).

By 29 October, the White House had reached an agreement with the Kremlin, putting an end to the crisis. With a week left before the election, the Republicans went again on the offensive and renewed their attacks against the incumbent arguing that Kennedy's policy left a communist country and a military ally of the Soviet Union in America's back garden. Even worse, by promising Khrushchev not to invade Cuba, Kennedy had, in the eyes of the Republican Party, essentially renounced the Monroe Doctrine.[18]

The 6 November election did not significantly modify Congress. The Republicans gained two seats in the House, where the Democrats retained the majority, and lost four seats in the Senate. Paterson and Brophy conclude that the Missile Crisis did not change the course of the election:

The crisis helped some Democrats and hurt some Democrats; it buoyed some Republicans and weakened some Republicans. In many instances Cuba was not even a conspicuous campaign issue. The historian cannot identify one election in 1962 decided by voter reaction to the missile crisis – not a single outcome where the Cuban issue made the difference between victory and defeat. The results of the House and the Senate races, in other words, are best explained by the mix of other factors ... personalities and their public images; local politics; domestic issues; reapportionment and gerrymandering; superior Democratic Party registration; and the nature of the 1960 election." (1986, 118)

Yet for a week between 22 October and 29 October the Republicans ceased their attacks against Kennedy. It was neither the most heartfelt nor the longest rally around the flag, but it did halt the Republican momentum. More importantly, it gave Kennedy an opportunity to demonstrate his leadership in the worst of times. Although he did not choose the hawks' preferred course of action – a more forceful response – Republican critics were silenced two weeks before voters were called to the polls.

CONCLUSION

Party politics does not always revolve around electoral objectives. Juliet Lodge and Avi Shlaim's write that "the greater the perceived probability of war, the greater is the freedom of key decision makers from domestic constraints" (1979, 74). Of course, the value of this set of historical examples is limited in several ways: only one country – and one political system – is taken into account and the timeframe is relatively narrow. More importantly, the selected events, because of their implications, represent cases where foreign policy events are most likely to influence the parties. Party behaviour during less intense crises must be less influenced by events outside the borders. In many ways this is what the first case study points out. In 1940 the United States was just a "neutral" bystander in the European military conflict, and political elites could look upon foreign policy as just another issue, albeit the most important one, in the presidential campaign. In 1956 a similar situation presented itself in the United Kingdom when Gamal Abdel Nasser decided to nationalize the Suez Canal. Conservative prime minister Anthony

Eden decided to seize back the canal through a military operation involving France and Israel. However, the Labour opposition, backed by a majority of the public opinion, opposed this intervention. The Conservative Party was itself split between those advocating an even tougher policy toward Egypt and those siding with Labour. This unequivocal position on the part of the Labour Party reinforced Nasser's as well as the US government's determination to oppose the British-led invasion and precipitated the failure of the operation. The crisis, despite its mainly economic implications, did not threaten the United Kingdom though it dismantled further an empire that had become a burden. The loss of Suez was symbolic of a vanishing supremacy. As a result, the Labour Party felt no qualms about opposing the government, particularly with public opinion very much against intervention.

The last two cases – Berlin Blockade and Cuban Missile Crisis – reveal a very different logic, particularly in the case of the 1948 election. Here, despite a looming election and an open road to victory, the opposition chose the national over the electoral interest. The loss of Berlin would have dealt a severe blow to the United States and its allies and would have put the next president – Dewey or Truman – in a difficult position. The 1962 Missile Crisis was another proof that when the going gets tough the tougher will rally. The rally only lasted a week, but it ended a mere eight days before the election. Had the Republican Party only had its best electoral interest in mind, it would simply not have stopped its attacks against Kennedy, not for a week, not even for an hour.

The idea of a shift from ordinary politics to extraordinary politics when the national security is threatened seems particularly relevant with regards to terrorism. The threat might be of a different scale, but as Michel Wieviorka and David Gordon White point out:

A terrorist movement at its height operates like a magnet, drawing attention to itself well beyond its terrorist acts per se. Overheating in the media, panic in the corridors of power, empty-handedness in the police and intelligence services, miscarriages in the halls of justice, and the human drama of victims and their families all combine to reinforce the image of the terrorist as an all-powerful figure. Conversely, disinterest reigns as soon as an incident has passed, and our memories are hardly jogged when we see these same terrorist actors, now portrayed as miserable figures, at the conclusion of an escapade. (2004, xxix)

If foreign policy crises can temporarily push electoral preoccupations aside and activate what Adam Smith calls the "patriotic imperative" (2006), then presumably the same holds for terrorist crises. The question then is one of trade-off between partisan interests and the national interest.

3

In the Shadow of the Flag

National Interest versus Partisan Interest

Love of the homeland is the civilized man's first virtue.

Napoléon Bonaparte, *Maximes et Pensées*

INTRODUCTION

On 14 September 2001, atop rubbles of concrete and mangled steel in what would be known as Ground Zero, President Bush grabbed a bullhorn and addressed a crowd of rescuers amid chants of "USA! USA!" His words mattered little. Here at Ground Zero, Bush the incidental president, became commander-in-chief of a nation at "war." The American people were invited to pray for the lost ones and support the troops. As for the US Congress, all it could do was stand still in the shadow of the flag and hope for a short war.[1] A week later Bush declared, "It [the war] will not end until every terrorist group of global reach has been found, stopped, and defeated."[2]

In his study of consociationalism, Arend Lijphart (1968; 1969) suggested that external threats provide political elites with an incentive to co-operate across partisan lines. Historical examples abound, not just in the United States, and tend to suggest that in times of uncertainty rallying around the government or the head of state is a common reflex, what John Mueller (1973) termed a "patriotic reflex." Yet examples to the contrary exist as well. The various ways in which elites and public opinions across the world reacted to the impending military invasion of Iraq in 2003 by US-led coalition forces are a case in point. Unfortunately, if an important literature exists on the behaviour of elites and public opinions during foreign policy crises, little has been written on the behaviour of parties during terrorist crises. Thus, one is left to wonder whether the aftermath of 9/11 is atypical or not. Do high-magnitude terrorist crises lead to massive rallies around the flag? If so, what exactly triggers this phenomenon?

This chapter's first section begins by addressing what constitutes a rally around the flag, then discusses the two main reasons why and how rallies develop. I look at how political elites, media, and public opinion might affect each other's reaction during critical times. In the second section, I examine the notion of the national interest and how it might take precedence over partisan interest, and I put forth my main hypothesis. The third and final section introduces the magnitude-repetition model, identifies key variables likely to influence the reaction of political elites to acts of terrorism, and presents a series of secondary hypotheses.

THE RALLY-AROUND-THE-FLAG PHENOMENON

Put simply, a rally around the flag is a very large movement of public support in favour of a government or whoever might be holding the executive power. Such a popular movement generally aims at defending the country in the face of adversity, a sort of *levée en masse* reminiscent only in spirit of this formidable army of ragged sans-culottes that coalesced in Valmy to defend the soon to be proclaimed republic.[3] In the following section I discuss the rallying phenomenon and differentiate it from other forms of support. I then look at why and how rallies develop. Finally, I assess the influence of political elites during critical times.

RALLIES AND OTHER FORMS
OF PUBLIC SUPPORT

As witnessed in the aftermath of 9/11, rallies around the flag are a powerful phenomenon that can literally bring party politics to a standstill and severely limit for a short time the flow of criticism from mainstream political elites and media outlets. However, the concept of rallies is often misunderstood and misused by scholars and pundits alike. Surges in approval ratings of the president or the head of the government are often seen as bona fide rallies when in fact they might only reflect a higher degree of appreciation within parts of the general population.[4] As a result, rallies around the flag are often seen as one-dimensional forces arising within the population and revealed by opinion polls. What constitutes a rally is then a matter of interpretation as to how steep, in terms of percentage points, the surge in the approval rating needs to be.

Approval ratings are only part of the story. Rallies cannot simply be equated with instant plebiscites in the polls; they must encompass other dimensions. Evidently the support must be massive but it must also come from different segments of society. I contend that a definition of a rally around the flag should incorporate this multidimensional aspect. I define a rally as a movement of widespread support in favour of the government within the mainstream political elite – crucially from the opposition parties – equally widespread support within the general population, and support from most media outlets.[5] What qualifies as "widespread support" is arbitrary, particularly with three indicators involved, and is discussed at length at the end of this section when I try to examine the interplay among media, elites, and the general population. The point, however, is that a rally should encompass more than just favourable public opinion polls.

This being said, we would not expect the support to be even across the full spectrum of a society's groups and subgroups. Someone, somewhere, is always going to disagree and refuse to join the rally no matter how severe the crisis is.[6] Radicals and fringe elites might have a different response reflecting a different political agenda. And yet, there are throughout history instances of near complete support for a government. The inception of major wars obviously provides the incentive to rally, even for radicals. A well-known example is of the French and German socialists in the run up to World War I, who despite their initial reluctance to support a "bourgeois" war eventually rallied around the flag – what the French called *union sacrée* – just days before the armies received their marching orders (Eley 2002).

WHY RALLY? TWO COMPETING EXPLANATIONS

John Mathews (1919, 213), in a pioneering article on political parties' attitudes during military conflicts, remarked shortly after the end of World War I that "one effect of war upon the party system ... is to bring about, at least for a time, a relatively greater stability of party control, if not complete quiescence of partisanship, either through coalition or through cessation of party opposition, or both." He concluded, however, that this union of political elites and parties was neither perfect nor durable: "While there may be practical unanimity upon the question of entering the war, there is more likelihood of a difference developing in the reaction of the parties toward the questions involved in the method of prosecuting it and of terminating it" (Mathews 1919, 214).

While the capacity of wars and diplomatic crises to trigger rallies has been acknowledged by many scholars (Polsby 1964; Waltz 1967; Mueller 1973; MacKuen 1983; Ostrom and Simon 1985; Brody 1991; Oneal and Bryan 1995; Hymans 2005; and many others), there is far less agreement as to how and why this rallying process comes about. Two main explanations have emerged over the years: the "patriotic-reflex" interpretation put forth by John Mueller (1973), and the "opinion-leadership" explanation put forth by Richard Brody (1991).

THE PATRIOTIC REFLEX

Although he was not the first one to detect a propensity among people to rally in times of crisis, John Mueller was the first to go beyond the passing remark and offer systematic insight into the phenomenon. To be fair, Mueller's seminal work *War, Presidents and Public Opinion* (1973) dealt with more than just rallies, and his contribution to understanding political behaviour is far more extensive than that. His reflections on rallies were part of a larger study on the causes of the downward trend of presidential popularity in the United States – rallies being studied as a case of temporary upturn.

Mueller (1973, 209) suggests that people will rally around the flag in the wake of specific, dramatic and sharply focused international events directly involving the United States and its president. They will do so in the hope of maximizing their nation's prospect in the crisis at hand. According to Mueller, six types of events have the potential to trigger rallies: sudden US military interventions abroad such as the Bay of Pigs (1961), major military operations in ongoing wars like the Tet Offensive (1968), major diplomatic developments such as the Berlin Blockade (1948) or the announcement of the Truman Doctrine (1947), dramatic technological developments like the launch of Sputnik (1957), meetings between the American president and his Soviet counterpart, and the start of each presidential term.

Interestingly, international terrorism was not listed as a potential catalyst. Yet terrorist attacks certainly fit the above description of events likely to trigger rallies, and it seems obvious that international terrorism could be added to Mueller's list of events alongside major military or diplomatic crises. Mueller's omission was likely because in the early 1970s international terrorism was still in its nascent phase and not yet a major security concern for the White House. The attack by the Palestinian organization Black September at the Munich Olympic Games had just happened and US citizens were still relatively safe within their own borders.[7]

Mueller also excludes domestic crises, which in his view are more "likely to exacerbate internal divisions" (1973, 209). In addition, he considers that only sudden events can trigger rallies, whereas the impact of gradual changes on public attitudes is likely to be diffused. Obviously economic recessions and chronic environmental degradations lack the suddenness of a declaration of war, but one could argue that even the most sudden foreign policy events often unfold over longer periods before they reach a breaking point. This being said, the argument of suddenness is far more compelling than the one about domestic events. Domestic events, such as the death of a political figure, or more joyful moments, such as celebrations, can trigger rallies just like international events.[8]

Mueller's pioneering work has spurred a host of studies based on the assumption that public support varies depending on how events unfold on the battlefield (i.e., the number of casualties). The "casualty hypothesis" holds that the more battle-deaths there are, the less people will support their government (Gartner and Segura 1998;

Gelpi, Feaver, and Reifler 2006; Karol and Miguel 2007). In the end, the general population will rally if the benefits of a successful war are perceived as greater than the costs.

The patriotic-reflex explanation has attracted a fair amount of criticism over the years for its inability to account for the fact that not all specific, dramatic, and sharply focused international events trigger rallies or have similar impacts on the president's approval ratings (Kernell 1975; Lee 1977). Still, hardly anyone would dispute the fact that elites' behaviour in such critical times is closely linked to the severity of the event. Mueller, however, stops short of explaining the process by which different groups of people will overcome their disagreements, perhaps even their enmity or distrust, to rally in support of their leader. In fact, he does not distinguish between the reaction of the political elite and that of the general population. In his view, the rally is the result of a patriotic reflex that encompasses all segments of society, decision makers, opinion leaders, and ordinary citizens alike.[9]

THE OPINION-LEADERSHIP EXPLANATION

Richard Brody fills the theoretical gap left by the patriotic explanation by adopting a different line of reasoning. Instead of looking at what kind of events trigger rallies in the first place, he focuses his attention on how rallies develop or rather how criticism of the government is subdued (Brody and Shapiro 1989; Brody 1991). Like Jong R. Lee (1977) and Karlyn Keene (1980) before him, Brody attempts to account for the puzzling fact that Americans, by and large, seem to rally around their presidents following major international events "regardless of the success or failure of the U.S. policy," while at the same time explaining the few instances when they do not rally (Brody 1991, 53). A rally when things go well and the president is a positive force seems natural, but what of rallies in support of faulty policies and blatant mismanagement by the executive branch of the government?

Unlike Mueller, Brody makes a distinction between different actors of public life, namely the political elite, the media and the general population. Brody suggests that in times of crisis, "when events are breaking at an unusually rapid pace, when the administration [i.e., the White House] has a virtual monopoly of information about the situation, opposition political leaders tend to refrain from comment or to make cautiously supportive statement" (1991, 63).[10] This restraint on the part of opposition elites is explained to some extent by a natural tendency to be supportive of the president when American interests abroad are at stake – Mueller's thesis. However, Brody insists that the decision of opposition elites to hold back is above all a consequence of being out of the loop – presumably only top White House officials are in it – and not having the necessary information to criticize the government. This means that during foreign policy crises the opposition is not able to provide the media with critical views on the government and its handling of the crisis. In turn, the media cannot use its traditional sources within the opposition elite to offer balanced news. In the end, this absence of criticism projects an image of a government doing a fine job and thus encourages the general population to rally as well. This situation prevails until the opposition elite makes such countervailing evaluation of the government's handling of affairs available to the media, and they in turn make it available to the general population.

Bruce Russett follows a similar line of reasoning and argues that "some of their [the leaders] best opportunities to insulate their actions from domestic politics occur in the realm of foreign and national security policy" (1990, 9). Russett remarks that "much foreign policy is literally and figuratively distant from most citizens; its interpretation is thus particularly subject to selective release of information and careful media presentation – a prime candidate for symbolic politics" (1990, 34). Cindy Kam et al., for their part, suggest that "political sophistication is likely to shape which citizens hear elite messages and to what extent they resist or accept them" (2004, 23). The argument, based on John Zaller's "reception-acceptance" model (1992), suggests that rallies will be largest among moderately politically aware individuals. Similarly, Adam Berinsky (2007) suggests that people, notably poorly informed ones, will take cues from the elite and that if they choose to support their government it is not because the war appears successful but because their elites chose to rally. Berinsky argues that the "elite-cue" theory explains why the mass public remained supportive of the US government all through World War II, even though casualties increased markedly from 1944 to April 1945.[11]

Others have been more critical of Brody's thesis. Matthew Baum (2002) finds that elite support for the president – especially from the opposition – while perhaps necessary, is not a sufficient condition for a rally. Baum and Groeling (2004) have gone as far as suggesting that elites do not in fact suspend partisan attacks in times of crises. Lian and Oneal (1993) argued similarly that there was no consistent rally effect following the use of military force by the president. Others have pointed out that Brody's understanding of the rallying phenomenon is incomplete; the argument being that the support offered by the opposition elite is often nothing more than a reaction to the popular mood (Hetherington and Nelson 2003). In other words, the mechanism is circular; the elite avoids criticizing the president because it believes public opinion is backing him.

Finally, at a contextual level, Robert Entman (2006) suggests that since the end of the Cold War, events taking place on the international scene have become more ambiguous and culturally less congruent, making it difficult for the White House to frame foreign policy news the way it wants. In other words, ambiguity opens space for dissent. However, Entman (2006, 18) argues that during culturally congruent crises, such as the multiple attacks of 9/11, elites, media and public will fall into line. Norris, Kern, and Just suggest that "in times of shared crisis, a sense of threat often means that journalists freely offer their collaboration. Even if journalists seek opposing views on government war policies, they are constrained by their dependence on government success in order to write the news" (2003, 296). Moreover "even if politicians and journalists have doubts or disagreements, they will probably suppress explicit criticism out of concern for damaging public morale or fear of public backlash" (Norris et al. 2003, 298).

PATRIOTIC LEADERSHIP?

William Baker and John Oneal (2001) conducted an assessment of both theoretical approaches and concluded that the opinion-leadership model accounted more accurately for the phenomenon than the patriotic-reflex model. In their view, "the public does not rally in response to crises in and of themselves, but rather to the president's handling and presentation of events" (Baker and Oneal 2001, 682). Cindy Kam and Jennifer Ramos (2008) reached a different and more nuanced conclusion by analyzing the evolution of public support for President Bush in the aftermath of 9/11. In their view, "rallies occur not just as a consequence of elite discourse (Brody 1991), but also as a consequence of patriotism – through renewed emphasis on national identity brought on by presidential rhetoric" (Kam and Ramos 2008, 641).[12]

Although they start from different premises, Mueller's and Brody's views are not necessarily incompatible with one another. For instance, Jacques Hymans (2005) adopts an approach midway between the patriotic- and opinion-leadership explanations by suggesting that four conditions are necessary for a rally to occur: a major international event or a disaster, mass patriotism, a substantial coverage by the media with a national framing, and the expectation on the part of public opinion that the country will prevail and come out of the crisis successful. Hymans considers that a rally cannot appear unless the feeling of belonging to a country is stronger among citizens than partisan feelings, and the framing and priming is orchestrated by the elite.[13]

Brody (2002) himself acknowledged that following Iraq's invasion of Kuwait in 1990, leaders of the Democratic Party decided at first to support President Bush because of patriotic considerations. Commenting on the events of 9/11, Brody declared, "It is likely that future analyses of the rally following the attacks on the towers of the World Trade Center and the Pentagon will also find that patriotism and opinion leadership affected public support for President Bush" (2002, 6–7).

Evidently neither Mueller nor Brody took specific interest in the impact of terrorism on political elites, yet their works do offer clues as to how these elites might react to terrorist attacks. The implications of terrorism for the national interest suggest a priori that this form of political violence offers a fertile ground for rallies. Terrorism ticks the same boxes as military and diplomatic crises. To paraphrase Mueller, it is dramatic – often more so than faraway military crises or opaque diplomatic disputes – it is usually specific, it is sudden and as a matter of national security it necessarily involves the president or head of the government. As for Brody's argument that in times of crisis when events break at an unusual rapid pace the government has a monopoly of information and the opposition is muted, it is well suited to terrorist events, which by nature unfold swiftly. In fact, terrorist attacks are far more sudden than foreign policy crises, which can develop over months if not years. As a result of this time compression, elites must react in an instant. Opposition elites do not have the luxury of time to appraise the situation and cannot rely on polls to assess the public's reaction to the event. Nor do they have necessarily an easy and by-the-minute access to classified information without which criticism of the government remains difficult.

ELITES, MEDIA, AND PUBLIC OPINION: WHO LEADS THE PACK?

Rallies around the flag in times of foreign policy crises are frequent but they are also ephemeral and not always characterized by massive surges in the president's popularity. Indeed, scholars have often chosen to consider rallies around the flag and spikes in the president's approval ratings as one and the same (Hetherington and Nelson 2003; Kam and Ramos 2008). Whereas a sudden surge in approval ratings can indicate the presence of a rally around the president within the general population, it does not necessarily indicate a rally within the political elite. Nor is it absolutely clear whether one follows from the other, though Brody goes some way into explaining how the two might interact.

George Herbert Walker Bush and his son provide an interesting case in point. In 1991, during the First Gulf War, the elder Bush enjoyed an 82 per cent approval rating in the polls, up from 64 per cent before the launch of Operation Desert Storm. His son enjoyed an even more impressive rise in his approval rating in the midst of the second Gulf War – from 51 per cent before the launch of Operation Iraqi Freedom to 86 per cent after the start of the war.[14] The two presidents, however, received a markedly different support from the Senate. Whereas 77 senators voted in favour of military action against Iraq in 2002 (and 23 against), only 53 senators approved the use of force some ten years before (against 47).

Beyond the semantic, what distinguishes a rally from a mere show of support remains debatable. How much of a surge should there be in the polls? How many members of Congress or any assembly of representatives should support the president or the government? Admittedly each and everyone can come up with thresholds. Perhaps the answers to these questions are better left to spin doctors. Let us simply acknowledge the fact that rallies differ in size and magnitude, and that public opinion and political elites will not necessarily offer a similar support.

Crucial, however, is the behaviour of mainstream opposition parties. Whereas surges in approval ratings are not uncommon, support from opposition elites is rare. After all, the confrontation between the government and the opposition is an essential aspect of party politics, a sort of default mode for elites. A show of support from the opposition elite, when it does happen, has tremendous symbolic and political value if, as Brody suggested, the elite's behaviour determines that of the general population. Hence, the importance of understanding the mechanism by which the political elite ceases, at least temporarily, to criticize the government.

Brody's contribution to understanding elite behaviour in the midst of fast-breaking international crises underlines the importance of the flow and distribution of information among different sets of actors including government, opposition, media, and public opinion. One of the essential points he raises is that when a crisis erupts elites need to react fast, a point made particularly clear in Charles F. Hermann's definition of a crisis: "a situation that (1) threatens high-priority goals of the decision-making unit, (2) restricts the amount of time available for response before the decision is transformed, and (3) surprises the members of the decision-making unit by its occurrence" (in Vasquez 1996, 192).

Despite this time constraint, governmental elites have an edge. By controlling the flow of information, the government is able, at least temporarily, to entice the support of the other actors, crucially that of the opposition. In other words, *ceteris paribus*, crisis situations favour the government by making it difficult for elites and media to dissent.

There are different degrees of threat, time constraints, and surprise depending on the type of crisis. Yet, as Boin et al. point out, "serious threats that do not pose immediate problems – think of climate change or future pension deficits – do not induce a widespread sense of crises" (2005, 3). Terrorism, unlike global warming, poses an immediate problem and does not allow for much time to react. Brody's argument is relevant here. By controlling the availability of sensitive information, the government is able to acquire the support of the opposition, the media, and of course the general public.

A rally depends on a chain of reactions between governmental elites, opposition elites, media outlets, and public opinion. The question Brody raises is whether the reaction of one of these groups sets in motion the reaction of the other ones and ultimately triggers a rally. Some suggest that the mechanism is circular and that much like a driver looking in the rear-view mirror before making a decision, the government will first evaluate the mood of the population. Kull and Ramsay, for instance, argue that policy-makers and elites are constrained by their perception or misperception of what the public deems acceptable (in Nacos et al. 2000, 95). The theory that "leaders follow masses" is based on the assumption that "societal interests shape the behavior of governments and therefore of states, because rational politicians adapt to the interests of society in order to assure reelection and stay in power" (Schuster and Maier 2006, 228). In other words, the government acts as a "transmission belt" (Moravcsik 1997, 518). John F. Kennedy's attitude during the 1962 Cuba Missile Crisis is a case in point. He chose to follow public opinion, which according to Gallup polls conducted at the time, was slightly in favour of tough actions against Castro's regime. In addition the Senate, including the opposition, also favoured a tough approach. With elections looming, the president chose the blockade and saw his job-rating rise sharply (Russett 1990, 36).[15] In that case, however, the crises lasted a couple of weeks and JFK could afford to wait for polls to come in.

Then again public opinion, no matter how vocal it is on issues of foreign policy, will not always be able to impact foreign policy. The 2003 invasion of Iraq is a good example. Most governments that supported the US military plan did so amid popular backing for a peaceful solution.

The question of who leads and who follows during critical times is complex. While foreign policy unfold over weeks, terrorist attacks are sudden. Government and opposition elites must react in an instant, leaving little time for the opposition to appraise the situation and gather information. Thus, siding with the government is the most likely reaction, at least in the short term. The same holds for the media. In-depth background information on the perpetrators might not be available, making the media dependent on what the government feeds them. Iyengar and Kinder (1987) suggest that they can influence the public in matters of foreign and security policy, and all things related to symbolic politics, but that they cannot on their own change attitudes. During tense periods such as terrorist crises, journalists are also likely to back the government in order to preserve their privileged relationship with the government or simply to avoid being accused of disloyalty (Norris et al. 2003).[16]

The debate is complex and far from over but there are reasons to believe that during terrorist crises the elite is leading the pack (at least in the short-run), and the media and general population have jumped on the bandwagon. Unable to access crucial information, the opposition is likely to support the government and thereby trigger a rally within other segments of society.

We turn now to the likely determinant of elite behaviour in critical times, namely the national interest.

THE PATRIOTIC IMPERATIVE

The rational choice school of thought posits that party behaviour reflects a preference or possibly a combination of preferences between basically three objectives: vote seeking, office seeking, and policy seeking. Yet historical examples, some presented earlier in the text, suggest that these preferences apply only to ordinary times.

Critical or extraordinary times generally make these electoral objectives less prevalent in the minds of our elites and give rise to another concern, namely the *raison d'état*. Faced with a foreign policy crisis, the political elite must then decide whether to think in terms of what is best for its party or best for the country, which might not necessarily be one and the same, particularly for opposition elites. Yet time and again mainstream political elites rally in support of their government, even if only for a brief period, to defend the national interest. We are reminded of Edmund Burke's definition of parties: "a body of men united, for promoting by their joint endeavours the national interest." Yet despite its capacity to bridge political differences and rally people, the notion of the national interest remains elusive. We all have an idea of what it means but would be hard-pressed to define it in precise terms.

The national interest is first and foremost a concept used by proponents of the realist school of thought in international relations to make sense of foreign policy-making in an environment that is anarchic and conflictual by nature, and in which countries are in a permanent state of insecurity (Smouts, Battistella, and Vennesson 2003). The national interest is influenced by the cultural context and political traditions, and thus each country is likely to have a slightly different take on what its national interest is (Morgenthau in Vasquez 1996). Yet there is a common denominator, at least among countries sharing similar cultures and values, which Hans Morgenthau captures in the following excerpt:

> In a world where a number of sovereign nations compete with and oppose each other for power, the foreign policies of all nations must necessarily refer to their survival as their minimum requirements. Thus all nations do what they cannot help but do: protect their physical, political, and external identity against encroachments by other nations ... Taken in isolation, the determination of its content in a concrete situation is relatively simple; for it encompasses the integrity of the nation's territory, of its political institutions, and of its culture." (in Vasquez 1996, 147–8)

Morgenthau goes on to suggest that "bipartisanship in foreign policy, especially in times of war, has been most easily achieved in the promotion of these minimum requirements of the national interest" (in Vasquez 1996, 148). Mueller (1973, 209) makes a similar point when he describes the type of event likely to bring political elites – and the general public – together. Clearly, most of the events Mueller refers to (Berlin 1948, the first Soviet atomic test 1949, Cuba 1962) would fall under the category "threats on physical, political, and external identity" of the United States – and other countries, for that matter.[17]

The notion of national interest and more exactly of threats thereon conjures up images of tanks crossing borders, sabre-rattling rhetoric by foreign leaders, or the occasional and more entertaining shoe-banging at the United Nations' General Assembly. Yet the national interest encompasses other threats besides those related to foreign policy crises. Shortly before becoming President Bush's national security adviser, Condoleezza Rice remarked that the national interest in the post–Cold War era must encompass conventional and unconventional threats, such as terrorism (Rice 2000). The idea that terrorism can threaten the survival of a state is still hard to fathom. Far-fetched scenarios involving the use of nuclear devices by terrorist groups have perhaps clouded our judgment one way or the other. Let us, however, bear in mind that the Tupamaros hardly relied on any fancy weapons to bring down democracy in Uruguay.[18]

Terrorism might not necessarily threaten the territorial integrity or the existence of democratic institutions, but it is a negation of the state's authority and monopoly of violence on its own territory. After all, homeland security is first and foremost about securing the borders and the territory against terrorist actions. David and Gagnon point out, "Terrorism reasserted the territorial dimension of national security" (2007, 1).[19]

More importantly, terrorism encroaches on people's daily life. I refer here to what Amitai Etzioni calls the "primacy of life," that "is the recognition that all people have an interest in and right to security, understood to include freedom from deadly violence, maiming, and torture" (2007, 1). Put differently, the national interest encompasses a human security dimension as well: "The condition under which most people, most of the time, are able to go about their lives, venture onto the street, work, study, and participate in public life (politics included), without acute fear of being killed or injured – without being terrorized" (Etzioni 2007, 2).

The security of a state is what makes it possible for its citizens to pursue their private interests (Smouts et al. 2003). Thus, political elites are likely to consider that the national interest encompasses terrorist threats as much as diplomatic and military threats. If and when the national security and more precisely the primacy of life is being threatened, the patriotic imperative is likely to overpower the partisan spirit. The frequent rallies around the flag following military or diplomatic crises suggests that a comparable phenomenon is likely to take place within mainstream political elites following terrorist acts. The logic should be similar. Political elites will stick together when the nation is under attack or is facing a threat. Crises threatening the interest of a country should not offer much room to manoeuvre. Parties are likely to think in terms of the national interest and thus offer a unified front. Hence the first hypothesis:

Hypothesis 1: Acts of terrorism cause mainstream opposition parties to rally in support of the government.

THE MAGNITUDE-REPETITION MODEL

Not all diplomatic or military crises trigger rallies and arguably the same is true for terrorist crises. The support given by the opposition to the government is not automatic and depends on a series of factors. I suggest that in the case of terrorist attacks, the reaction of the political elite depends to a large extent on two variables: the magnitude of the terrorist act in terms of fatalities, and the repetition of these acts over time. The magnitude-repetition model presented here is completed by a number of secondary variables likely to influence party and elite behaviour. Each primary and secondary variable presented below introduces a new hypothesis on the reaction of political elites to terrorist acts.

CASUALTIES AND TRENDS

Doughery and Pfaltzgraff remind us that "it is difficult to give operational meaning to the concept of national interest" (1981, 125). Obviously, not all terrorist acts result in a genuine menace on human security. Whereas human tragedy is always a likely outcome of any terrorist action, more often than not the end result will rarely raise an eyebrow among politicians. The impact on human security and on the ability of people to go about their life must be manifest to elicit a reaction. The number of fatalities, much like battle-deaths in war, is a particularly relevant indication of how serious the terrorist crisis is and one to which political elites are likely to pay attention.

Terrorism is a tragedy, and the human tragedy is quintessential to the way elites and other segments of society react. Terrorism is what Mark Juergensmeyer calls "performance violence" (2002, 3), an act of communication meant to affect the public. The more lives are threatened or taken, the more people are affected and the deeper the crisis.

Acts of terrorism are essentially rated according to their destructiveness or lethality. Media are particularly sensitive to this aspect, with tabloids and quality newspapers alike splashing their front pages with deaths counts, and news networks doing very much the same with their news banners. Societies, at least in the Western world, have come to evaluate the newsworthiness of terrorist attacks by the numbers of victims, which after all is the way most catastrophes are evaluated. The total number of casualties is a proxy for the severity of the attack. In fact, the literature on conflict often considers casualties as the most salient cost of conflict. Thus, the impact of casualty rates and casualty trends on political behaviour and decision making is nothing new. Essentially, the longer and deadlier the crisis becomes, the less people are ready to support their government (Gartner and Segura 1998; Gartner, Segura, and Barratt 2004; Boettcher and Cobb 2006; Gartner 2008). The rate at which the bodies of US soldiers were flown out of Vietnam accounts to a large extent for the growing unpopularity of the war and the decision to cease America's involvement in that conflict (Mueller 1973; Zaller 1992). The same applies for the post-9/11 military operation in Iraq (Gartner 2008).

A similar logic is likely to apply to terrorist crises. The response of mainstream political elites to terrorist acts should depend to a large extent on two variables: the magnitude of the act (measured by the number of fatalities) and the repetition of the acts (measured by the number of previous terrorist events). For instance, opposition parties and elites should be less inclined to openly criticize the government when an event has high casualty rates. In those cases, one would expect parties to think in terms of the national interest rather than particular interests, and thus offer a unified front. However, the magnitude of the crisis is just part of the story. Just like the duration of a military conflict affects the behaviour of elites, we expect the repetition of terrorist acts to have a significant influence on elites' behaviour. Those in charge of governing the country are expected to limit the occurrence of terrorist acts. If they fail, those in the opposition who wish to replace them in government will likely criticize them. The duration of the crisis, that is the failure to end the crisis, will activate the partisan (electoral) interest and encourage opposition parties to break away from the rally. Put differently, rallies have an expiry date. Mainstream opposition parties will likely be patient when the government faces its first terrorist acts and therefore be supportive. However, this support will fade if terrorist acts are repeated. In other words, more fatalities can mean less support if the acts continue. The magnitude-repetition model suggests the two following hypotheses:

Hypothesis 2: Political parties and elites are more likely to rally around the flag as the terrorist act causes a larger number of fatalities.

Hypothesis 3: The repeated occurrence of acts of terror under a same government (and same mandate) makes a rally around the flag less likely.[20]

RALLYING AROUND THE STATE

Although the magnitude and repetition variables might account to a large extent for the reaction of the mainstream political elites, other secondary variables are likely to play a role as well. First among these potentially influential variables is the target of the attack, particularly when the gun sight is pointed at a representative of the state. Obviously corporatism beyond political divides might render members of the political elite particularly sensitive to acts targeting one of their own and as a result more susceptible to rally.

If rallying around the flag means rallying around its symbols and representatives, then political elites will likely rally promptly when one of their own is targeted because of his or her position within the state apparatus. One of the main reasons for rallying under such circumstances is the risk of being perceived as disloyal to the country if one abstains from rallying. A terrorist might hide a bomb in a public place with the intention of killing as many bystanders as possible, but the actual target is the wider public, those bewildered and frightened television viewers and newspapers readers. With attacks on public officials and other state representatives, the logic is slightly different. Here too terrorists attempt to scare many, but their choice of a state target reveals another objective: to demonstrate that they can target living embodiments of the state and what it stands for, like law and order. Put differently, terrorists are usually unable to conquer land or aim at the territorial integrity of a state, but they can strike at its human representatives. An act aimed at such a symbol challenges the government's authority, especially its monopoly of physical force on the national territory.

The necessity to appear loyal should be particularly strong when the state is targeted, as disloyalty or perceived disloyalty in times of crises can be severely reprimanded by the voters. For instance, Regens, Gaddie, and Lockerbie (1995) demonstrated that members of Congress who voted against America's entry into World War II had a lower probability of re-election than those who voted in favour.[21]

The fourth hypothesis follows:

Hypothesis 4: *Ceteris paribus*, terrorist acts aimed at symbols of the state are more likely to trigger a rally around the flag.

THE THREAT FROM WITHIN
VERSUS THE THREAT FROM ABROAD

If the target matters, then arguably the perpetrators identities could also influence the reaction of the political elite. Attacks coming from abroad could be perceived as more threatening to the national interest than attacks originating from within. The political elite might perceive such an attack as not only a menace on human security but also as a threat on the national interest in the traditional realist sense of the word. The likelihood that foreign terrorists might be supported financially and logistically by foreign states reinforces the sense of threat. Moreover, terrorist acts perpetrated by foreigners might be perceived as targeting the country as a whole, hence making it difficult for political elites to openly disagree with one another. Acts committed by homegrown terrorists, on the other hand, might exacerbate existing divisions within the political elite; for example, disputes might surface if the terrorists are ideologically closer to one or the other party. This suggests the following hypothesis:

Hypothesis 5: When confronting a terrorist attack originating from abroad (or perceived as such) the mainstream elite is more likely to rally.

RALLYING AROUND THE HAWKS?

If the perpetrators' identities influence the behaviour of the political elite, the reverse could be true as well. The party in power might influence terrorist activities. The terrorists could avoid committing acts when the party with the toughest antiterrorist approach is in government. By concentrating their activities when the party with the softest approach is in power, the terrorists might be able to create disunion within the elite and encourage those with a tougher approach to criticize the government for being too lax. For instance, Claude Berrebi and Esteban Klor (2008) argue that in Israel the occurrence of terrorism increases popular support for right-wing parties. Berrebi and Klor (2006) also found that the level of terrorism in Israel is higher when the left is in power. Therefore, it appears possible that in certain cases terror organizations choose the timing and location of an attack because of the expected reaction of the elite.

Some studies suggest that right-wing parties are more hawkish than their left-wing counterparts (Budge and Hofferbert 1990), while others have suggested that the rally effect will be probably strongest for tough actions (Russett 1990). For instance, in the United States the public often sees the Republican Party as better able to deal with issues of national security than the Democratic Party.[22] In 1986, during Ronald Reagan's presidency, 56 per cent of Americans trusted the Republicans to do a better job in dealing with terrorism, whereas only 25 per cent trusted the Democrats (Nacos 2007, 187).[23] The immediate post-9/11 period revealed a similar trend with 50 per cent of Americans trusting the Republican Party to do a better job at handling terrorism and only 31 per cent trusting the Democrats.[24] And in September 2014 a Gallup poll revealed that 55 per cent of respondents believed the Republican Party would do a better job at protecting the country and only 32 per cent believed the Democratic Party would.[25]

This demonstrates a right-wing ownership of security-related issues. The idea is that on some issues parties are more credible than others (Damore 2004). Parties on the Right of the political spectrum are perceived as more capable of dealing with issues of national and public security, whereas parties on the Left are perceived as having more credibility on social and environmental issues. According to the theory of issue ownership, parties and their candidates put forward issues on which they appear more credible than their political adversaries. Voters then use issue ownership as a cue to evaluate parties.[26] This being said, reputations are not frozen and can evolve. Parties can try to steal an issue – what David Damore (2004) calls "issue-trespassing," such as when Democrat Bill Clinton successfully took away from the Republicans the issue of crime during his first presidential campaign (see Holian 2004).[27]

These days, terrorism and security issues are hot commodities on the political and electoral market. Among the policy benefits that voters seek and leaders can promise is security, which of course parties will want to advertise as one of their paramount concern when seeking votes. Berrebi and Klor (2006) have demonstrated that from 1991 to 2003, the Israeli Labour party was forced to be tougher in its policies than Likud, precisely because the latter was perceived by the population as better qualified to deal with terrorism. Thus, left-wing parties might be tempted to appear more credible on issues pertaining to national security by adopting a tougher stance. If both right-wing and left-wing parties adopt similar approaches, the likelihood of a disagreement over the handling of terrorism might diminish. As a result, a right-wing opposition should find it more difficult to criticize a left-wing government for being too soft. This suggests the following hypothesis:

Hypothesis 6: Rallies are not less likely when the Left is in power.[28]

RAILING AGAINST THE MAINSTREAM ELITE

So far I have considered mainstream parties only. But what of radical parties and fringe elites? Do they have a different rationale when it comes to partisan interests versus national interest? The American Left, particularly its intellectuals, were quick to point out that the World Trade Center and the Pentagon as symbols of capitalism and modern warfare got what they deserved. Even Reverend Pat Robertson, a conservative Southern Baptist and hardly Noam Chomsky's soulmate, was initially as critical as Gore Vidal and company, though for entirely different reasons; Robertson saw the attacks as a sign of God's displeasure with American "sins," such as abortion and same-sex marriage.

Much like the socialists of yesteryear who railed against the bourgeoisie's penchant for war, today's radical elites are likely to follow a different logic than their mainstream counterparts. It is not at all impossible that they will seize the opportunity created by terrorist attacks to criticize not only the government but also the whole political system. Unlike mainstream elites, radical elites are unlikely to be deterred by the prospect of looking disloyal to the state. Hence my seventh hypothesis:

Hypothesis 7: Radical parties do not rally around the flag following acts of terror and are on the contrary outspoken in their criticism toward the government.

THE 9/11 EFFECT

The events of 9/11 profoundly influenced international affairs, but to what extent did they influence domestic politics in the United States and in Europe? Following the fateful events of 2001, political elites across the Western world rallied in support of the American president.[29] This compassion eventually subsided, yet 9/11 left a scar: national unity would be perceived as crucial in the struggle against terrorism. Mainstream opposition elites might feel that they have less room for manoeuvre than prior to 9/11, and that to avoid being lambasted as disloyal, they must rally. This suggests the final hypothesis:

Hypothesis 8: Mainstream parties have a greater probability of rallying in the post-9/11 period.

CONCLUSION

This chapter challenges the notion that the behaviour of political parties is always determined by partisan interests and the electoral agenda, and suggests that during dramatic events when the national interest is being threatened, the patriotic imperative might prove too much to brush aside, particularly for mainstream opposition parties. The rally-around-the-flag phenomenon is traditionally associated with events such as military and diplomatic crises. I have argued here that during terrorist crises the need to defend the security of its citizens is a powerful incentive for the elite to support the government. The magnitude-repetition model suggests that elites will be likely influenced by the magnitude of the attack and the repetition of terrorist acts. I also suggest that secondary variables, such as the target of the attack or the origin of the perpetrators, are also likely to influence the reaction.

Next, I take up Michael Shermer's advice that "there is only one surefire method of proper pattern recognition, and that is science" (2011, 62) by describing in the following chapter the data and method of analysis used to test my hypotheses, and presenting my findings.

4

Politicians in the Aftermath
of Terrorist Attacks

A Statistical Analysis of the Rally-around-the-Flag
Phenomenon in Five Democracies

Our government has kept us in a perpetual state of fear – kept us in a
continuous stampede of patriotic fervor – with the cry of grave national
emergency. Always there has been some terrible evil at home or some
monstrous foreign power that was going to gobble us up if we did not
blindly rally behind it by furnishing the exorbitant funds demanded. Yet,
in retrospect, these disasters seem never to have happened, seem never to
have been quite real.

 General Douglas MacArthur, address to the annual stockholders meeting,
Sperry Rand Corporation, 30 July 1957[1]

Cold-blooded mass murder requires cold-blooded analysis, the careful
selection of words to convey precise meaning uncluttered by emotional
rhetoric.

Brian Jenkins, *The Organization Men*

INTRODUCTION

Ariel Merari once remarked that "terrorism is a study area which is
very easy to approach but very difficult to cope with in a scientific
sense" (in Schmid and Jongman 1988, 179). Of particular concern to
him was the lack of "precise and extensive factual knowledge" necessary for any kind of scientific inquiry into the field of terrorism.

The first extensive databases on terrorist events – the Pinkerton Global Intelligence Services (PGIS) database and the RAND database – were launched in the early 1970s but were until very recently available only to a select few. This meant that a majority of studies on terrorism had to be qualitative.

My own research is based on a two-step approach integrating quantitative and qualitative methods of analysis. At the core of this study is an original dataset on terrorist events and the reaction of political elites to them. The purpose of the quantitative analysis is to establish through both descriptive and inferential statistics a pattern of behaviour among mainstream political elites, and indicate whether these trends and findings can be generalized outside of the sample. The qualitative approach is then used to complement, through in-depth case studies, and nuance the statistical findings.

REACTION TO TERRORISM IN DEMOCRACIES

The study of the reaction of political parties and their elites to terrorism implies certain restrictions. First, political parties must be free to oppose their government. The rally, if they choose to rally, can therefore not be forced upon them by the government or any other authority. The choice to rally must always be theirs. Therefore countries selected for this study have been stable democracies for at least the last thirty years. Autocracies, even those operating under the veil of democratic institutions, cannot be considered. Second, terrorism must be nothing new for the selected countries, for there is no point in studying the reaction to terrorism if the phenomenon is absent or of such low intensity that it remains unnoticed by the elites. Finally, these countries must be relatively peaceful and cannot be in the midst of a civil war or any other enduring military crisis. In other words, ordinary politics as defined in chapter 2 must be the rule. These restrictions mean that neither Israel nor Russia nor India were included in this study.

The countries that meet these criteria are France, Germany, Spain, the United Kingdom, and the United States. They have been stable democracies for the past thirty years, with political parties that are free to oppose the government.[2] Although terrorism might have been a more acute phenomenon in recent years in some countries (e.g., Spain and France) than in others (e.g., Germany), it remains a recurring problem for all of them.

Finally, this study is also limited in time. Of particular concern was the need to avoid any overlap with the Cold War, a period that could have influenced the reaction of political elites. For instance, the Soviet Union and its allies were often blamed for providing support to terrorist groups, such as Palestinian and Western European groups. Among others, Claire Sterling in *The Terror Network* (1981) fuelled the notion that Russia conspired to destroy the West through an international network of terrorists. Although proof of this support is murky at best, it is not improbable that certain segments of the political elite, particularly right-wing politicians, gave credence to this accusation. As a result, the period under scrutiny will be stretching from the end of the Cold War in 1990 to 2006.[3] The post-9/11 period during which the five countries had troops on the ground for prolonged military operations in Iraq and Afghanistan is also potentially problematic. Again, in order to differentiate the effects of terrorism from other foreign and security-related crises, overlaps with wars must be limited. As pointed out in chapter 2, the world is never at peace but the period between Operation Desert Storm (1991) and the 9/11 attacks represent a relatively more peaceful period for France, Germany, Spain, the United Kingdom, and the United States.

SELECTING A DATABASE FOR TERRORIST EVENTS

An increasing number of databases on terrorism are available, however, none of them provide information on the reaction of political elites to terrorist events. Thus the dataset necessary for this project had to be created by using an already existing database of terrorist incidents and adding the data on the reaction of political elites.

The selection of a database on terrorist events is a delicate matter not the least because a great deal of what is included in it depends on what the original developer considered to be terrorist in nature and intent. Thus, by choosing a certain database we also accept the definition of terrorism that comes with it (see chapter 2). The definition used will in turn have an impact on the number of observations that are being recorded. Ideally a large number of observations is preferable but a dataset that is too inclusive is also less desirable as it tends to include cases that might only be remotely connected to terrorist activities (e.g., criminal activities and street protest). The objective remains the study of the reaction to terrorism, not to political violence in general.

After careful examination of what several databases had to offer, the Terrorism Knowledge Base (TKB) developed by the RAND Corporation in co-operation with the Oklahoma City National Memorial Institute for the Prevention of Terrorism (MIPT) was selected. The TKB emerged from a database of terrorist events developed and maintained by a team of researchers at the RAND Corporation from the early 1970s onwards, among them respected scholars such as Brian Jenkins and Bruce Hoffman. This chronology was used exclusively by RAND experts until the end of the 1990s, then in 2001 the project was given a new impetus with a grant from the MIPT. The resulting MIPT Terrorism Knowledge Base is divided into two datasets:

- The RAND Terrorism Chronology for incidents collected between 1968 and 1997 includes cases of international terrorism; that is, acts perpetrated by individuals coming from abroad to strike their target, domestic targets associated with a foreign state, or attacks on airline passengers or equipment.
- The RAND-MIPT Terrorism Incident Database, which records domestic and international terrorist incidents from 1998 onwards. Domestic terrorism is here defined as incidents perpetrated by local nationals against a purely domestic target.

The TKB was constructed on the premise that not every act related to political violence should be regarded as terrorist and that "terrorism is defined by the nature of the act, not by the identity of the perpetrators." This means that a criminal act perpetrated by a known terrorist organization would not have found its place in the database. Equally important, an exchange of fire between a terrorist organization and a regular army would not have been considered terrorist.[4]

SELECTING A DATA SOURCE FOR REACTIONS

Neither TKB nor any other existing databases on terrorist events include information on the reaction of political elites. This information is, however, available in most major media outlets such as national and international newspapers. Choosing media outlets as a source is not only practical but also logical in view of the symbiosis that exists between terrorism and media.

Political elites' reactions to terrorist acts have been gathered using national newspapers. For each of the five countries chosen for this study one national newspaper has been selected: *Le Monde* for France, *Frankfurter Allgemeine* for Germany, *El País* for Spain, *The Times* for the United Kingdom, and the *New York Times* for the United States. These five newspapers are renowned and respected sources of information, thus concerns with their impartiality and accuracy in reporting should be minimal. It should be noted that reactions reported by these newspapers are often based on press releases from the parties themselves. Furthermore, in order to avoid reporting bias, opinion editorials have not been taken into account. Finally, a limited review of other leading national newspapers in France and the United States has been carried out to further verify that reactions are reported accurately and check for any discrepancies. The analysis of the coverage of thirty randomly selected terrorist events (fifteen in France and fifteen in the United States) in the database by four additional newspapers – *Libération* and *Le Figaro* for France; *Washington Post* and USA *Today* for the United States – indicates that the coverage of the elite's reaction is very similar to that of the selected papers (*Le Monde* and the *New York Times*). All these newspapers seem to report the same reactions, even though their interpretation of these reactions sometimes differs.

CREATING THE DATABASE

After limiting the countries and period under consideration, another limitation had to be set in: the magnitude of the terrorist events. Indeed a preliminary survey revealed that most low-magnitude incidents, that is those causing a minimal number of wounded, simply did not register on the media's radar and did not elicit any reaction from the political elite. Including these acts would have brought no valuable information and would have lengthened considerably the process of data gathering. Therefore, it was decided that acts that had caused no fatalities and wounded fewer than six people would not be included in the database.

In chapter three, I defined a rally around the flag as a movement of widespread support in favour of the government from the mainstream political elite (crucially from the opposition parties), from the general public, and from most media outlets. It does not help determine, however, what qualifies as a rally within the political elite. What we need here is an operational definition for this group. For the purpose of this study a rally around the flag within the political elite is said to exist whenever the mainstream opposition parties support the government. This support can either be explicit (i.e., support made public by a spokesperson or a leading figure of the opposition) or implicit (i.e., silence implying consent). A rally involves at best a truce in party politics, or total support of the government, and at least an absence of criticism on the part of mainstream parties as far as the government's reaction to the terrorist act and to the issue of national security is concerned.[5] In order to constitute a rally, this support must last a minimum of five consecutive days following the terrorist event.

I assume, like Richard Brody (1991), that silence implies consent. In other words, if the elite remains silent, I consider it as an instance of rallying.[6] Silence might not have the symbolic weight of a public declaration of support, but it indicates that the opposition does not intend to argue with the government. Silence might be motivated by reluctant support or a need to appear loyal, but it is still a sign of support. Parties always have the choice to remain critical and signal their disagreement with how the government handles national security–related issues such as terrorism. The absence of criticism, that is a deliberate decision by the opposition to stay mute and to break from traditional partisan politics, is in itself sufficiently unusual to be considered as a show of support. Although different from a jingoistic rally, silence represents consent, a sign that a common purpose, in that case the national interest, must prevail.[7] Even in the immediate aftermath of 9/11 not all members of the US Congress chose to voice their support of the government;

many simply decided to stay mute and avoid partisan politics for the good of the country. In other words, regardless of whether the support is explicit or implicit, what really matters is that political criticism is subdued.[8]

Put somewhat differently, there is a rally when none of the mainstream opposition party either through a leading figure or spokesperson blames the government for the act or makes public criticism of its handling of national security. Furthermore, the decision to focus on the first five days following an act is not arbitrary. Indeed, preliminary research suggested that elites react very soon after the event, sometimes only a few hours after the attack took place, and that the bulk of reactions to a terrorist act appear during the five days following the act. Important terrorist acts will typically fall off the front pages of the newspapers by the third or fourth day. By the fifth day, parties have taken a stance and are either supporting or criticizing the government. Of course rallies have an expiry date, but studying the duration of rallies is not the objective here.[9]

For each act recorded in the database, I carried out a content analysis of elite discourse. I looked at how mainstream political parties reacted and determined whether there was criticism from the opposition, expressed either by a spokesperson or a leading figure of the party – isolated criticisms from backbenchers where not taken into account. In other words, I have not been looking for explicit declaration of support but for explicit criticism. Furthermore, since the present study deals exclusively with the reaction of political elites at the national or federal level – and their support or lack thereof for the government – criticisms voiced by political representatives at the provincial, regional, or local level were not taken into account. Criticisms from trade union leaders were not considered either.[10]

To understand how the mainstream opposition behaves in the absence of terrorism, I have also compiled the reactions of political elites five days prior each of the terrorist attack included in the database. The proximity to the terrorist act means that all variables in the comparison group – except for those related to the terrorist act itself – are the same. Yet one should remember that this study is concerned primarily with party behaviour during critical times. Therefore, this compilation of reactions during ordinary times prior to a terrorist attack provides a benchmark and allows some simple comparison. The dynamics of behaviour are likely to be very different. For instance, silence in the five days prior to the act does not have necessarily the same meaning as during the five days after the act. Perhaps the silence of the elite before the attack is for other reason, such as summer break in Parliament, absence of events worth debating, and so on. Whereas in the aftermath of a terrorist act the issue of national security is likely to be prevalent – sometimes to the point of being the only issue discussed by the elite – during a "normal" period national security will be just one issue among many others.

A FEW WORDS ON THE QUALITATIVE ANALYSIS

The qualitative analysis will focus on two sets of cases: deviant or outlier cases, that is cases where the reaction of the mainstream political elite did not conform to expectation with regard to magnitude and repetition; and cases outside of the period studied in the quantitative analysis. This approach makes it possible to uncover other variables. Alexander George and Andrew Bennett remind us that "statistical analysis can help identify outliers or deviant cases, and case studies can then investigate why these cases are deviant, perhaps leading to the identification of omitted variables" (2005, 35). In order to determine which cases are deviant, I create an ideal-type model based on the magnitude-repetition model presented earlier, and which rests on the assumption that the behaviour of mainstream political elites depends primarily on two variables: magnitude and repetition of terrorist acts. It implies four different scenarios (see table 1, page 82):

1 Low repetition and high magnitude: the opposition is expected to support the government.
2 High repetition and high magnitude: the opposition is expected to offer no support to the government.
3 High repetition and low magnitude: the opposition is unlikely to support the government particularly because of the low magnitude.
4 Low repetition and low magnitude: no reaction from the opposition or from the government is expected, and the media are

Table 1
The impact of magnitude and repetition on the reaction of the opposition

	Low magnitude	High magnitude
High repetition	Unlikely support	No support
Low repetition	No reaction	Support

unlikely to report the act. In other words, the terrorist act simply does not register on the radar.

Of course this ideal-type model is not a carbon copy of the reality but rather a simplified schematic of how mainstream political elites are likely to react in the event of a terrorist attack.

Of particular interest in chapter 5 are instances that do not conform to the ideal-type model; for example, event X scored high in terms of magnitude and low in terms of repetition, but failed to trigger a rally. In order to determine which cases conform or do not conform to the ideal-type model, I assign a threshold for the magnitude variable and another one for the repetition variable. I rely here on the thresholds used in the logistic regression presented in the appendix:

- Two fatalities or fewer are considered an instance of *low magnitude*, whereas three fatalities or more are considered a case of *high magnitude*.
- When five acts in a row or more occurred before the act being considered for analysis, we consider it an instance of *high repetition*, and if four acts or fewer occurred before we consider it an instance of *low repetition*.

Obviously the division is slightly arbitrary but a cut-off point is needed.

The qualitative analysis and case studies serve many purposes. As George and Bennett point out, case studies have the "ability to accommodate complex causal relations such as equifinality, complex interactions effects, and path dependency" (2005, 22). A qualitative approach makes it possible to analyze the effect of other variables which could not be tested in the statistical analysis. Furthermore, a qualitative approach, particularly the use of detailed case studies, makes it possible to analyze the interaction between government and opposition and the evolution of their attitude, and assess the extent of the rally; that is, public or silent support from the opposition. This approach makes it also possible to broaden the range of observations by analyzing the reaction to events outside the selected period. Historical depth can provide useful insights, particularly if there is an element of path dependency. Finally, through this approach, I intend to test hypothesis 7 (page 72) and address the role of radical elites. In the end, the qualitative analysis might confirm most of the statistical results, but it might also nuance some of these results.

This qualitative analysis will focus exclusively on France and its experience with terrorism from 1980 to 2015. The decision to select France rather than any of the other four countries studied is threefold: France has had the most wide-ranging experience of terrorist groups in terms of diversity (revolutionaries, separatists, religious, etc.); the ideological difference between right- and left-wing parties is wide; and radical parties and elites are forces to be reckoned with.[11]

STATISTICAL FINDINGS

Out of the nearly two hundred terrorist attacks analyzed here, 22 per cent do not register on the media radar and do not initiate any public reactions on the part of the spokespeople or leaders of the mainstream parties (see table 2). Part of the explanation for the lack of interest (and of coverage) for certain terrorist acts lies with their magnitude in terms of fatalities. Terrorist acts with low human costs are unlikely to elicit much interest from media outlets, unless they involve public figures, such as presidents or members of governments, in which case they might become more "newsworthy." On the other hand, the selected newspapers almost never ignore acts causing three fatalities or more (see table 3). Another explanation points to the type of target. The newspapers report attacks against state targets 91 per cent of the time, but report attacks on other targets only 72 per cent of the time.[12] Finally, country-specific reporting attitudes may also play a role. France and Spain have higher reporting numbers (89 per cent and 98 per cent respectively) of all terrorist acts reported in the selected newspapers. In comparison, rates in the other three countries range from 55 per cent in Germany and 57 per cent in the United Kingdom to 68 per cent in the United States. To some extent, Spain's high reporting rate is to be expected in a country where terrorism, particularly Basque-related, has been at the centre stage of public life for the better part of the last forty-five years. Germany, on the other hand, has been spared terrorist acts since the late 1980s; consequently its media might have been less interested in pursuing terrorist-related stories.

As postulated in hypothesis 1 (page 66), political elites tend not to criticize their government in the aftermath of terrorist attacks. More precisely, table 2 shows that following reported acts of terrorism, political elites have been critical of the government only 16 per cent of the time – or rallied 84 per cent of the time. It is worth remembering that this 84 per cent rallying rate includes cases when the elite remained silent throughout the five-day period under scrutiny and did not explicitly support the government. As discussed, silence might not imply a massive and enthusiastic rally; yet by putting its criticisms on hold, the opposition indicates that it supports the government. This point is made more apparent by the striking difference between the behaviour of the political elite before and after the attack. Table 2 suggests that during the "normal" five-day period before the terrorist act, political elites in the five countries criticize the government 67 per cent of the time, compared to 16 per cent after an attack. Prior to attacks, the elite is particularly critical in the United States (82 per cent) and Spain (76 per cent), whereas it is relatively less disapproving in the United Kingdom (53 per cent). This suggests that the advent of terrorism has an impact on parties' attitude. Yet as I remarked earlier, these are two very distinctive periods. The comparison provides merely an idea of the contrast. But it is inherently difficult to compare an "ordinary" period to an "extraordinary" one. The rules of behaviour are not the same, and the nature of the political debate itself changes dramatically. Thus, I am reluctant to read too much in this statistical difference.

Table 2 also reveals that in the aftermath of a terrorist act, French and Spanish political elites rally less often than their German, Amer-

Table 2
The rallying phenomenon

Country	Total number of attacks	Criticism prior to the attacks (%)[1]	Number of news-paper[2] report attacks[3] (and %)	Number of reported attacks with criticism (and %)
France	36	64	32 (89)	7 (22)
Germany[4]	11	73	6 (55)	0 (0)
Spain	59	76	58 (98)	12 (21)
Spain (no Pact)[5]	33	82	32 (97)	11 (34)
United Kingdom	53	53	30 (57)	2 (7)
United States	22	82	15 (68)	1 (7)
Total[6]	181	67	141 (78)	22 (16)

Notes:

1 For each terrorist act, the occurrence of criticism from mainstream parties was evaluated during the five days preceding the attack for comparison purposes.

2 Newspapers used to define media reporting are *Le Monde* (France), *Frankfurter Allgemeine* (Germany), *El País* (Spain), *The Times* (United Kingdom), and the *New York Times* (United States).

3 Factors affecting newspapers reporting include targets (state targets are reported 91 per cent of times versus 72 per cent for other targets) and size of the attack (acts with more than two victims are almost never ignored in the media).

4 The sample for Germany is restricted to attacks occurring after 1 January 1993 due to limited access to newspaper archives.

5 Spain (no pact) uses only attacks occurring outside the antiterrorist-pact period (December 2000 to March 2004) during which governing (PP) and opposing parties (PSOE) agreed to present a unified front toward terrorists.

6 Total statistics exclude Spain (no pact).

ican, and British counterparts, with respectively 22 per cent and 21 per cent of reported attacks with criticisms. The context might account for this difference: France and Spain experience more reported terrorists acts than Germany or the United States. As a result, opposition parties in those two countries might be less patient toward their government.[13] The fact that the French and Spanish presses cover terrorism so abundantly makes it easier for political elites in these two countries to be more critical; the issue never vanishes, making it easier for elites to discuss it.

THE MAGNITUDE EFFECT

The findings support hypothesis 2 (page 68). The magnitude of the terrorist act (the number of fatalities) plays an important role in the reaction of the mainstream political elite. The more fatalities there

Table 3
The magnitude effect

	Number[1] of attacks (%)	
	Fewer than 3 deaths	3 or more deaths
Attacks not reported in the press	39 (28)	1 (7)
Attacks without rally (criticism)	20 (14)	1 (7)
Attacks with rally (no criticism)	81 (58)	13 (87)
Total	140 (100)	15 (100)

Note:
1 Attacks in Spain during the antiterrorist-pact period are not included in this analysis in order to control for the artificial rallying effect of the pact.

are, the more rallies and fewer criticisms there are. Table 3 shows that 87 per cent of all terrorist acts causing three fatalities or more trigger a rally in support of the government, whereas among attacks causing fewer than three fatalities, only 58 per cent elicit support for the government. Moreover, giving credence to the motto "if it bleeds it leads," 28 per cent of attacks causing fewer than three deaths are ignored by the media altogether, whereas only 7 per cent of ter-rorist acts causing three or more fatalities are not reported by the media. Among media reported attacks only, 80 per cent of the at-tacks with fewer than three fatalities resulted in rallies, versus 93 per cent for attacks causing three or more deaths.

THE REPETITION EFFECT

As proposed in hypothesis 3 (page 68), terrorism can represent a se-vere test of resilience for a population, but it is also very much a test of aptitude for those in government. If the government cannot maintain order and security, the political opposition will grow im-patient and increasingly critical. Table 4 supports this hypothesis and indicates that following the first three terrorist acts, opposition parties have always supported their government (100 per cent rally-ing rate), but that they were less inclined to do so when the acts are repeated. After attack number eight, the rallying rate drops to 75 per cent, suggesting that the opposition is monitoring the government's

Table 4
The repetition effect

Frequency of attacks[1]	0–3	4–7	8 or more
Attacks leading to rallies / Total number of attacks[2]	28 / 28	17 / 20	48 / 64
Percentage of rallies (%)	100	85	75

Notes:
1 Number of attacks under same government (and same mandate).
2 Attacks in Spain during the antiterrorist-pact period are not included in this analysis in order to control for the artificial rally effect of the pact.

performance and success in the fight against terror. The continuation of attacks makes it possible for an opposition party to criticize its government without the fear of being labelled disloyal.

THE TARGET EFFECT

The findings do not support hypothesis 4 (page 69). The bull's-eye has been placed on state representatives in 31 per cent of the cases (see table 5). However, contrary to expectation, aggregate data for the five countries do not indicate that more rallies occur when the state is targeted by the terrorists. On the contrary, the rallying rate is at 70 per cent when the state is hit and at 86 per cent when other targets are struck. Hypothesis 4 holds for France and the United States where attacks on symbols of the state trigger more rallies (83 per cent and 100 per cent respectively) than attacks on other targets (77 per cent and 92 per cent). This result might not be surprising since France is the embodiment of a centralized state. One would expect French political elites to strongly condemn attacks on its symbols or representatives, or at the very least to refrain from criticizing those in charge of the state. For its part, the United States does not share this Jacobin tradition yet rallies massively around their leaders when the state is targeted. However, the United States has a tradition of strong support for the state when it comes to its military and policing roles, though there is more suspicion, especially on the part of the Republicans, when it comes to its domestic economic role.

Table 5
Target effect

Country	Total number of attacks	Percentage of attacks with state[1] targets	Percentage of reported attacks with rally	
			State targets	Other targets
France	36	7	83	77
Germany[2]	22	3	n/a	100
Spain	59	38	78	81
Spain (no pact)[3]	33	20	58	77
United Kingdom	9	1	100	100
United Kingdom – Ulster	44	7	75	95
United States	22	3	100	92
Total[4]	192	59	70	86

Notes:
1 State targets include government, military, and police.
2 Information regarding rallies is limited to the eleven attacks that took place after 1 Janaury 1993 for the German sample due to limited access to newspaper archives. The total number of attacks and number attacks with state targets, however, include all attacks in Germany from 1990 to 2006.
3 Spain (no pact) uses only attacks occurring outside the antiterrorist-pact period (December 2000– March 2004) during which governing (PP) and opposing parties (PSOE) agreed to present a unified front toward terrorists.
4 Total statistics use France, Germany, Spain, the United Kingdom, United Kingdom–Ulster, and the United States for total number of attacks and number of attacks with state targets. Statistics regarding percentages of attacks with rallies, however, use only attacks outside the pact period in Spain to control for its rallying effect.

THE RIGHT-WING EFFECT

The findings support hypothesis 6 (page 72). From 1990 to 2006, right-wing parties and left-wing parties were in government almost an equal number of years.[14] In the database, 55 per cent of the attacks occurred under a right-wing government. Overall, right-wing parties did not benefit from more rallies – or less criticisms – when they were in government (see table 6). In fact, the rallying rate for the Right and the Left is remarkably similar: right-wing governments' was 84 per cent, 1 percentage point less than for left-wing governments. However, one should be careful in interpreting these overall results as the number of attacks under right-wing governments differs markedly from one country to the other. In addition, right-wing parties in France, the United Kingdom, and the United States bene-

Table 6
The right-wing effect

Country	Total number of attacks	Number of attacks with right-wing party[1] in government (and %)		Percentage of reported attacks with rally	
				Right	Left
France	11	18	(50)	93	67
Germany[2]	36	9	(82)	100	100
Spain	59	54	(92)	77	100
Spain (no pact)[3]	33	28	(85)	59	100
United Kingdom[4]	53	7	(13)	100	93
United States	22	11	(50)	100	88
Total[5]	181	99	(55)	84	85

Notes:
1 Right-wing parties include RPR (and then UMP) and UDF for France; CDU-CSU for Germany; PP for Spain; the Conservative Party for the United Kingdom; and the Republican Party for the United States.
2 Information regarding rallies is limited to the eleven attacks that took place after 1 January 1993 for the Germany sample due to limited public access to newspaper archives.
3 Spain (no pact) uses only attacks occurring outside the antiterrorist pact.
4 Ulster included.
5 Total statistics use France, Germany, Spain, the United Kingdom, and the United States for total number of attacks with state targets. Statistics regarding percentages of attacks with rallies, however, use only attacks outside of the pact period in Spain to control for its rallying effect.

fited from more rallies than their left-wing counterparts, whereas in Spain the Left benefited from more rallies.

THE 9/11 EFFECT

The findings support hypothesis 8 (page 73). The average yearly number of attacks prior to 9/11 was 23.5 (see table 7).[15] In the period that followed 9/11, the average number of attacks for our five countries dropped to 8.2 per year. More importantly, the rallying rate followed a different trend. In the period before 9/11, there were 77 per cent of reported attacks with rally; whereas in the period that followed 9/11, the percentage of rallying increased to 94 per cent. This trend is impressive for France and Spain where the rallying rate increased by 45 points and 16 points respectively. These figures suggest that political elites felt more compelled to unite after the events of 9/11. Of course, 9/11 was unique by most accounts, but these

Table 7
The 9/11 effect

Country	Total number of attacks (>1998)	Average yearly number of attacks		Reported attacks with rally (%)	
		Pre 9/11[1]	Post 9/11	Pre 9/11[1]	Post 9/11
France	17	2.9	1.1	55	100
Germany[2]	2	0.5	0.0	100	100
Spain	57	10.1	3.6	73	89
Spain (no pact)[3]	31	6.1	1.5	55	88
United Kingdom	2	0.3	0.2	100	100
United Kingdom – Ulster	41	8.3	1.9	90	100
United States	12	1.3	1.3	100	100
Total[4]	131	23.5	8.2	77	94

Notes:
1 The pre-9/11 statistics are based on the 1998–2001 period to avoid confounding due to the higher proportion of international attacks in the database prior to 1998. The post-9/11 statistics correspond to the 2001–06 period.
2 Information regarding rallies is limited to the eleven attacks that took place after 1 January 1993 for the Germany sample due to limited public access to newspaper archives.
3 Spain (no pact) uses only attacks occurring outside the antiterrorist pact.
4 Total statistics use France, Germany, Spain, the United Kingdom, and the United States for total number of attacks with state targets. Statistics regarding percentages of attacks with rallies, however, use only attacks outside of the pact period in Spain to control for its rallying effect.

results seem to indicate that the effects of large terrorist crises can cross borders. Both the magnitude of this attack and the perceived proximity of the targeted country and its victims (culturally if not geographically) probably played an essential role.

The events of 9/11 mark a turning point, not least because of the ensuing "war on terror" that saw the United States and its allies embark on two lengthy military operations: Operation Enduring Freedom in Afghanistan from October 2001 to December 2014 and the Iraq War from March 2003 to December 2011. These two wars make it difficult to determine whether rallies are a reaction to a terrorist act or more generally to the ongoing military operations.

THE INTERNATIONAL TERRORISM EFFECT

Table 8 suggests, as hypothesized, that political elites are less critical of their government when the attack is perpetrated by a group orig-

Table 8
The international terrorism effect

	Number[1] of attacks (and %)		
	Domestic	International	Unknown
Attacks not reported in the press	17 (14)	3 (14)	26 (49)
Attacks without rally – criticism	52 (21)	2 (9)	2 (4)
Attacks with rally – no criticism	80 (65)	17 (77)	25 (47)
Total	80 (100)	22 (100)	53 (100)

Note:
1 Attacks in Spain during the antiterrorist-pact period are not included in this analysis in order to control for the artificial rallying effect of the pact.

inating from abroad than when the act is caused by a domestic group. As I discussed, a foreign threat is likely to trigger the same defensive mechanism regardless of whether the threat is military, diplomatic, or terrorist. The fact that attacks perpetrated by terrorists originating from within generate more criticism could also be linked to the duration of the crisis. Domestic groups have often been carrying out their terror campaign for longer periods than groups from the outside. Therefore, cases of domestic terrorism – particularly for groups whose raison d'être is secession of part of the national territory – can be perceived by members of the elite as security issues that have been dragging on for too long and have not been adequately managed by those in government.

MULTIVARIATE ANALYSIS

A logistic regression is used to jointly model the impact of the repetition and magnitude of attacks on the likelihood of witnessing a rally (that of having no open criticism toward the government) in the five days following these attacks. This analysis also controls for the unifying effect of the Spanish pact, whereby the two main parties pledged to support one another in the fight against terrorism, and that of diplomatic and military crises. The type of group perpetrating the attack is also accounted for, thereby providing a control for domestic terrorism. I also include controls for the 9/11 effect and country effects.

Results shown in table 9 confirm that the repetition of acts significantly increases the chances of open criticism toward the government regardless of the magnitude. For events taking place after the initial five, probability of dissention are increased by roughly 22 percentage points compared to the first five events.

The magnitude of the act is, as expected, a unifying factor. As acts cause more victims, rallies are more likely to be observed. An attack causing three or more fatalities translates into an approximate 16 percentage-point increase in the probability of witnessing a rally compared to attacks with two fatalities or less.

The unifying effect of the Spanish pact is important and statistically significant, as one would expect. Acts taking place in Spain during the corresponding period result in a probability of open criticism that is reduced by more than 21 percentage points compared to acts observed during ordinary times.

The probability of rally is 15 per cent less when the group claiming the act is a domestic group. Diplomatic or military crises, as well as the 9/11 effect, are not statistically significantly correlated with the probability of a rally, although both coefficients are positive as expected.

Various robustness checks were performed. Results remained qualitatively the same for potential alternate specifications of the model, including removing country controls, restricting the time period and varying the cut-off points for the magnitude and repetition variables. Conclusions were also stable when removing controls that were not statistically significant, or adding a control variable indicating whether the government was criticized in the five-day period preceding the attack (not statistically significant either).

COUNTRY-SPECIFIC REPORTS

Spain

Of the five countries included in this study, Spain has the highest number of recorded events, the highest percentage of reported events (2 per cent of terrorist acts were not reported by *El País*), and the lowest rallying rate (66 per cent). Even when including the period covered by the antiterrorist pact, whereby the Partido Social-

Table 9
Factors affecting the probability of rally

Variable[1]	Parameter estimate	Probability change[2] (%)	p-value[3]
Intercept	1.48	–	0.27
First five attacks	3.66	22.1	0.003
Pact (Spain)	3.34	21.5	0.004
Magnitude	1.6	16.0	0.045
Domestic	−1.9	−15.4	0.03
Post 9/11	1.23	9.9	0.24
Crisis	0.22	2.0	0.89
France	−1.61	−16.2	0.21
United Kingdom	1.3	10.7	0.34
Spain	−1.21	11.9	0.32

Notes:

1 The repetition variable (the first five attacks) takes value 1 if the attack was one of the first five, and value 0 if the attack was number six or more. The pact (Spain) variable takes value 1 if there was a pact and value 0 if there was no pact. The magnitude variable takes value 0 if there were two or fewer deaths involved in the attack (but at least six were injured) and value 1 if there were three or more fatalities. The domestic variable takes value 1 if the attack was perpetrated by a domestic group and value 0 otherwise. The post 9/11 variable takes value 1 if the attack took place before 9/11 and value 0 if it took place afterwards. The crisis variable takes value 1 if there was a major military or diplomatic crisis at the time of the attack and value 0 otherwise. The France variable takes value 1 if the attack took place in France and value 0 otherwise. The UK variable takes value 1 if the attack took place in the UK and value 0 otherwise. Finally, the Spain variable takes value 1 if the attack took place in Spain and value 0 otherwise.

2 Changes in the probability of a rally are marginal effects calculated from the regression estimates by measuring the average simulated impact of a change in the relevant variable across all observations.

3 N = 141. Model fit: Likelihood ratio test was statistically significant at the 0.0001 level. R-Square = 24 per cent. Adjusted (Nagelkerke) R-Square = 42 per cent. C statistic = 87 per cent.

ista Obrero Español (PSOE) pledged to support the conservative Partido Popular (PP) government in its fight against Basque terrorism, the overall rallying rate was just 79 per cent.[16] Part of it has to do with the fact that terrorism has become an election issue over which the main parties try to gain the upper hand. The attempt by José Maria Aznar's conservative government to blame the ETA for the March 2004 bombings of commuter trains in Madrid just days before the legislative elections is a case in point.

Most attacks in Spain are directed at state targets, far more than in the other four countries – 61 per cent outside the pact compared to 19 per cent in France and even less elsewhere. This is due in large part to ETA, which traditionally targets people representing the Spanish state. The rallying rate following attacks against the state is the lowest (58 per cent when there is no pact) of all five countries. Even during the period covered by the antiterrorist pact the rate was only 78 per cent.

The PP, which was in power for most of the acts included in the dataset, did not benefit from more rallies than the PSOE. In fact, with a rallying rate of 59 per cent outside of the pact, the PP, had the lowest rallying rate of all right-wing parties in the study.

Finally, like the other four countries, Spain experienced more rallies in the post 9/11 period (89 per cent) than it did before (73 per cent).

France

France and Spain have the same low rallying rate (78 per cent). Although France has experienced fewer terrorist acts between 1990 and 2006 than Spain or the United Kingdom, it has been targeted by a more diverse range of terror groups than its two European neighbours. The French political elite has been prompt to rally when symbols of the state were targeted (83 per cent).[17]

The right-wing effect is particularly strong in France. The Right and the Left have experienced the exact same number of attacks when in power, but right-wing governments have enjoyed far more rallies than their left-wing counterparts: 93 per cent of reported attacks with rally for the Right; 67 per cent for the Left. To some extent this difference might be due to the perceived permissiveness of the Left and to the traditional ownership of security-related issues by right-wing parties.[18]

Finally, the 9/11 effect has been especially impressive in France with a rallying rate going up from 55 per cent prior to 9/11 to 100 per cent afterward.

Germany

Terrorist activities since 1990 have been less intense in Germany than in any of the other four countries included in this study. With the exception of a 1996 arson attack on a refugees hostel in Lübeck, which killed ten and injured another thirty-eight, most attacks claimed two fatalities or fewer, many causing only injuries. Most of these terrorist acts were either racially motivated or perpetrated by people with no clear political cause (except for the Kurdish activists) and were as such borderline cases. Faced with low-intensity terrorism with sometimes unclear messages, the *Frankfurter Allgemeine* and the German political elite have usually ignored those attacks.[19] Only 55 per cent of terrorist acts were reported, leading to a 100 per cent rallying rate. Overall, the small number of observations for Germany makes it difficult to establish patterns of behaviour.

The United Kingdom

The United Kingdom has both the lowest percentage of reported events (less than 60 per cent) and one of the highest rallying rates (93 per cent). The fact that the opposition is rarely critical following attacks can be explained by the bipartisan approach to terrorism.[20] In other words, the relative agreement of the main parties on the aims and methods to deal with terrorists (mostly Ulster-related terrorism) ensures a more or less constant support from the parliamentary opposition.

The right-wing Conservative Party has benefited during its years in power from the complete support of the opposition Labour and Liberal Democrats, whereas the left-wing Labour Party has enjoyed a slightly lesser rallying rate (93 per cent). Finally, the post-9/11 period has witnessed an increase in the rallying rate (from 90 per cent prior to 100 per cent after).

The United States

Despite the horrific events of 9/11, terrorist attacks have been rare in the period studied, at least among those causing a minimum of six injured (the limit set for being recorded in the database). Between 1990 and 2006, there were twenty-two attacks of at least this magnitude (the second-lowest tally among countries selected for this study). These attacks were committed by a variety of groups including Christian extremists, militias, white supremacists, and Islamic extremists.

Rallying around the president in times of international crises is common and so is rallying around the president during a terrorist crisis (93 per cent of rallying rate). However, only 68 per cent of terrorist attacks are reported in the *New York Times*. Democrats and Republicans were in power for the exact same number of terrorist events; however, the Republicans benefited from a 100 per cent rallying rate, whereas the Democrats had an 88 per cent rallying rate in their favour. Unfortunately, the 9/11 effect cannot be assessed as all terrorist acts taking place in the United States after 1998 triggered rallies.[21]

CONCLUSION

Rallying around the flag following terrorist acts is frequent among the political elites of the five countries covered by this study, though more so in some (Germany, the United Kingdom, and the United States) than in others (France and Spain). Overall, the results show that the repetition of acts of terror is a strong factor affecting parties' responses to terrorist acts, as repetition is more likely to prompt criticism. The magnitude of the act is also associated with a rallying effect as larger attacks are more likely to result in a unified front across parties. Mainstream political elites are also more likely to rally when a foreign group perpetrates the terrorist act. Finally, the existence of a formal antiterrorist pact between the parties, such as the one that existed in Spain, increases the likelihood of rallies.

The results reported here are both limited in time (1990 to 2006) – and scope (five countries), but indicate at the very least a tendency among mainstream parties and elites to be less critical of the government in the aftermath of terrorist attacks.

The Reign of Terror

An Account of Terrorism in France
from 1980 to 2015

In the blinding flash of exploding bombs, the contours of political parties and the dividing lines of the class struggle disappear without a trace.

Leon Trotsky, *Bankruptcy*

INTRODUCTION

The statistical analysis conducted in chapter 4 revealed several important trends in the reaction of mainstream political parties to terrorist acts. Two variables in particular stand out: the magnitude of the attack in terms of fatalities, and the number of terrorist acts prior to the act under consideration. The results suggest that mainstream opposition elites are less inclined to criticize their government in the immediate aftermath of a terrorist attack that claims many victims, as long as the occurrence of terrorist acts is limited. The statistical significance and explanatory power of these two variables fits well with the casualty hypothesis developed by other scholars regarding public support for wars and military operations. Yet it does not mean that other influencing factors are not at work as well. An electoral context, for instance, could shed light on the behaviour of political parties whose raison d'être is a priori to win elections, although the national interest might be the guiding principle in troubled periods.

This chapter considers a host of other variables that could not be included in the statistical model. A qualitative analysis, and in particular case studies, makes it possible to detail the reactions of the political elite by analyzing the interaction between the government and its opposition. Indeed, the statistical analysis cannot capture the dynamic of the political debate, nor can it capture the extent of a rally. Are we in the presence of a weak support from the mainstream opposition parties, or do we have a full-blown jingoistic rally that has taken over the country as a whole? Admittedly, determining the extent of a rally is difficult if not impossible mainly because exhaustive data on the behaviour of all segments and sub-segments of society (general population, media, elites, etc.) are not available, but that does not preclude trying to assess the prevalent mood among the elite and within society. In other words, I acknowledge that the magnitude and repetition variables do not necessarily tell the whole story and that other variables can help make sense of parties' reactions in critical times. In addition, this chapter looks beyond the mainstream political elite analyzing the behaviour of fringe parties and radical elites, which do not necessarily share the same objectives as their mainstream counterparts, and which might not necessarily support their government in the aftermath of terrorist attacks.

This chapter focuses exclusively on France. In many ways, the French experience with terrorism is unique, not just compared to the other four countries studied here but among Western democracies. Obviously, the modern significance of the word *terrorism* owes in large part to the revolutionary period known as "La grande terreur," but even the subsequent period and particularly the last seventy-five years have provided France with arguably the most wide-ranging experience of terrorism or terrorist-related activities in the West: state terrorism under the Vichy government and guerrilla warfare during the Nazi occupation[1] (1940–45); anticolonial terrorism across its overseas empire, and during the Algerian War (1954–62); the closely related ethnic-separatist or regionalist terrorism in Corsica and the Basque Country; revolutionary and counter-revolutionary terrorism; and finally the latest incarnation, transnational terrorism particularly in its jihadist form.[2] Unlike the British with the IRA or the Spanish with the ETA, the French experience with terrorism is not associated with a particular type of terror, let alone a particular terrorist organization. Equally important, terrorism has been recurrent without being a constant threat. In other words, terrorism has not become an unending issue of the kind that could possibly distort the way party politics is conducted, as is often the case in Israel. Finally, France with its wide array of political sensibilities provides the possibility to analyze the impact of variables such as the ideological divide between Left and Right, and the reaction of radical and fringe elites.

This chapter begins with an overview of the terrorist groups that have been active in France during the last forty years and then offers a similar overview of French political parties over the same period of time. The period under consideration is extended so as to shed light on the so-called *années de plomb* or "years of lead," which preceded the period 1990–2006 investigated in chapter 4, and cover the latest attacks in Paris in January and November 2015.

TERRORISM IN FRANCE

One of the most inexorable forms of terrorism against the French state has come from separatist or autonomist groups operating in Corsica, and on a smaller scale in the Basque Country, in Brittany, and in the overseas French territories.[3] First among separatist organizations, in terms of resilience and resources, are the Corsican groups, many of which are splinter groups from the Front de Libération Nationale de la Corse (FLNC). Initially the first Corsican activists were autonomists seeking more land for local farmers, and opposing the development of mass tourism on the island. However, early setbacks and heavy-handed response from the authorities opened the door to more radical groups advocating the independence of Corsica through the use of force. The FLNC was formed in 1976 to reclaim the Corsican territory from France and became thereafter the standard-bearer for all separatists. Their slogan, "la valise ou le cercueil" ("the suitcase or the coffin"), left no doubt as to what their intentions were.[4]

During its "opening act" on 5 May 1976, the FLNC perpetrated sixteen attacks in one night. This type of operation, known as *nuit bleue* ("blue nights"), would become a trademark for Corsican groups. By the early 1980s, FLNC attacks had become almost daily or nightly routines. In 1982, Corsican terrorists perpetrated eight hundred attacks, ninety-nine in a single night. Although most operations were carried out on the island, FLNC activists did occasionaly venture on the mainland, most notably on 31 May 1979, when the organization struck twenty-two targets in Paris. Most attacks were usually aimed at administrative buildings, and private properties or resorts owned by "continentals" (non-Corsicans). Although targeted buildings were usually vacant at the time of the attacks, keeping casualties rates low, the FLNC never committed itself to a policy of zero casualties, as far as representatives of the French state were concerned.[5]

In March 1992, the nationalists obtained around 25 per cent of the vote at the local elections, yet most Corsicans were becoming disillusioned with the terrorist groups.[6] At first these groups had been seemingly fighting a battle for the Corsicans – more land for the locals, fewer resorts on the coast – but by the 1990s the difference between the nationalist struggle and outright banditry had become slim. The extortion, through the revolutionary tax, and the killings conjured up images of mafia-like organizations, and the worsening of the island's reputation abroad jeopardized the tourist industry.[7]

The assassination of French prefect Claude Erignac on 6 February 1998, served as a wake-up call for the population and the political elite both on the island and on the mainland. Shortly after Erignac's murder, the government of socialist prime minister Lionel Jospin stepped up its efforts to reach a political solution. In a show of good-will, most clandestine nationalist organizations announced a cease-fire, and in July 2000 the Assembly of Corsica approved the Jospin plan, known as the "processus de Matignon," to give the islanders more legislative power and promote the Corsican language. However, this plan provoked tensions within the Jospin-led government, and by August 2000 Minister of Interior Jean-Pierre Chevènement had resigned, accusing the government of threatening France's integrity. Meanwhile, President Jacques Chirac opposed the transfer of legislative power to the Corsican assembly, arguing that this was tantamount to transforming the unitary French republic into a "federation of regions."[8]

In a referendum held in July 2003, 51 per cent of Corsicans chose to reject the proposed new territorial assembly – a plan which had received the support of all nationalist groups – a clear sign that a majority of residents were opposed to more autonomy, let alone sovereignty. Although figures on the number of Corsicans supporting full independence are hard to come by, some have projected it to be around 20 per cent of the island's population – about 200,000 people (Sanchez 2008).

Terrorism in Corsica never reached the intensity of terrorism in Ulster or in Spain, and as a result casualties have always been kept at a relatively low level. Still, as of 2014 when the FLNC announced its intention to disarm, the organization had been responsible for more that 10,000 attacks, killing more than 220 people and injuring thousands more.

Though nowhere close in terms of operational capacity and political weight to the FLNC, let alone to their "brothers in arms" of the ETA south of the border, the Basque separatists of Iparretarrak (IK, "those of the north") have been at times lethal and disruptive since their creation in 1973. Between 1975 and 1988, when its leader Philippe Bidard was arrested, IK committed more than fifty attacks, killing four people (all from the *gendarmerie*), injuring hundreds more, and damaging countless buildings and homes (Gregory 2003). Much like the Corsican separatists, IK targeted the French state and the tourist industry. Its objectives were twofold: the defence of the Basque language, and the self-determination of the Basque people. Throughout the 1980s, IK also provided logistical support and refuge to ETA members. However, the organization has been dormant since the late 1980s when its main leaders were arrested, though it did resurface in the late 1990s and the beginning of 2000.[9] Electorally, the independentists have never received more than 5 or 7 per cent of the vote (Moruzzi and Boulaert 1988).

The least known of the main separatist organizations fighting against the French state is also the oldest. The Front de Libération de la Bretagne (FLB) was created in 1964 and its military branch, the Armée Révolutionnaire Bretonne (ARB), in 1971. Unlike the Corsican or Basque organizations, the ARB never engaged in the sort of operation that could spill blood, instead targeting infrastructures, most notably the regional office of former prime minister Lionel Jospin in 1999. They did, however, unintentionally kill the manager of a McDonald's restaurant in April 2000. As a response to this tragic event, a number of prominent separatists asked the ARB to cease its activities. Denis Riou, an imprisoned activist, summed up the mood among separatists by declaring that if the people of Brittany have been led to fear the ARB, then this organization has failed in its mission.[10]

Although the decolonization process was completed by the early 1960s, France retained a number of overseas territories – *les confettis de l'empire* ("the empire's confetties") – in the Caribbean and the Pacific where supporters of independence undertook terrorist activities in a last attempt to oust the French state. During the 1970s and early 1980s, these groups carried out bombings in Guadeloupe and Martinique, as well as in French Guyana. However, by the late 1980s police operations and political adjustments put an end to these activities. A similar process took place in New Caledonia where the Front de Libération Nationale Kanak et Socialiste (FLNKS) was trying to loosen France's grip. The FLNKS, which benefited from the operational and financial backing of Libya and the Corsican FLNC throughout the 1980s, obtained a political autonomy deal from Paris. Although less murderous and destructive than the FLNC, the FLNKS campaign ended in a bloodbath in 1988 following a hostage crisis that left twenty of its members dead.

From the early 1970s to the mid-1980s, French authorities also dealt with a revolutionary brand of terrorism targeting the state and the capitalist establishment. This movement had taken Western Europe by storm, particularly in Italy with the Brigate Rosse (BR) and in Germany with the Rote Armee Fraktion (RAF) and the Bewegung Zwei Juni (B2J).[11]

In France, Action Directe (AD) became the standard-bearer for what was also known as Euroterrorism. AD targeted the French state and corporate business. Among its most infamous *fait d'armes* were the point-blank assassinations of General René Audran in January 1985 and Renault chairman Georges Besse in November 1986. Yet AD's resources and labour remained small in comparison to those of the BR and the RAF. Despite this limited operational capacity, AD members struck the headquarters of the Organisation for Economic Co-operation and Development (OECD) and of Interpol. By 1981, AD had split into four different groups operating under different names, some working on the international scene with the RAF or the Belgian Cellules Communistes Combattantes (CCC), some focusing on domestic targets. In the end, the movement proved far less durable than the Corsican FLNC. Particularly problematic was its social and intellectual depth, or lack thereof. AD never received the kind of support enjoyed by similar groups in Italy and Germany, and throughout the 1980s, the organization relied increasingly on bank robberies to finance its activities. By the end of the decade, its last members were arrested and imprisoned, generally for life.

Reactionary and neo-fascist groups such as the Faisceaux Nationalistes Européens (FNE) and the Fédération d'Action Nationale et Européenne (FANE) have caused far less trouble compared to similar organizations in Italy and Germany where right-wing extremists have carried out murderous operations.[12] They have never reached the intensity of the Organisation Armée Secrète (OAS) during the Algerian War (1954–62). Amateurish and logistically incapable of threatening the French state, the FNE and the FANE have made the headlines by either desecrating cemeteries – usually Jewish tombs – or setting fire to housing centres for North African guest workers. On 14 July 2004, Maxime Brunerie, a young neo-Nazi, attempted to kill President Chirac during a military parade on the Champs-Élysées.

Another unrelenting source of terrorist activities within its borders or against its interests and citizens abroad has to do with France's colonial past as well as its meddling in international affairs, particularly in the Middle East. For much of the 1970s and 1980s, the most acute problem came from pro-Palestinian activists. No stranger to the Arab-Israeli conflict, France became a destination of choice for Arab terrorists particularly after General Charles de Gaulle resuscitated France's Arab policy (*politique arabe*) in an attempt to reclaim the position of influence it had lost in the Middle East following the Suez crisis in 1956. Chief among these groups operating on French soil was the Lebanese-Palestinian Comité de Solidarité avec les Prisonniers Politiques Arabes et du Proche-Orient (CSPPA), which targeted both Israeli and French individuals and interests, the latter as a means to force the liberation of Arab prisoners detained in French jails on terrorist offences. The CSPPA targeted the Eiffel Tower and the high-speed train between Paris and Marseille – both attempts failed. However in September 1986, the CSPPA set the streets of Paris ablaze with five bombings in the space of ten days, killing 9 passersby and wounding more than 160 others. Meanwhile, French nationals abroad were targeted either through assassinations or kidnapping.[13]

Palestinian terrorism in France disappeared shortly after the 1986 wave of attacks but was soon replaced by Algerian terrorism. Having sided with the ruling Front de Libération Nationale (FLN) party in Algeria in an attempt to quell the Islamic upsurge – the Front Islamique de Salut (FIS) was on its way to winning a majority of votes at the December 1991 general election – the French government soon faced a new terrorist threat aimed at ending its meddling in Algerian affairs. The Islamists' cause was taken over by former FIS members who, in 1992, formed the Groupe Islamique Armé (GIA). Over the following decade, the GIA became infamous for its murderous acts in Algeria where more than 50,000 people died, and for various attacks on French soil.

The GIA's first actions against France took place on 24 December 1994, with the hijacking of an Air France Airbus from Algiers to Paris. The hostage takers killed three passengers before French special forces stormed the plane in Marseille, killing all the terrorists.[14] The hijacking was followed a few months later by a wave of attacks reminiscent of the one that hit Paris in 1986. By the end of October 1995 the bombings – mainly in Paris but also in Lyon – had claimed the lives of ten people and had injured close to three hundred more.

Other groups or individuals have imported their conflicts to France over the last thirty-five years, such as the Armenian Secret Army for the Liberation of Armenia (ASALA). Its most tragic *fait d'armes* killed 8 and wounded 60 when a bomb exploded at Orly airport (1983). The Iranian Secret Services and the infamous Carlos the Jackal also featured prominently throughout the 1980s. Although often cited by Bin Laden as a target, France had been relatively spared by al Qaeda operatives.[15] This respite came to an abrupt end on 7 January 2015, when two gunmen claiming to act on behalf of al Qaeda killed 12 people within and close to the offices of *Charlie Hebdo*, a satirical weekly magazine. A three-day man hunt ensued during which two other attacks were perpetrated by another gunman, killing 5 people. A few months later, ISIS would claim responsibility for the multiple attacks of 13 November that left 130 people dead. These headline-grabbing events had been preceded in March 2012 by two attacks in Toulouse and Montauban, which claimed the lives of 7 people. Here too the culprit, Mohammed Merah, allegedly acted on behalf of al Qaeda.

Overall, France has been targeted over the past thirty years by a variety of terrorist groups. Homegrown organizations, such as the Corsican FLNC and AD, have been active over longer periods than most foreign groups operating on the French territory, but attacks by the latter have usually been far more lethal.

POLITICAL PARTIES IN FRANCE

The terms *Left* and *Right*, which originate from the French Revolution, initially reflected the seating plan within the newly created National Assembly, with those favouring the *ancien régime* and the king seated on the right side of the hemicycle, and those keen on limiting the powers of the monarch seated on the left. Although the meaning of *Left* and *Right* has changed over the centuries, the current seating plan still reflects basic ideological differences: the party on the left side being what François Goguel called the "Party of movement" and the party on the right side being the "Party of order." Historically, the "Party of movement" embraced values such as secularism and social justice, whereas the "Party of order" looked at social reforms with skepticism, shared many of the values defended by the Catholic Church, and believed in strong political leadership. The difference between Left and Right has now shifted toward socio-economic considerations; however, France never had a bipartisan system.

The following section presents the main political forces in France over the last thirty years and underlines their stance on terrorism and national security. I start with mainstream parties, and then proceed with radical and fringe parties.

THE SOCIALISTS

The Parti Socialiste (PS) was created in 1971 on the remnants of the Marxist Section Française de l'Internationale Ouvrière (SFIO). Over the next decade, and with François Mitterrand at its helm, the PS slowly supplanted the Parti Communiste (PC) as the main political force on the left of the political spectrum. In 1981, for the first time under the Fifth Republic, the presidential election was won by a left-wing candidate, namely Mitterrand. Many on the Right were bewildered by Mitterrand's victory, he who a mere seventeen years before had denounced the Fifth Republic as de Gaulle's ploy to carry out a *coup d'état permanent*, "a permanent coup." Adding insult to injury for the right-wing Gaullists, Mitterrand appointed four members of the PC – de Gaulle's nemesis – to his first government.

Although Mitterrand remained president of the republic until 1995, he was forced to share power with right-wing governments on two occasions following socialist defeats at legislative elections – 1986–88 and 1993–95. These periods known as *cohabitations* were marked by intense terrorist activities.

Initially, the socialists were brought to power to "break with capitalism" and implement far-reaching reforms based on a "Keynesian dash for growth" (Frears 1991, 73). Humanism was the order of the day and quickly led to a series of symbolic measures, such as the abolition of the death penalty. The 110 measures on which Mitterrand had been campaigning in 1981 had a distinctively pacifist feel with, among other proposals, the withdrawal of Soviet troops from Afghanistan, peace in the Middle East, progressive disarmament of the Western and Eastern blocs, and an end to nuclear dissemination. Yet, with the socialists barely a year in power, *realpolitik* made a flashing return to the top of the agenda. After abandoning the socialists' Keynesian stimulus plan, Mitterrand went back on a number of foreign policy–related promises concerning weapons sales and the installation of US Pershing missiles on European soil. The participation of French military forces in the US-led Operation Desert Storm in 1991 further demonstrated that Mitterrand was no dove, even though some of his closest political allies within the PS were reluctant to follow a hawkish policy.[16]

With regards to terrorism, the socialists made a series of gestures sympathetic to certain former activists, notably an amnesty law, which led to the liberation of two AD leaders. In 1985, Mitterrand went still further by establishing what would be known henceforth as the "Doctrine Mitterrand," pledging not to extradite former left-wing Italian terrorists and BR members. During that same year the Direction Générale de la Sécurité Extérieure (DGSE)[17] sank the *Rainbow Warrior*, flagship of the environmental organization Greenpeace, to prevent its crew from reaching French Polynesia where nuclear tests were carried out.[18] The socialist government, it appeared, had greenlighted the use of enforcement terrorism to protect the country's interests.[19]

After a seventeen-year hiatus, during which the PS failed to win the presidential election, the socialists under François Hollande's leadership returned to power in 2012.[20] Like Mitterrand, Hollande has shown his willingness to intervene abroad as demonstrated in the Central African Republic and in the Middle East, where the French airforce is engaging ISIS as part of the US-led coalition and, in fact, increased its involvement following the 13 November 2015 attacks in Paris.

THE GAULLISTS

The Rassemblement pour la République (RPR) was founded in 1976 to rekindle the Gaullist movement and regain leadership of the Right that had fallen in the hands of non-Gaullist Valéry Giscard d'Estaing, and offer support to Jacques Chirac in the electoral campaigns that lay ahead. Ideologically, the *gaullisme chiraquien* resulted at first in an "aggressive, populist, anti-European, anti-free-market rhetoric" and toward the mid-1980s in an "aggressive pro-free-market rhetoric" amid internal disagreement on the issue of Europe (Knapp and Wright 2006, 226).

After an initial term as prime minister (1974–76) under President Giscard d'Estaing, Chirac returned to the Hôtel Matignon – the prime minister's official residency – in 1986 after a right-wing victory (RPR and UDF) at the legislative elections. During this first cohabitation period, Chirac's government tried to undo some of the more symbolic measures adopted by the socialists, such as privatizing some previously nationalized companies, but was frustrated by President Mitterrand's refusal to ratify some of these policies.[21]

The RPR, which had been very critical of the socialists' handling of terrorism earlier in the decade, was soon tested by a terrorist campaign carried out by Palestinian activists that claimed the lives of nine people in September 1986. Shortly thereafter, Georges Besse, president of the state-owned carmaker Renault, was shot dead by members of Action Directe. Meanwhile several French citizens were abducted in Lebanon, and most of them were eventually freed.[22] Chirac ended his last mandate as prime minister with a heavy-handed policy in New

Caledonia where nineteen independentists were killed during an operation by French special forces to free hostages.

The RPR returned to power between 1993 and 1995 with Édouard Balladur in the prime minister's seat. Balladur's mandate was marked by several terrorist acts perpetrated by Algerian jihadists. On a more symbolic level, Carlos the Jackal, who had masterminded several terrorist operations throughout the world in the 1980s, was arrested by French police in Sudan.

In 1995 upon becoming president, Chirac faced a particularly intense wave of attacks perpetrated by Algerian terrorists, and in the end was widely praised for dealing effectively with this particular threat and for dismantling its operational base. However, dealing with the separatist menace proved a more daunting task and by 1998, the Corsican separatists were again making headlines with the assassination of Claude Erignac, France's highest civil servant on the island.

In 2002 Chirac secured a second presidential mandate and changed the name of the Gaullist party from Rassemblement pour la République to Union pour un Mouvement Populaire (UMP). Five years later, Nicolas Sarkozy, his successor at the head of the UMP claimed victory in the presidential election. The party changed its name again in 2015 and is now called Les Républicains.

THE PRO-EUROPEAN RIGHT-WING

The Union pour la Démocratie Française (UDF) was founded in 1978 to support Valéry Giscard d'Estaing's re-election bid and counter Chirac's rising influence within the Right. Eventually, the UDF relinquished its dominant position within the Right, though its distinctive pro-European stance made it more of a centre-right political force anyway. The UDF took part alongside the RPR in each of the first two cohabitation governments and again in each right-wing government under Chirac's (1995–2007) and Sarkozy's (2007–12) presidencies.[23]

Perhaps wary of endangering its *politique arabe*, Giscard's government proved less resolute with Palestinian terrorists than with left-wing radicals.[24] In January 1977, Giscard authorized the release of Abu Daoud after the known terrorist had served just ten days' detention, despite Daoud's involvement in the operation against the Israeli delegation at the 1972 Olympic Games in Munich. Similarly his government offered a safe passage to Iraq to CSPPA activists responsible for taking hostages at the Orly airport.

Finally, Giscard's government set up the Plan Vigipirate in 1978. This national emergency plan is intended for exceptional crises, such as terrorist attacks, and involves coordinated operations by the army, the gendarmerie, and other police forces to protect public and sensitive sites, such as airports, railway stations, and nuclear power plants.

THE RADICAL PARTIES

After more than thirty years in the opposition, the PC returned to power in 1981, albeit in a junior role, and embraced most of the policies advocated by the PS, particularly its leniency toward left-wing activists. By 1984, however, the communists had left the government only to return in 1997 following another socialist victory. However the PC, which represented close to a quarter of the electorate at the end of the 1970s, fell well below the 10 per cent mark in the 1990s. Throughout these years the communists maintained a rather permissive stance regarding terrorism.

The first electoral breakthrough for the far-right Front National (FN) came in the early 1980s. The party led by Jean-Marie Le Pen became known for a tough rhetoric on crime and terrorism, insisting for instance that the death penalty be reinstated for terrorists. Following the 1986 legislative elections, the FN won thirty seats in the National Assembly.[25] Though the party lost most of these seats two years later, the FN remained a force to be reckoned with whether at local elections or at presidential elections. The FN's popularity peaked in 2002 when Le Pen reached the second round of the presidential election after making security the number one issue during the campaign. Since 2011, Le Pen's daugher, Marine, has taken over the reins and has attempted, rather successfully, to make it appealing to a larger number of voters by deradicalizing its rhetoric and courting the more moderate right-wing electorate.

Although right-wing parties, in particular the RPR, might have had the ownership of the twin issues of national security and terrorism, it is fair to say that right-wing governments were at times as permissive with terrorists as left-wing governments. The socialists might have been more lenient with leftist radicals, but the RPR and UDF hardly set the example with terrorists originating from the Middle East. In fact, Walter Laqueur in *The Age of Terrorism* considered France to be the "most permissive" of all Western European countries in its handling of terrorist groups (1999a, 289).[26]

We now turn to the period known as the "years of lead" and examine how both the Left and the Right handled various terrorist crises.

THE "YEARS OF LEAD"

The expression "years of lead," or *années de plomb*, came to describe the peak of left- and right-wing terrorism in Western Europe throughout the 1970s and early 1980s.[27] Yet whereas the phenomenon was particularly acute in Italy and Germany, France's experience was noticeably different although equally ruthless. From the mid-1970s to the mid-1980s, France became the target of various domestic groups (revolutionaries, separatists, etc.) but also foreign-based groups originating from Palestine, Lebanon, Iran, and Armenia. Assassinations of public figures, shootings in public places, and explosions in busy streets were common occurrences.

This section presents a series of case studies covering the most important attacks during this period: the synagogue bombing on rue Copernic in October 1980, the wave of attacks between March and September 1982, the wave of attacks in September 1986, and the Georges Besse assassination in November 1986. This selection of cases is based on five criteria: the magnitude of the attack, the repetition of attacks, the type of target, the identity of the perpetrators, and the party in power. In other words, I have selected the attacks with the highest fallout in terms of victims but also made sure to include attacks and waves of attacks with different targets (from civil servants to passersby) perpetrated by different groups (domestic and international), and taking place during periods with right-wing and left-wing governments. In so doing, I can analyze the impacts of five key variables on the reactions of mainstream and radical elites. Furthermore, the international context of that particular decade (the Cold War and tension in the Middle East) provides an interesting background to the decision-making process and behaviour of French political elites. I conclude this analysis by focusing on attacks taking place between 1990 and 2015.

For each case study, I follow the same procedure. The first part describes the event and the political situation at the time of the attack. The second part examines what the magnitude-repetition model suggests will happen, details the reaction of both mainstream and radical elites, and compares it to what the model predicted.

Who's to Blame? A Case of Mistaken Identity: The Synagogue Bombing, Rue Copernic, Paris, 3 October 1980

On 3 October 1980, in the late afternoon, a bomb exploded in front of a Paris synagogue killing four people and injuring another twenty-two. The tragedy could have been far worse had the terrorists been able to implement their original plan, which was to place the device inside the premises where more than three hundred worshipers were attending a religious service on the eve of Shabbat. However, the presence of a security guard led the terrorists to dispose of the bomb outside of the synagogue. Responsibility for the attack was claimed straight away by the FNE, a far-right group linked to the FANE, which had been dissolved by the French government a month before the attack. Marc Fredriksen, former leader of the defunct FANE, quickly issued a press release disclaiming responsibility for the act. The police remained unconvinced, particularly since the rue Copernic bombing followed a series of anti-Semitic attacks in France and across Europe, notably in Bologna where eighty-four perished on 2 August 1980, and Munich where twelve died on 27 September 1980. As a result, dozens of people within neo-Nazi circles were arrested in the ensuing days.

In the following week, *Le Monde*, and most other French newspapers, maintained throughout their editorials and articles that the attack had been the work of far-right terrorists. Eventually, as the police investigation proceeded, the blame shifted toward Abu Nidal, a "hired gun" for Syria, Iraq, and Libya whose prime purpose was to make money out of terrorist activities (Hoffman 2006, 259). The French authorities later identified five Palestinians as prime suspects.[28] However, in the heat of the moment and in the days that followed, the reaction from the elite as well as from the main media outlets was based on the assumption that the attack was the work of neo-Nazis.

President Giscard was in the last year of his seven-year mandate. Presidential elections were scheduled six months later and re-election was far from certain. Although the right-wing coalition had been victorious at the 1978 legislative elections, Giscard's party (the centre-right UDF) came in second behind the Gaullist RPR led by Jacques Chirac, Giscard's former prime minister.[29] The rivalry between UDF and RPR turned especially sour when Chirac claimed that the UDF was "le parti de l'étranger," meaning both the party from abroad and the foreigner's party – a clear attack on Giscard's pro-European policies. The split between the two right-wing parties was confirmed in the following weeks when the RPR representatives in the National Assembly refused to vote in favour of government bills. Meanwhile, the situation on the left of the political divide was heating up. The PS and the PC after a brief alliance returned to their old rivalry with the communists accusing the socialist of taking a "virage à droite," a conservative turn.

The end of Giscard's mandate was marred by foreign policy crises and controversial decisions, such as the sanctuary offered to Ayatollah Ruhollah Khomeini shortly before his return to Iran to lead the Islamic Revolution, and the government's mild criticism of Moscow following the invasion of Afghanistan.[30] The economic situation was even worse with the second oil crisis pushing inflation and unemployment rates up.

The rue Copernic explosion was an instance of high magnitude and high repetition. Therefore, the magnitude-repetition model leads us to expect criticisms from mainstream opposition parties. Radical parties for their part are expected to criticize both the government and mainstream opposition parties.

Leaders of the Jewish community in France were the first ones to react to the attack and thereby set the tone. They deplored the tameness of the authorities and the indifference of the government.[31] Le Monde took a similar stance and in a front-page editorial blamed the state for its permissiveness (complaisance) and for being too lenient with far-right extremism.[32]

The opposition was quick to capitalize on the controversy surrounding the perceived laxness of the government. PS leader François Mitterrand underlined the fact that this terrorist attack was part of a long series of similar acts.[33] He bemoaned the government's impotence and its inability to take into account the warnings. On a more personal level, Mitterrand pointed out that far-right activists had been working as security agents for Giscard during the 1974 presidential campaign and had subsequently won seats in the National Assembly under the UDF banner. Mitterrand's point was that Giscard needed the far-right to govern and therefore was not at liberty to strike at neo-fascist groups when needed. In a similar vein, Gaston Defferre (leader of the socialist group at the National Assembly) remarked that by minimizing the danger posed by far-right extremists, the government would never be able to control them.[34] By 7 October – four days after the explosion – the socialists asked for Christian Bonnet's resignation as minister of the interior.

UDF spokesperson Michel Pinton deplored the attempt by the socialist opposition to politicize the issue. Unfortunately for the government, criticisms were also voiced within conservative ranks, particularly among Gaullists.[35] Bernard Pons, RPR secretary general, asked the government to finally realize the danger posed by right-wing extremists. Michel Debré, de Gaulle's former prime minister, was far less subtle and criticized the government for its hesitation and lack of audacity. Chirac for his part refrained from openly criticizing the government.

Surprisingly, radical parties did not seize the opportunity created by the attack to strongly criticize the government or the political system. Georges Marchais, PC secretary general, issued a mildly critical statement asking the government to finally take all measures necessary to arrest and condemn the criminals and asked that a debate on terrorism be organized in the National Assembly.[36]

FN leader Le Pen also refrained from criticizing the government. However, he used the opportunity to redirect the blame on the communists, claiming that this criminal act was part of a provocative strategy that could only benefit communist subversion.[37] He accused the KGB of wanting to destabilize the West.[38] He also remarked that repeated warnings of a renewed Nazi scare would only deflect attention from the imminent Soviet invasion of Poland and from the various political scandals in France, notably those involving Giscard and Marchais.[39] Elsewhere Le Pen used the opportunity to restate two key points in his electoral platform: the need to re-establish severe controls at the border, and to reinstate the death penalty against terrorists.

As an instance of high magnitude (four people killed) and more importantly high repetition (this was the latest in a long list of terrorist attacks), it does not come as a surprise that the opposition was critical of the government in the aftermath of the rue Copernic bombing; indeed, Mitterrand reminded everyone of this fact. In that respect, the magnitude-repetition model withstands the test. Yet to be fair, a number of other factors made sure that the Left and even part of the Right would avoid the rally. First, the act was perceived – wrongly as it eventually turned out – as part of a wave of far-right attacks that the government had failed to stop. (*Le Monde* put the number of anti-Semitic attacks in France at about 120 since 1975.) This could only reinforce the feeling that the government was not handling the right-wing threat well enough. In addition, the reaction of the main Jewish organizations, echoed by the press, fuelled public dissatisfaction and resulted in several demonstrations across the country. As often in the aftermath of deadly attacks, a rally in support of the victims quickly developed. Thus, the socialists and the Gaullists joined the chorus of disapproval. The government, for its part, was unable to control the flow of information and impose its own framing on the events. Whether or not a rally would have been triggered had the perpetrators been correctly identified remains impossible to determine. Yet we do know from the statistical analysis conducted in chapter 4 that attacks originating abroad are more likely to trigger rallies.

The electoral variable cannot be discounted either. With a presidential election a mere six months away, the political elite had an opportunity to strike at the incumbent. More importantly, they could do so without any fear of their loyalty to the nation being questioned. After all the wave of criticism toward the government's permissiveness with right-wing fanatics was coming from all political directions and all quarters of civil society. Interestingly, a right-wing government was criticized for being too soft on terror.

What was perhaps more surprising was the behaviour of the main radical parties, the PC and the FN, neither of which were particularly critical of the government, certainly not more than mainstream parties. One of the reasons for this apparent leniency might have to do with the fact that criticizing the government could have been perceived as siding with the rest of the mainstream elite. There was clearly nothing to be gained at being more critical than the rest of the opposition. With elections less than six months away, the communists were keen to distance themselves from the socialists. The FN for its part could hardly side with the critics and ask that the government be ruthless with far-right activists, many of which were FN sympathizers or even members.[40] On the contrary, Le Pen found it more profitable to deflect the blame toward the communists at home and abroad, and to demand a reinstatement of capital punishment against terrorists.

In the end, the high number of casualties coupled with the (mis)perception that this was the latest in a long list of acts committed by far-right terrorists left the government little chance to escape the crisis unscathed, particularly with presidential elections looming.

Seeing Red! Blame Game between a Socialist Government and a Conservative Opposition: Wave of Attacks, Paris, March to September 1982

Between March and September 1982 a wave of attacks swept France, killing 12 people and injuring more than 200. The first attack, an explosion on the Paris–Toulouse train, took place on 29 March. Five passengers were killed and another 27 wounded. Ilyich Ramirez Sanchez, alias "Carlos the Jackal," was blamed for the attack although no official claim was issued. The second attack took place on 22 April and targeted the Paris office of the Lebanese newspaper *Al Watan Al Arabi* (*The Arab Nation*) on rue Marbeuf. The explosion killed 1 person and injured another 64. Syrian secret services were blamed for the attack on this pro-Iraqi publication.[41] On 9 August, 6 people were killed and another 22 were wounded on rue des Rosiers in Paris. At the time, the shooting was thought to be the work of Abu Nidal or possibly Action Directe.[42] Finally, on 17

September an explosion near Lycée Carnot in Paris claimed no lives but injured 91 passersby. Although these attacks were thought to be linked to Middle Eastern groups, the eclectic nature of terrorist groups operating in France at the time made it difficult to blame one organization or the other.

After more than twenty-three years in opposition, the Left was finally back in power. François Mitterrand (PS) had beaten his arch-rival Valéry Giscard d'Estaing (UDF) in May 1981 to become the Fifth Republic's first socialist president. A month later a landslide victory at the legislative elections gave the socialists a majority of seats at the National Assembly. For the Right, which had been in power since May 1958, the defeat was bitter, particularly for the Gaullist party (RPR) of Jacques Chirac, which considered the Fifth Republic its creation. To add insult to injury, Mitterrand and most of the elite on the left of the political divide had been initially bitterly opposed to the new constitution, which many of them viewed as autocratic and dangerous for democracy. Thus, many right-wing politicians felt that Mitterrand did not deserve the extensive power bestowed upon him by a constitution he rejected so forcefully. Worse still for the Right was the inclusion of four communists in the government of Prime Minister Pierre Mauroy.

After a long drawn-out battle in Parliament that ended shortly before the attack on the Paris–Toulouse train, the socialists kept their election promises and undertook major reforms: nationalizing five of France's largest industrial groups, thirty-nine banks, and two financial companies; transferring substantial power to regional councils; and abolishing the death penalty. However, by early 1982, economic setbacks were already putting the socialist plan for a "new society" in peril. The revival of the economy through Keynesian inspired policies never materialized and increased massively the budget deficit, the public debt, and the trade balance deficit. As a result, the French currency underwent a series of devaluations. Meanwhile, the inflation rate remained high at 14.1 per cent between March 1981 and March 1982 in comparison to other European countries, and the unemployment rate was rising too.[43] By June 1982, the government had abandoned its bold plan and was returning to the austerity measures they had vowed never to use. As a consequence of this economic downturn, the approval ratings of both President Mitterrand and his prime minister decreased from 74 and 71 per cent respectively in June 1981 to 57 and 58 per cent in December 1981 (Becker 2003, 194).[44] By September 1982, the president's popularity plummeted, with 42 per cent satisfied of his actions and 45 per cent dissatisfied (Becker 2003, 194). This decline was confirmed electorally at the beginning of 1982 when the socialists lost three seats to the right-wing opposition following legislative by-elections. This string of electoral setbacks carried on with a major defeat for the Left at the cantonal elections in March 1982.[45]

According to the magnitude-repetition model the elite should have supported the government in the aftermath of the first attack (high magnitude and low repetition). Thereafter, the repetition factor following the second and fourth attack (both low magnitude) made a support unlikely. As for the third attack (high magnitude and high repetition) the opposition was expected to be critical of the government inability to end the wave of attacks.

The first attack, an explosion on the Paris–Toulouse train, was not initially perceived as terrorist in nature. Even though Carlos the Jackal was mentioned in the news reports because of an ultimatum he had given to the French government days before the explosion, other scenarios were put forth in the media, such as gangsters or autonomists transporting explosives.[46] Within a few days a host of organizations claimed responsibility for the explosion: several far-right groups, among them an organization asking for the exclusion of the communist from the government; far-left groups; and Carlos himself.

Initially the elite was slow to react to what was essentially the first major attack since Mitterrand's election. Christian Bonnet (UDF) himself, whose resignation from the Ministry of the Interior had been demanded by the socialists less than two years before (see page 113), declared that terrorism was not a new phenomenon and that it would be unfair to lay the blame for recent terrorist activities on any particular government.[47] Besides, the absence of serious claims created a murky situation, and making sense of what had happened rather difficult. In addition, the particularly dense flow of events on the international scene (intensification of the Iran–Iraq War, and the Argentinean invasion of the Falkland Islands) – deflected part of the elite's attention.

The second attack elicited far more reactions from the opposition. Chirac (RPR) merely asked the government to endow the security forces with the necessary resources to combat terrorism, but Pons (secretary general of the RPR) went on the offensive accusing the government of letting people known for their connections with terrorist organizations free and of failing to take action despite knowing the whereabouts of those responsible for the attacks.[48] Even more critical, the UDF declared that the "socialist-communist" government had neglected the warnings it received from the opposition and shut its eyes on the rise of insecurity and violence, and concluded, "We were expecting actions, all we had were new victims."[49]

Criticisms were also widespread within right-wing leaning newspapers. Max Clos in Le Figaro claimed that the government was too permissive and thus responsible for the crisis; Pierre Charpy in La Lettre de la Nation asked for the dismissals of Claude Cheysson (minister of foreign affairs), Gaston Defferre (minister of the interior) and Robert Badinter (minister of justice). Surprisingly, the government refused to respond to these criticisms and accusations of carelessness, and simply indicated that using this drama for political gains was indecent.[50]

During the following days, criticisms against the government continued with the same level of intensity. Senator Charles Pasqua (one of the leading figures of the RPR) and Jacques Toubon (close adviser to Chirac) claimed that terrorist groups were creeping into France, and accused the government of supporting violent organizations in other countries.[51] Chirac commented on the government's lack of resolve to tackle the security problem.[52] However, the most damning criticism yet came from Claude Labbé (president of the RPR group in the National Assembly): "I say this with solemnity and a certain brutality, we must ask those in charge of governing to leave. This is our role as opponents. Let them go, they are useless."[53]

In response to the uproar provoked by this declaration within socialist ranks, Pons remarked that though the declaration was excessive in its form, it did indicate a concern about the way the government had handled the national security so far.[54] A few days later Bonnet and Labbé called again for the prime minister's resignation, openly condemning what they considered to be a "rotten intellectual circle" within the Parisian Left, a group of "conscientious objectors."[55]

The socialists, through Georges Sarre, expressed dismay at the use, or abuse, by the Right of the terrorist issue for political gains: "I pity those on the Right who in order to make a political gain did not hesitate to make intolerable and abject declarations against the government of the Republic ... The truth is plain. You are spurred on by a genuine rage to destroy. You only seek an electoral revenge, and to reclaim your lost power."[56]

Labbé, who launched the initial verbal attack, maintained his declaration and even questioned the legitimacy of the socialist president:

I do not consider that we are really in a situation where the Left has the power. By claiming on day one of his mandate to be a socialist President, François Mitterrand committed a major blunder and limited his capacity to be recognized as the President of all French people. By embarking on a programme of major disruptions that are not in accordance with what a majority of French people want, the government did not respect the continuity of power that defines periods when government changes hand.[57]

Labbé and others were not just voicing criticisms but literally indicting the president and declaring him unfit to run the country.

Faced with mounting accusations of permissiveness, the Left remained for the most part stoic, although Defferre accused the Right of negligence when it was in power, reminding the public that right-wing governments had in the past released known terrorists.[58]

On 8 August, more than three months after the rue Marbeuf explosion, Paris was again hit by terrorists. This time it was a shooting aimed at the Jewish community and occurring at a time of extreme tension in Lebanon where an Israeli military operation was underway. Less than two years after the rue Copernic attack, the Jewish community set the tone again (see page 112). Mitterrand, who shortly before the shooting had become the first French president to travel to Israel on an official visit, was given a chilly welcome by the residents while visiting rue des Rosiers to pay his respects to the victims. The booing that greeted Mitterrand was reminiscent of Giscard's cold reception in the aftermath of the rue Copernic terrorist attack.

The UDF and the RPR renewed their criticisms of the government's alleged laissez-faire attitude regarding terrorist activities.[59] This time, however, criticisms toward the government remained limited, in large part because many felt that France was being wrongfully accused of anti-Semitism by the Israeli government. Isreali prime minister Menachem Begin had raised the possibility of asking French Jews to organize their collective defence if the French state failed to protect them. Rejecting any accusations of anti-Semitism, right-wing-leaning newspaper *Le Figaro* declared:

> We cannot accept that France, albeit a socialist France ... is accused of being anti-Semitic ... To designate the President of the Republic, a man who has been legitimately elected by a majority of French people – even though we think that this was an aberration – as the instigator, even the accomplice, of the massacre rue des Rosiers, is a vile accusation that nothing can justify.[60]

Pons (RPR) remarked that in view of the many casualties caused by the last attack, it would be scandalous to try and take advantage of this act for political gains.[61] However, yet again the rally failed to materialize as once more the UDF issued criticisms of the government's handling of affairs. The government's perceived negligence regarding security matters was again stigmatized. More surprisingly, Jean-Claude Gaudin (president of the UDF group in the National Assembly) asked the socialist government to cease its anti-Israeli stance. Others within the opposition argued that the socialists were making France a target for international terrorism, and underlined the weakening of justice and police under the socialist government.[62]

The fourth and final attack took place on 17 September and was thought to be the work of the Fraction Armée Révolutionnaire Libanaise (FARL), a Palestinian group based in Lebanon. Although the explosion did not cause any fatalities, more than ninety people were injured, and its proximity to a school raised serious concerns, particularly as several of the victims were teenagers. The mild criticisms still underlined the perceived inadequacy of the government's response. UDF president Jean Lecanuet complained that the government talked a lot but failed to act decisively. For his part, former prime minister Raymond Barre (UDF) was far more incisive and claimed that the socialists had set terrorists free and had weakened France's capacity to respond to terrorism.[63] Others criticized the socialists for governing with what they perceived to be anti-Israeli communists.[64] Chirac, as usual, was far less aggressive and, as mayor of Paris, simply asked for a meeting with Mitterrand to discuss counter-terrorist measures.[65] It should be noted that ever since his defeat at the presidential election, former president Giscard remained on the sideline and refrained from making any public comments on the attacks. Chirac had therefore become the de facto leader of the right-wing opposition.

Despite being in the line of fire again, the government did not respond to the accusations of carelessness. Prime Minister Mauroy simply pointed out that unlike Germany or Italy, France was facing a brand of terrorism originating from abroad.[66]

Throughout the crisis, the communists supported the government, demanding only a severe response against the terrorists.[67] This support was manifest following the third attack when the PC decided to postpone a planned demonstration against the Israeli intervention in Lebanon, and instead condemned vigorously the rue des Rosiers shooting.

The FN went on the offensive against the government. Le Pen blamed the recent attacks on the presence of the "subversive" communists in the government and on the passive complicity of their socialist allies.[68] Toward the end of the crisis, the FN raised again the spectre of an international conspiracy, arguing that the terrorists were on Moscow's payroll, and that France was slowly descending into chaos.[69] The FN also claimed that the government's policies regarding immigration, asylum seekers, border controls (or lack thereof), and the death penalty were favouring the rise of terrorist activities on French soil.[70]

The magnitude-repetition model explains to a large extent why the mainstream elite rallied in support of the government following the first attack (high magnitude and low repetition). The right-wing opposition parties recognized that the government could hardly be blamed for what was the government's first major terrorist crisis. In addition, the lack of certainty as to who had carried out the attack made it all the more difficult for the opposition to criticize the government. The attack also coincided with the unfolding of two international crises with potentially serious implications for France: the Argentinian invasion of the Falkland Islands, and a major Iranian victory at the expense of the Iraqi Army. The French political elite was thus less likely to show disagreement on matters pertaining to the security of the country.

The model proved conclusive for the first attack (support following high magnitude and low repetition) and the second attack (no support following low magnitude and high repetition). In all fairness, the second attack was just a pretext for many within the opposition to lash out at the government. Ever since the election of Mitterrand, prominent figures within the RPR and UDF felt that the Left did not deserve to be in government and had no real legitimacy. In their view, Mitterrand had forfeited his right to lead the republic after claiming to be a socialist president. More importantly, the Right called into question the moral values of the Left and asked whether the government had what it took to lead the country through a terrorist crisis; hence, the call by some for the government to step down. The consensus among many right-wing politicians was that the socialists lacked the resolve necessary under these stressful times; they were doves, when France needed hawks. Personal agendas cannot be discounted either, as when Christian Bonnet asked the prime minister to step down, merely two years after being himself targeted by the socialists in similar circumstances.

The model is conclusive for the third attack (high magnitude and high repetition), which resulted in additional criticisms. After being so critical following the second attack, the opposition could hardly rally whole heartedly around the government. Yet the right-wing parties, particularly the RPR, were more lenient this time around. Accusations of France being an anti-Semitic country convinced part of the Right to tone down its criticisms. Begin's threat to call for French Jews to defend themselves clearly gave the political elite a common purpose. Yet many within the Right, particularly within the UDF, remained critical of the government's perceived permissiveness.

The fourth and final attack (low magnitude and high repetition) was an instance where the opposition was again expected to be critical. As was the case throughout this wave of attacks, the RPR remained less critical than its right-wing partner, the UDF. The UDF and Giscard had been the main victims of the socialist victory in 1981, hence perhaps their hostility toward the government. For his part, Chirac (RPR) refrained from going on the offensive. Rising tension in Lebanon with the entry of Israeli forces in west Beirut, and the ensuing massacre of Sabra and Shatila probably helped mellow the debate somewhat. Yet with municipal elections looming and the *rentrée politique* ("return to politics") in full swing (a period after the summer break traditionally known for its heated debates), the Right had every intention of remaining critical of the government.[71]

The communists, for their part, played the role of faithful coalition partners and constantly rallied to the support of the socialist majority. The FN's reaction on the other hand was more consistent with expectations regarding radical parties. Le Pen instrumentalized the crisis by blaming the socialists and their communist allies, using the opportunity to present his party's electoral platform: return of the death penalty, tougher immigration laws, and so on.

In the end, the magnitude-repetition model proved conclusive for all four attacks. More importantly, partisan and electoral politics played an important role and influenced the behaviour of the opposition, particularly after the second attack. Prominent right-wing politicians, who felt that Mitterrand had no legitimacy to occupy the position once held by Charles de Gaulle, resented the presence of a socialist at the Élysée Palace and were simply unwilling to rally around this controversial figure regardless of the situation. In all fairness, the socialists had set a precedent by being particularly vindictive of Giscard's government in the aftermath of the rue Copernic attack (see page 111).

Let's Not Rally! When the Governing Majority Blames the Opposition: The Wave of Attacks, Paris, September 1986

Between 8 and 17 September 1986, Paris was hit by a series of five explosions that set ablaze streets, department stores, and subway trains killing 9 people and wounding another 163, making it the worst wave of terrorist attacks in the capital since 1982. All of these attacks were linked to the Comité de Solidarité avec les Prisonniers Politiques Arabes et du Proche-Orient (CSPPA), an organization set up following the imprisonment in France of Georges Ibrahim Abdallah, leader of the FARL, for complicity in the murders of an American and an Israeli diplomat.[72] At the time, France was targeted not just by international groups but also by homegrown terrorists such as Action Directe. As a result, terrorism became a prevalent issue during the 1986 legislative election campaign, with more attacks occurring on 17 March, the day after the election; and on 20 March, two days after Jacques Chirac's appointment as prime minister.[73]

Turmoil in the streets was followed by constitutional turmoil when for the first time under the Fifth Republic, a president and a prime minister from different sides of the political divide, namely François Mitterrand (PS) and Jacques Chirac (RPR), were forced to share the executive power. A cohabitation became unavoidable following the socialists' narrow defeat at the March 1986 legislative elections. Adding to the feeling of unrest was the controversy surrounding Mitterrand's decision to switch from a majority runoff system to a proportional one, a decision that handed the far-right FN an unprecedented thirty-five deputies in the National Assembly – as many as the PC, which for its part was reaching a new low.

The magnitude-repetition model leads us to expect criticism of the government (unlikely support) following the four initial attacks (each of them low magnitude and high repetition) and the last attack (high magnitude and high repetition). However, considering the chronological proximity of these attacks (nine days separating the first and fifth attack) and the overlapping of reactions, a more logical approach might be to consider these attacks collectively rather than individually. The first attack on 8 September might still be considered separately, but the remaining ones – 12, 14, 15 and 17 September – are too clustered to differentiate the effects of repetition.

Following the 8 September attack, the socialist opposition lost no time rallying around the government. PS leader Lionel Jospin declared that the national community had to come together and the political forces had to display their will to overcome this challenge.[74] Likewise, Laurent Fabius, Chirac's predecessor in the prime minister's seat, gave his successor his complete support: "I approve wholeheartedly the Prime Minister's attitude. The entire population, as well as all political parties must back those in charge of governing the country. For my part, I will support them."[75]

Despite a heated debate on some of the reforms proposed by the new government, such as *redécoupage électoral* ("gerrymandering"), the call for union was by and large respected. The example was set by none other than President Mitterrand who made public his support for his right-wing prime minister. Edouard Alphandery (UDF) summed up his colleagues' state of mind, on the Left and the Right, by declaring, "We will not bicker with the government over the limits of counties while bombs are exploding; the people would not understand it."[76]

Yet some within the Right felt the need to avoid a domestic backlash for the attack and preserve the Right's reputation on national security issues by claiming that the socialists were responsible for the crisis.[77] The socialists did not counter this but simply asked for decency and an end to the controversy that they themselves had by and large avoided. In fact, the socialist opposition seemed eager to maintain the rally and declared once more that this was a time when the nation had to demonstrate unity.[78] As a result, the relative truce between the government and the opposition was maintained after the second attack on 12 September during which forty-one people were wounded.

After the third and fourth attacks on 14 and 15 September killed three people and wounded more than fifty, Mitterrand reiterated his earlier call for unity by declaring that the fight against terrorism concerned the whole nation, and by giving his support to a host of antiterrorist measures proposed by the government: visa requirement for nationals from outside the European community, increased border controls by the army, and "secret actions" against terrorists or those helping them.[79] Again the socialists gave their full support, merely insisting that these measures should respect people's rights:

> The Socialist Party has always made it clear that the terrorist
> issue should not be a pretext for domestic controversy ... One
> should not divide the national community at a time when it
> must demonstrate its solidarity in the face of aggressions that
> aim at coercing France. The citizens expect the government to
> be responsible and resolute in its action while respecting the
> rule of law.[80]

Yet former prime minister Mauroy, who had been severely criticized
by the right-wing opposition in 1982 (see page 115), deplored the
Right's inability to adopt a similar attitude of national concord.[81]

The explosion at the Tati department store, which killed six people and injured more than fifty on 17 September, nine days after
the first strike, was the last of the series.[82] Again some prominent
right-wing politicians blamed the Left for their handling of affairs
in the past, and again the Left replied that this was not a time for
polemics.[83] Jospin (PS), still supportive of the government, argued
that in order to enhance the cohesion of the political elite, the opposition parties should not be left out of the loop on matters pertaining to the crisis.[84] As a show of goodwill, Chirac agreed to meet
the parliamentary leaders of all groups, including the PC and FN.[85]
Following the meeting, all parties expressed their support for the
government with the exception of the FN, which demanded the appointment of a government of public safety.[86] Despite reiterating
his support and his call for national unity several times throughout
the crisis, Jospin warned the Right about giving out lessons on how
to handle terrorist crises.[87]

The wave of attacks coincided with a significant rise in the popularity of Chirac and Mitterrand, with 47 per cent of respondents
approving the prime minister's actions at the end of September (up
from 40 per cent in August 1986) and 57 per cent approving the
president's actions (up from 51 per cent).[88] Nevertheless throughout the crisis Prime Minister Chirac appeared as the stronger of the
two heads of the executive, and as the de facto president.[89] As *Le
Monde* remarked, Mitterrand who was known for his hands-on attitude in times of crisis was now leaving his prime minister in
charge:[90] "Today the Prime Minister guarantees the national unity,
he is the figure around which people rally and to whom the polit-

ical elite and foreign governments show their solidarity ... Within the executive couple, Chirac appears today as the one who holds all the power."[91]

As an ultimate sign of appeasement and in order to preserve the national unity, Mitterrand decided, after months of heated debates on the proposed project of *redécoupage électoral*, to postpone his decision for after the crisis.[92]

The radical parties were far less supportive than their mainstream counterparts. PC leader Georges Marchais condemned the first attack vigorously but did not explicitly support the government.[93] By the second attack, Marchais was railing against the government's antiterrorist measures, which he claimed were only a pretext for racist campaigns and an attempt to limit individual liberties. Furthermore, Marchais considered that the confusion between war and terrorism only served to legitimate the arms race and acts of war committed by Israel and the United States.[94] Alain Krivine, leader of the Trotskyist Ligue Communiste Révolutionnaire (LCR), shared a similar opinion and considered that these attacks allowed the government to pass measures endangering civil liberties.[95]

As in 1982, the FN remained opposed to any kind of rally, but suggested that it would accept to join a government of public safety:

> The Front National will never adhere to a consensus based on sabre-rattling and a series of half measures taken in a hurry ...
> We do not trust Chirac to implement an effective anti-terrorism policy. The only way to take the necessary measures to fight this war would be to set up a government of public safety including the Front National and backed by a real majority.[96]

Already in March 1986, shortly after the legislative elections, Le Pen had ridiculed the teary condemnations of the "gang of four" (the PS, PC, RPR, and UDF), which he found ineffectual.[97] By September, Le Pen was particularly critical of the antiterrorist measures, which he considered dated, mediocre, and inefficient.[98] In his view, these attacks were acts of war and required the re-establishment of the death penalty.[99] Interestingly, a poll conducted at the beginning of the crisis confirmed Le Pen's rising support on issues of security and justice: 29 per cent approved of his stance on those issues in

October 1985; 34 per cent did so at the beginning of the September 1986 crisis.[100]

The analysis of this case study within the established theoretical framework presents two important challenges. First, the line that separates the government from the opposition is blurred. Though in the opposition, the socialists still have one of their own at the highest echelon of the state and therefore still share part of the executive power regarding national security matters, which are traditionally the domain of the president. Even the National Assembly is almost evenly split with the right-wing parties having only a two-seat majority. Second, the series of attacks take place over a relatively short period of time (nine days), making it difficult to tell apart the reactions.

Throughout the crisis, the socialist "opposition" demonstrated its readiness to support the government. In that respect the model, which predicted criticism, is not conclusive. Yet this truce in party politics was only relative as the right-wing "majority" never showed a real desire to rally alongside the socialists. In fact, RPR and UDF members repeatedly blamed the socialists for the situation. However, none of the major figures of the government criticized the socialists. More importantly, Prime Minister Chirac avoided the controversy and never criticized publicly the opposition or President Mitterrand. On the contrary, the two heads of the executive cooperated throughout the crisis.

The high occurrence of attacks since the Right's return to power could have been interpreted by the socialists as a sign that the government was not handling national security well; hence, encouraging the opposition to be critical. Yet the opposition – and the media – knew full well that the group responsible for this series of attacks, CSPPA/FARL, had already committed several terrorist acts on French territory before the March legislative elections. Both the Right and the Left shared responsibility concerning French foreign policy in the Middle East. Under these circumstances the socialist opposition could hardly afford to criticize the government. Besides, foreign policy is traditionally the president's domain, even during periods of cohabitation. Any criticism of the government could have been perceived as a criticism of Mitterrand.

Criticisms coming from the RPR and the UDF served one purpose: to protect and maintain their ownership of the national security issue, especially with senatorial elections at the end of September.[101] The series of measures taken in the aftermath of the second attack served to reassure the people but also re-establish the Right's credibility. As it turned out, the Right gained seats in the Senate and the socialists lost a few.

The attitude of some right-wing politicians also confirms a recurrent unwillingness to side with the socialists under any circumstances; a pattern of behaviour noticeable during the 1982 wave of attacks. The fact that the Left was no longer in power in 1986 mattered little to some within the Right who still resented the election of a socialist president. Accusations of permissiveness also served to delegitimize Mitterrand.

Radical parties behaved as expected. The PC, despite being critical of any form of terrorism, was even more critical of the government's reaction and what it perceived to be curtailing basic civil liberties. The FN, as it had done before under similar circumstances, used the events of September to push its electoral program – a pro-FN demonstration was organized in Paris amid chants of "Le Pen Président!" – and criticize the RPR for failing to live up to its promises. The assault on the RPR's ownership of security-related issues could not be clearer.

The Assassination of Georges Besse: Paris, 17 November 1986

Two months after the series of attacks masterminded by the CSPPA, Action Directe committed its most infamous feat: the assassination of Georges Besse, CEO of the state-owned car manufacturer Renault.[102] Besse was the second high-ranking official to be killed by AD after General René Audran's murder in 1985.

The political situation was very similar to the one described in the previous case, with one important difference: after letting Chirac take centre stage following his electoral victory, Mitterrand was trying to regain the upper hand. As a consequence, the cohabitation with Chirac and his right-wing government became tenser.

The model suggests that following this act of terror (low magnitude and high repetition), the opposition was unlikely to support the government. Yet beyond the model, the identity of the target (a state representative) favoured a rally.

Mitterrand, abroad on an official visit, asked all political forces to unite in the fight against terrorism.[103] From Chirac to Jospin, the political elite paid its respect to a man who gave his career to public service.[104] The elite was undeniably in shock, yet aside from the traditional marks of respect, it was politics as usual. However, on 19 November following an intervention by Le Pen (FN) in the National Assembly during which the far-right leader asked the government for more actions and less rhetoric, Minister of the Interior Charles Pasqua replied by blaming the socialists once more for their carelessness and permissiveness with terrorism, reminding everyone in the assembly that the socialists had released more than three hundred members of the Italian Brigate Rosse.[105] Yet for the most part, the political elite remained silent on national security matters. By 21 November, Le Monde stopped running articles on Besse's murder; instead, reporting on the rising tension between Mitterrand and Chirac.[106]

Despite being labelled an anti-capitalist terrorist organization, the Far Left had no empathy for AD's latest operation. The PC condemned the assassination vigorously and L'Humanité, the party's newspaper, remarked that the blood of a CEO would not solve the class struggle.[107] Even more meaningful under the circumstances was the reaction of the Confédération Générale du Travail (CGT), a trade union close to the PC, which declared that this act of violence was against everything this union stood for. As a sign of respect, the CGT called off a demonstration against the restructuring plan designed by Besse shortly before his death that would have laid off numerous factory workers at the Renault plants.[108]

Le Pen, always very critical of the mainstream parties in similar circumstances, asked for a national union against terrorists.[109]

By and large the French political elite behaved as expected following Claude Besse's assassination, with expressions of sympathy coming from all sides of the political spectrum, from the Far Left to the Far Right. As hypothesized in a previous chapter, the murder of a well-known and well-respected agent of the state hardly represented an opportunity to criticize the government. However, the lingering resentment on part of the Right vis-à-vis the Left led a prominent member of Chirac's government to once more lambaste the socialists for being too permissive with terrorists. Interestingly, this criticism of the socialist legacy came in response to a similar critique directed by the FN leader toward Chirac's government, further confirming that the Right's credibility on national security was a sensitive subject matter. Yet by November 1986, the French political elite had grown weary of terrorist acts, and the controversy did not last.

THE PERIOD FROM 1990 TO 2006 RECONSIDERED

The previous section has tested the validity of the magnitude-repetition model for a selection of terrorist attacks not included in the database. By and large the model withstood the test, and the analysis of four case studies supports the claim that both the magnitude and repetition variables are linked to the decision to support or be critical of the government. Yet these two variables represent only part of the story. Other contextual factors, such as foreign affairs and the electoral timetable, have an effect on party behaviour too, even in the midst of a terrorist crisis. More importantly, the analysis suggests that party behaviour, at least in France, might be influenced by more general political considerations, such as the perceived legitimacy (or lack thereof) of the government and head of state. To some extent the behaviour of political elites is also determined by previous attitudes under similar circumstances. Thus, taking into consideration the reaction to past events might shed light on subsequent behaviour. These four case studies are therefore particularly informative for the period under consideration, 1990–2006.

The following analysis focuses on cases where the reaction of the mainstream political elite did not fully conform to expectations; that is, cases where other variables besides the magnitude and the repetition variables influenced their behaviour.

FRANCE AND THE ALGERIAN CIVIL WAR:
THE GIA ATTACKS OF 1995–96

The following case study illustrates that political elites react not only to the terrorist event but also to the management or perceived mismanagement of the crisis by the government.

France Unites:
Explosion on Avenue Friedland, Paris, 17 August 1995

A gas-canister bomb filled with nails and bolts and planted in a trash bin on avenue Friedland, near the Arc de Triomphe, exploded late afternoon 17 August, injuring seventeen people, including four children. The Algerian GIA-Commandement Général claimed responsibility for the bombing, which was linked to a series of terrorist attacks, including an explosion at the Saint-Michel subway station three weeks before, taking seven lives. Elites reacted on the assumption that this event was part of a wave of attacks perpetrated by the same terrorist organization.[110]

After two failed attempts Jacques Chirac (RPR) had been elected president in May 1995, two months before the series of attacks started.[111] More importantly, after fourteen years in opposition, interrupted by two brief spells in a cohabitation, the Right was once again in charge of the executive and legislative branches of the state, with Prime Minister Alain Juppé (RPR) heading a right/centre-right coalition made up of the RPR and UDF. The PS, which had lost the 1993 legislative elections in dramatic fashion (retaining only sixty-eight seats, hence the second cohabitation), remained the main opposition party in Parliament. On top of these pressing national security concerns, the government was facing international condemnation for announcing its decision to carry out nuclear tests in the Pacific.

The government reacted swiftly. Prime Minister Juppé arrived at the scene an hour after the explosion with a hands-on attitude, marking a noticeable change from the government's immediate reaction following the explosion at Saint-Michel three weeks before.[112]

Support for the government was massive. Predictably, the RPR, through its secretary general, indicated it had complete trust in the government's ability to face this violence.[113] More importantly, Jean Glavany (PS) declared that the socialists intended to demonstrate their sense of responsibility by supporting the government in its fight against terrorism.[114]

No dissenting voices from the mainstream political elite surfaced during the week that followed. Lionel Jospin (PS), who had been defeated by Chirac in the second round of the presidential election a few months before, uttered a few criticisms but none of them were directed at the government's response to terrorism. In fact, Jospin unambiguously declared that the national community should be united against the terrorist threat. *Le Monde* spoke of an "esprit républicain" ("a republican spirit"). However, Jospin was keen to remind everyone that back in 1982 when France was hit by a similar wave of terrorist attacks, the Right had failed to rally around the socialist government.[115] Jospin's own willingness to support the government was, in fact, not infinite, and he lost little time to remind his socialist colleagues that they had a duty to oppose the government on other issues.[116] He stigmatized in particular Chirac's economic conservatism and his rhetoric of social exclusion.

None of the radical parties broke the apparent unity of the political elite. PC leader Robert Hue declared that such odious acts can only trigger a unanimous condemnation, adding that the victims could count on the complete solidarity of the French communists.[117] FN leader Jean-Marie Le Pen was less polemical than on other occasions, though he declared that once more the French people were taken hostage in a conflict to which they were fundamentally strangers.[118]

By the end of August 1995, it was clear for both the elite and the public that France was under attack by a resolute group of terrorists most likely associated with the GIA.[119] This was not just a repetition of unconnected or loosely connected acts; this was a wave of attacks orchestrated by the same group over a narrow time period. Rather than separate occurrences, this was a two-month long crisis; therefore, it is likely that the number of previous attacks did not influence the reaction. The repetition effect was also offset by the fact that

Juppé's conservative government had been in power for less than three months when the attacks started. This short timeframe made it difficult for the opposition to blame the government for any shortcoming in the fight against terror. In other words, the government received the benefit of the doubt.

It is also likely that the French political elite chose to rally around the victims as much as around the government. The presence of children among the victims only heightened the necessity for opposition leaders to show their solidarity. This need to project an image of responsibility and compassion probably accounts for the behaviour of radical parties such as the FN, which toned down its traditional rhetoric of blame. The communists were keen to be seen as supporting the government. A member of the *national comity* reasoned that a purely negative attitude toward President Chirac would not make the PC win anything. Their reaction was part of a larger strategy of constructive opposition aimed at differentiating themselves from the socialists and giving Chirac the benefit of the doubt.[120]

Yet despite unanimous support, Jospin reminded everyone that the Right had opted out of the rally in 1982 and suggested that the rally was conditional on the Right reciprocating the next time a socialist government faced a similar situation. Eventually Jospin signalled that this was a limited rally and that being critical on other aspects of the government's handling of affairs, such as the economy, was very much a duty for the opposition.

A Tale of Two Presidents and a Controversial Meeting That Never Was: Explosion in a Subway Train Near Station Musée-d'Orsay, Paris, 17 October 1995

By the end of October 1995, France had experienced what was arguably one of the worst waves of terrorist attacks to hit the country since World War II. The series of attacks masterminded by Algerian terrorists that had started in early July had claimed ten lives and wounded more than two hundred people. One last explosion, the eighth since the beginning of the crisis, aboard a subway train during morning rush hour injured another twenty-nine people.[121]

The situation is very similar to the one described previously, with the RPR and UDF in power, and the PS in opposition. However, by October 1995, the honeymoon period had run its course and public dissatisfaction with the government was growing, eventually triggering massive demonstrations throughout France.

After a long and murderous summer during which the left-wing opposition never once failed to support the government, a certain weariness was taking hold of the political elite. Signs of impatience with the government's inability to stop the attacks were becoming more ominous, especially among backbenchers. More importantly, just a few days before the explosion near the Quai d'Orsay, the headquarters of French diplomacy, the opposition vehemently criticized President Chirac for scheduling a meeting with Algerian president Liamine Zéroual during a United Nations summit in New York. Many within the opposition feared that this meeting would further demonstrate that France was meddling in Algerian affairs and signal that the French government had thrown its weight in favour of the incumbent for the upcoming Algerian presidential election.[122]

As an instance of low magnitude and high repetition, criticism of the government was likely. Yet if the opposition's recent behaviour was any indication, this outcome appeared unlikely as the leading figures in the PS had rallied after the previous seven attacks. Yet in the midst of the controversy surrounding the Chirac-Zéroual meeting, the latest attack could also embolden critics of the government's policy toward Algeria.

Prime Minister Juppé reacted swiftly to news of the latest attack and addressed the deputies present at the National Assembly merely hours after the explosion. His intentions it seems were to raise the flag and ask the opposition to rally around it, as they had done after each previous attack since July. After a brief opening address in which Philippe Séguin (RPR), president of the National Assembly, announced the unanimous condemnation of the attack by all deputies,[123] Juppé declared, "I call upon the solidarity of everyone. I want to thank the leaders of all political parties who since the beginning of this crisis have shown through their actions a spirit of responsibility ... There are times in the life of a nation when the citizens gather to face together challenges that could jeopardize the country's supreme interests."[124] Mindful of the existing controversy, Juppé reminded the deputies that the meeting between Chirac and Zéroual was not a sign of support for one of the candidates, but merely an indication that Algeria's difficulties could only be resolved through dialogue.

Juppé's appeal was initially successful and managed to dampen criticisms. The opposition displayed both its solidarity with the government and its respect for the victims. Addressing the deputies after the prime minister, Laurent Fabius (president of the socialist group in the National Assembly) rallied unambiguously: "I would like, Mr. Prime Minister, bearing in mind lessons from the past, and being fully aware of the disagreements that exist between us, to tell you that during moments such as this one we wish, beyond all disagreements, to see national solidarity prevail in the struggle against this unacceptable violence."[125]

Lionel Jospin, although less eloquently than Fabius, asked for the complete solidarity of the national community.[126] PS spokesperson François Hollande remarked that his party had voiced its doubts about the meeting between Chirac and Zéroual but that today, faced with a new attack, the socialists should not say anything that could prove dangerous for the national community.[127] This display of solidarity was concluded by Michel Péricard, speaking for the RPR, who predictably declared that in moments such as this, union behind the prime minister and the president is the only one that counts.[128]

This unity was displayed again when Prime Minister Juppé and the leaders of all parliamentary groups met to discuss the situation. Yet backbenchers were still voicing their skepticism regarding the Chirac-Zéroual meeting,[129] and former socialist prime minister Pierre Mauroy came out publicly against this meeting.[130]

By the following day (two days after the terrorist attack), the unified front was collapsing. Jospin insisted that Chirac should not be meeting with Zéroual.[131] Soon after, the leader of the socialists in the Senate, as well as other prominent socialists, expressed similar concerns.[132] Meanwhile, other leading socialists such as former ministers Claude Cheysson and Jean-Pierre Chevènement expressed their disagreement with their colleagues, arguing that a meeting between two heads of state was normal.[133]

The meeting became more controversial after a London-based, Saudi-financed newspaper, *Asharq Al-Awsat*, reported that in exchange for the end of their terrorist campaign, the GIA had allegedly asked the French government to cancel the meeting between the two presidents.[134] Some within the RPR claimed that by opposing the meeting, the socialists were submitting to the terrorists.[135] Finally, two days before the meeting was due, the Algerian authorities cancelled it, providing the socialists with more ammunition to criticize the government. Fabius, who less than a week before had received a round of applause from the right-wing deputies for his support, declared that the government's handling of the Chirac-Zéroual meeting epitomed bad decision-making.[136]

As it had done previously during this crisis (see page 133) the PC backed the government, pointing out through Alain Bocquet (leader of the communists in the National Assembly) that democrats must join forces to defeat terrorism.[137] With regards to the Chirac-Zéroual meeting, PC secretary general Robert Hue claimed that there was nothing wrong about heads of state meeting one another, adding that France's policy could not be changed under the pressure of terrorists.[138]

The FN remained on the offensive, blaming the government for trying to deliberately implicate France in the Algerian conflict,[139] and claiming that contrary to declarations made by members of the government terrorism was on the rise.[140] After the cancellation of the Chirac-Zéroual meeting, the FN through Bruno Mégret (number two in the party hierarchy) declared that Chirac had not only ridiculed and humiliated France but also proven his incompetence.[141]

The magnitude-repetition model, in view of the above declarations, is conclusive. Despite sympathetic declarations by prominent opposition leaders, the rally did not last more than a couple of days. This initial support, as well as the auspicious behaviour of the opposition throughout the crisis, suggests that the socialists were not becoming impatient with the government. In fact, the repetition variable was probably not a factor in the decision by prominent left-

wing figures to break away from the rally. After all, the GIA-led terrorist campaign was perpetrated in retaliation to an Algerian policy shared by left-wing and right-wing governments alike.[142] French
meddling in Algerian affairs was a collective responsibility. Apart
from the FN, none of the parties blamed the government for its inability to end the attacks. The rally ended because prominent members of the Left felt that Chirac's meeting with Zéroual was ill-timed
and ill-advised considering the ongoing crisis. The controversy and
in particular the abrupt decision by Algerian authorities to cancel
the meeting presented the socialists with an opportunity to criticize
the government for its lack of judgment without being perceived as
disloyal to the country. Thus, the key factor in ending the rally was
not the duration of the crisis – or the repetition of attacks – much
less the magnitude, but rather a basic disagreement as to how to
handle relations with Algeria. To be sure, the difficulties experienced
elsewhere by the government, such as with the economy, and its
growing unpopularity with the population were conducive to criticisms of its handling of foreign affairs.

The FN again used the opportunity to ridicule the RPR on its own
turf, regarding national security. In addition, the identity of the terrorists played into the hands of a party bent on curbing immigration
from North Africa. The PC behaved unexpectedly. Not only did the
party refrain from criticizing Juppé's right-wing government but
they were openly supportive throughout the crisis and even backed
Chirac's decision to meet with Zéroual. To some extent this surprising behaviour was part of a wider strategy whereby the communists would try to offer constructive rather than systematic
criticisms, which meant siding with the government on occasions.
Besides the party had decided to give Chirac the benefit of the doubt
during his first few months in office.[143]

The Unlikely Rally:
Explosion at Port-Royal Subway, Paris, 3 December 1996

This latest GIA attack provides a unique and intriguing case with a
rally occurring despite the magnitude-repetition model predicting
otherwise. The attack, which killed 4 and injured another 128 people, was preceded by twenty-five other terrorist acts, all happening

during Prime Minister Juppé's term. Both high magnitude and high repetition were conducive to criticisms of the right-wing government, yet instead the opposition gave its support. Former socialist prime minister Laurent Fabius received a round of applause from right-wing MPs by declaring at the National Assembly, "We have always backed antiterrorist actions taken by the authorities, and we have rejected any political exploitation. We will not behave any differently today."[144]

Another socialist leader, Jospin, remarked in similar fashion that the socialists must work to bring the population together.[145] François Bayrou (UDF) and Jean-François Mansel (RPR), for their part, declared that this moment called for all French people to rally behind the president.[146]

The communists gave a limited and essentially silent support by expressing through their leader, Robert Hue, their utmost indignation.[147] However, the FN, as usual, went on the offensive and denounced the inconsequence and weakness of an inept government.[148]

More than a year after France was hit by a wave of attacks orchestrated by the GIA, this was obviously a severe setback for the government, particularly at a time when President Chirac and Prime Minister Juppé were facing constant criticisms for their decision to embark on a policy of economic austerity to meet the criteria set by the European Commission for the entry into the eurozone. With the unemployment rate rising, and the president and the prime minister at their lowest in the polls, the government was particularly weak and thus an easy prey for opposition parties. Yet surprisingly the socialists avoided criticizing the government that was becoming more unpopular by the day and decided to be openly supportive.

The socialists' attitude is less puzzling if one considers the magnitude and the sheer atrocity of the attack (4 dead and 128 injured), which made it one of the worst terrorist acts in recent decades in terms of overall casualties. Did the magnitude variable offset the effects of the high number of previous attacks? This is an interesting working hypothesis. It implies that a large number of victims (dead and injured) might trigger a rally, regardless of whether fatalities are numerous and regardless of the duration of the crisis and the number of previous attacks.[149] This suggests that deaths and injuries should be factored into a magnitude index. The explosion at Port-

Royal station was meant to kill as many people as possible. Although many escaped, the threat to national security must have been obvious to most members of the political elite; hence, their unequivocal support of the government.

The French political elite was also working under the assumption that this latest attack was the work of Algerian jihadists, possibly even of members of the GIA, a group responsible for the 1995 series of attacks. As discussed, Left and Right shared responsibility for French meddling in Algerian affairs and were unlikely to criticize one another for what was arguably a byproduct of this meddling. In any case, the socialists had little to gain by criticizing the government over its handling of terrorism. The cost of being perceived as unsympathetic to the many victims and even disloyal in the face of an external threat was not inexistent. The government was in enough trouble as it was, digging its own grave by pursuing widely unpopular economic policies.

The FN, on the other hand, was at liberty to criticize this failed Algerian policy and call into question the government's credibility on matters of national security, unlike the PC, which, as it had done throughout the 1995 wave of attacks, refrained from criticizing the government.

FRANCE AND CORSICAN SEPARATISTS

As a general rule, low-magnitude terrorist attacks, much like foiled attacks, are unlikely to be reported by the media, let alone trigger any kind of rally.[150] Obviously there are exceptions and certain low-magnitude acts will resonate enough to register on the media radar and elicit a political response. A number of reasons can account for this outcome. The first rests on a wider definition of magnitude that includes fatalities and wounded. As discussed, a high tally of wounded could signal an elevated national security threat, which would have the same effect on the political elite as a high number of fatalities. The perpetrators most certainly intended to kill as many as possible, thus the *potential* number of deaths that these explosions could have caused is here more relevant than the *actual* number. Media outlets like *Le Monde* often treat these attacks like any other high-magnitude attack, with front-page and in-depth coverage: "if it bleeds, it leads." Faced with destruction and mutilation, mainstream political elites are likely to react by rallying, even if no one died as a result of the attack.

Another explanation for this atypical outcome points to the target, particularly state representatives, as with the assassination of Claude Erignac, which is discussed below. However, the attack on a state representative need not be particularly "successful" to elicit support. The failed assassination attempt on President Jacques Chirac on 14 July 2004 is a case in point. The incident involving a lone gunman was sufficient to trigger a wave of sympathy, albeit a limited one, even though Chirac was neither injured nor in any danger of being hurt.[151] Yet the combination of the target (head of state), the date (Bastille Day) and the location (Champs-Élysées) – three powerful symbols for the French republic – made it impossible for any politician on either side of the political divide – even among radical elites – not to express their support.

The Assassination of Claude Erignac: Ajaccio, Corsica, 6 February 1998

On the evening of 6 February 1998, shortly before he was to join his wife at a concert in Ajaccio, Claude Erignac, the prefect of Corsica, was shot point-blank on a sidewalk. Erignac, who had chosen not to have bodyguards with him, died at the scene. Corsican nationalists were blamed for the assassination.

For the third time under the Fifth Republic, France was governed by a president and a prime minister from different sides of the political divide. However, unlike the two previous cohabitations, this time a right-wing president, Jacques Chirac (RPR), shared power with a left-wing government headed by Prime Minister Lionel Jospin (PS).[152] In addition, whereas the two previous cohabitations had occurred at the end of the president's seven-year tenure, this third cohabitation started relatively early in the president's mandate and would continue for another five years until the next legislative election in 2002.

The PS had more seats than any other party, but was still short of the absolute majority in the National Assembly. As a result, Jospin was forced to govern with coalition partners: the PC and les Verts ("the Greens"). Much to the surprise of pundits and political analysts the cohabitation was running relatively smoothly, and both Chirac and Jospin enjoyed relatively high approval ratings in the polls (Becker 2003). Erignac's assassination was the first serious terrorist act since the socialists' return to power.

According to the magnitude-repetition model, the assassination of the prefect (low magnitude and low repetition) should have elicited no reaction from the political elite, and yet it resulted in one of the largest rallies in recent years.

Since 1975, Corsican separatists targeted the French state several times, but never before had one of these factions succeeded in murdering such a high-ranking official; indeed, the highest-ranked civil servant on the island. The attack was considered so serious that President Chirac reacted in person, rather than through his spokesperson. On the front steps of the Élysée Palace, Chirac solemnly told the press that the assassination of a state representative was a barbarous act of extreme gravity and without precedent in French history.[153] Echoing Chirac's statement, Prime Minister Jospin said that the nation as a whole had been hit, and that the state had to present a unified front.[154] Other majority leaders reacted in similar fashion. Laurent Fabius (PS), president of the National Assembly, called for the strongest possible condemnation by the national community.[155]

The mainstream opposition was unanimous in its condemnation. Philippe Séguin (RPR president) declared that the state must chase after the assassins in order to defend the republic and preserve national unity.[156] Adding his voice to the chorus, former prime minister Alain Juppé insisted on the necessity to come together as a nation to guarantee Corsica's civil peace. François Bayrou in the name of the UDF (centre-right wing) declared that such an event must rally people beyond political differences.[157]

The rally among mainstream elites was complete, with the three main parties calling explicitly on everyone to unite.

A week after the tragic event, during a ceremony organized in Ajaccio and attended by leaders of the Left and the Right, Chirac declared, "Beyond our differences, beyond political cleavages, we represent a unanimous France, a France standing tall. France is one and indivisible."[158] A similar unanimity was displayed the following day during question period at the National Assembly.[159]

The only dissenting voice on the Left came from Michel Charasse, former minister under Mitterrand and a renowned loose cannon, who declared that in the last thirty years the state and the republic had not been doing their jobs and were effectively the true assassins of Claude Erignac.[160] For his part Jean-Louis Debré (RPR), former minister of the interior, criticized Jospin for not sending more police to the island. However, both Charasse and Debré were by then minor political players, with no real impact on the debate.

The two main radical parties reacted in different ways. PC leader Robert Hue declared that the republic had been targeted and that the entire national community had to denounce this odious crime.[161] Jean-Marie Le Pen, who incidentally was not invited to the ceremony in Ajaccio (unlike Robert Hue), voiced strong criticism at the political elite, declaring that the assassination was proof that the nation's social fabric was falling apart and disorder was on the rise.[162] He concluded by accusing the different governments (Left and Right) of connivance with the Corsican terrorists.

What is interesting about the reaction to this terrorist act is that the distinction between opposition and majority was blurred once again. The RPR and UDF (right and centre-right) were the main opposition parties in the lower house, but still retained a sizable share of the executive power through President Chirac; thus, both the socialists and their right-wing opposition stood to gain from a rally. As it turned out, the Left's call for unity was reciprocated by the Right. In addition, the very nature of cohabitation made a rally more likely, regardless of the specificities of the terrorist act, the unwritten rule being that on matters of foreign affairs and security policy a cohabitation government speaks with one voice.[163]

The breadth of the rally in terms of support across the political spectrum is also a consequence of the inclusiveness of the coalition government led by Jospin. Despite having the largest number of MPs, the socialists governed with five junior partners in what has been termed a *majorité plurielle* ("plural majority").[164] To be fair, these parties' commitment to the government was at times

questionable; many programmatic differences and even incompat-
ibilities existed within this plural majority, notably between the ecol-
ogists and communists. Yet this tragic event provided an
opportunity to project an image of cohesion within government.

Neither the Right nor the Left had over the years been able to
deal with Corsican nationalists and put an end to terrorism on the
island, so neither were in a position to criticize. The rhetoric across
the board was similar and did not pit the hawks against the doves.
Softer and tougher approaches had been tried over the years by left-
and right-wing governments to little avail. Jospin, for instance, declared that negotiation was no longer an option: "[I]l n'y a rien à né-
gocier en Corse" ("[T]here is nothing to negotiate").[165] Furthermore,
the Jospin government had only been in power eight months when
Erignac was assinated, so criticism from the Right was unlikely.

The shortcomings of the magnitude-repetition model are not surprising under these circumstances. The French political elite has always been quick to rally whenever the state was targeted (see table
5), a likely outcome in a country with a strong Jacobin tradition. To
be fair, the rally was perhaps not so much around the government
as around the republic and what it stands for. The need to uphold
the state's authority and defend its territorial integrity was the over-
riding concern, even for the PC, which was part of the governing
coalition. Yet this is exactly what prompted Le Pen (FN) to criticize
the political elite and discredit its record regarding Corsica. The FN
had little to gain from rallying around Chirac, who was Le Pen's
sworn enemy and its ideological nemesis, and had little to lose from
underlying the inability of the Left and the Right to solve the Corsican problem once and for all. Whereas all parties seemed to behave in the best interest of the state, the FN behaved in the best
electoral interest of itself and cared little for the patriotic imperative.

FRANCE AND POST-9/11 JIHADISM

The Charlie Hebdo *and Kosher Supermarket Shootings:*
Paris, 7–9 January 2015

Since the 9/11 attacks, France has been one of the primary targets for
various jihadi groups operating in Europe, but unlike Spain and the

United Kingdom, was for nearly fifteen years remarkably successful at foiling these potentially large-scale attacks. Already in December 1994, in an act foreshadowing the events in Manhattan seven years later, Algerian terrorists hijacked an Air France plane with the probable intention to crash it into the Eiffel Tower. And in December 2000, an attack against the Strasbourg Christmas Market by terrorists close to al Qaeda was foiled at the last minute. However, Mohammed Mehra's killing spree in March 2012 in which seven people, including three children, were murdered in Toulouse and Montauban, served as a reminder that none of the counterterrorist measures, not even the well-tested Vigipirate plan, could keep all terrorists at bay, even homegrown ones. In fact, Mehra's actions prefigured the events of January 2015. Like the Kouachi brothers, Mehra operated on his own, claimed to act on behalf of al Qaeda, and claimed to have trained in Afghanistan (Saïd Kouachi claimed to have trained in Yemen). Vengeance was their avowed goal; dying as "martyrs," their chosen fate.

At 11:20 a.m. on a brisk winter day, Saïd and Chérif Kouachi were armed with Kalashnikovs and approached the offices of the satirical weekly *Charlie Hebdo* in downtown Paris. After initially attempting by mistake to enter the building next door, they made their way to 10 rue Nicolas-Appert where they killed a maintenance worker, Frédéric Boisseau, before proceeding to the second floor where the *Charlie Hebdo* offices were located. Shouting "Allah Akbar!" the two men made their way toward a room where the contributors were holding their weekly meeting. Five minutes later ten more people were killed: renowned cartoonists Jean "Cabu" Cabut, Stéphane "Charb" Charbonnier, Phillipe Honoré, Bernard "Tignous" Verlhac, and Georges Wolinski; columnists Elsa Cayat and Bernard Maris; copy editor Mustapha Ourrad; visitor Michel Renaud; and Charbonnier's bodyguard, Franck Brinsolaro. Three *Charlie Hebdo* contributors were wounded.

By 11:30 a.m., a police unit was on its way and the two gunmen exited the premises shouting, "We have avenged the prophet. We have killed Charlie Hebdo!" and killed another policeman point-blank in an adjacent street. After a two-day manhunt, the Kouachi brothers were killed while charging the police special units (GIGN) that surrounded their hideout in the north of Paris.

A day after the *Charlie Hebdo* shooting, as the Kouachi brothers were still on the run, their accomplice, Amedy Coulibaly, killed a policewoman at point-blank in the south of Paris. The media did not immediately perceive the murder as terrorist, much less link it to the events of the previous day. But by the next day, Coulibaly's identity and his intent were made plain as he entered a Jewish supermarket in Paris and shot four people dead before holding another sixteen hostage. A few hours later Coulibaly was killed in a police assault launched minutes after the one against the Kouachi brothers.

The murderous three-day rampage killed seventeen, making it one of the deadliest terrorist attacks on French soil since 18 June 1961 when the OAS, a pro-French Algeria terrorist group bombed a Strasbourg–Paris train, killing twenty-eight.

The subsequent rally described below corresponds to what the magnitude-repetition model predicts in the case of a high-magnitude act preceded by fewer than five attacks (low repetition).

An hour after the attack, French president François Hollande stood in front of the *Charlie Hebdo* building, condemning an act of "exceptional barbarism" and calling for national unity.[166] Nicolas Sarkozy as leader of the UMP, France's main opposition party, reciprocated by calling on French people to unite and urging the government to take measures to fight terrorism.[167] In similar fashion, François Bayrou (now leader of the centre-right Mouvement Democrat, or MoDem, formerly UDF)[168] declared, "We have one duty, unite."[169] François Fillon (prime minister during Sarkozy's presidential mandate) summed up the mood across the mainstream political spectrum: "Criminals hope to intimidate us [French people], but they reinforce our courage. They hope to divide us, but reinforce our unity! ... To the terrorist criminals, let's oppose or national unity, our composure, our relentless determination."[170]

The UMP, through its Senate leader, Bruno Retailleau, underlined the need to avoid confusing the jihadists responsible for those attacks with French Muslim citizens. And in the same vein, former prime minister Jean-Pierre Raffarin (UMP) reminded everyone to preserve a harmonious life between communities.[171]

When Jean-Louis Debré (UMP) addressed the political elite, he recalled past struggles against terrorism from 1995 to 1996 during his term as interior minister: "There must be a national union and solidarity. Now is not the time anymore to be critical of one another. Let us be all united in order to fight against those terrorists."[172]

And in case anyone still doubted the necessity to rally in the wake of such a horrendous act, PS leader Jean-François Cambadélis said, "There will be a before and after January 7. This is a situation which on the scale of France is equivalent to September 11, 2001 in the United States."[173]

The more radical-minded PC called for a rallying of all republican forces beyond political and religious differences.[174] Even Jean-Luc Mélenchon, leader of the far-left Parti de Gauche (PG) and a vocal opponent of mainstream parties, declared that "we must demonstrate that we are capable of sticking together, of being a united people, which will not be divided."[175]

Yet words of caution abounded. Emmanuelle Cosse, national secretary of les Verts, warned that despite the horror of this terrible act, one must not let fear take over. She referred in particular to " a unhealthy climate that exists in our society: many confusions, amalgams" and warned against a fictitious rally.[176] For his part, Nicolas Dupont-Aignan, leader of Debout la France (DLF) – a resolutely anti-European party attempting to win over FN voters – asked in a tweet shortly after the attacks why Vigipirate was not at its highest level, and demanded an explanation by the government. Dupont-Aignan asked for more border control and a suspension of the Schengen Agreement, which allows citizens and residents of various European Union (EU) countries to cross borders freely.[177]

The FN's response was less homogenous. Its leader, Marine Le Pen, talked about "a nation united to say that us, French people of all origins, will not accept threats on our lives and our freedoms."[178] Yet at the same time, one of the FN's vice-presidents (and Le Pen's spouse), Louis Aliot, stuck to a more traditional FN script:

National unity means nothing, these are merely words. We have solidarity and compassion for the families. For the rest, the duty of the president and his government is to protect the citizens against a known menace. Until now, they have tried to put things into perspective. Our country is the main purveyor of troops to the jihadists and ISIS ... This criminal episode will reignite the debate on the presence of Islamism in our suburbs and the entire French territory.[179]

In the hours following the attacks, Prime Minister Manuel Valls contacted Sarkozy to discuss the organization of a march in Paris the following Sunday, 11 January, and made the gesture publically known. The point of contention was the failure to agree on whether or not the Front National and its leader Marine Le Pen should be invited to march alongside the other party leaders in what was being advertised as a republican rally. The UMP was in favour of the FN joining the march, but the PS was split. In the end, Le Pen was not invited to the march and denounced a "shabby political manoeuvre" that excludes millions of French people.[180] The rationale behind this decision was that the FN was simply not a republican party and never belonged to this tradition of party politics. Some within the republican mainstream Right disagreed. Laurent Wauquiez, UMP secretary general, announced that "it isn't acceptable to exclude the Front National from a national unity demonstration," to which FN vice-president Florian Philippot replied that "under those conditions, the UMP should not accept to take part in this little sectarian demonstration" adding that this is not a march of national union but a march for the system in place.[181]

Symbols of unity abounded in the days that followed the march. On 14 January, for the first time since 1918 and the end of World War I, all members of the National Assembly spontaneously sang "La Marseillaise." A few minutes before, Claude Bartolone, the socialist president of the assembly, had addressed his peers: "[N]ational unity is the shield that protects our society from division."[182] Reflecting on those "magnificent demonstrations of unity" witnessed throughout France a couple of days before, Bartolone asked that the collective interest takes precedence over private interests.[183]

The rally was massive, both within the elite and among the general public. A large swath of the French Muslim community condemned vigorously the various attacks and joined the republican rally. The messages of support were often directed at the victims, their families, and their co-workers, as well as to the various French police forces involved in chasing the terrorists.

The mainstream parties behaved as expected. The sheer atrocity and magnitude of the attacks were enough to convince most of the French political elite to rally. The targets (journalists, the police, and the Jewish community) as well as the terrorists' identities and their likely sponsors (al Qaeda and ISIS) reinforced the urge to present a unified front across all parties. Radical parties, particularly on the Left, behaved in similar fashion.

Despite being initially sympathetic to the idea of a rally, the FN quickly realized that the Left, in particular the governing PS, had serious misgivings about including the Far Right in a republican march. Yet to Marine Le Pen this public affront was not necessarily a bad news. After all, did she want to be seen marching alongside the leaders of what she had denigrated time and again as the "UMPS"; that is, the parties of the system? And yet for the past five years, she had tried to normalize the political organization founded by her father, hoping to transform a radical movement into a mainstream party. Having failed to be accepted as such in the aftermath of the attacks, Le Pen did what her father had done in similar circumstances: portray herself, her party, and her supporters as victims of the system, and used the attacks to once again put forth her political agenda: curb immigration, present Islam as a threat, and so on. In the end, Le Pen distanced herself from the rally: "I do not ask to be integrated into the national union. The national union is not a blackmail, where joining is conditional on shutting up. I do not intend to be subjected to this blackmail. The concept [of rallying] is distorted. They [the government] will have to bear the electoral consequences."[184]

The 13 November Attacks:
Paris and Saint Denis, 13 November 2015

The prevailing mood in Saint Denis on this November evening was celebratory as some 80,000 spectators gathered in the Stade de France to watch France take on Germany in a friendly soccer game. President Hollande was in attendance, and many millions were watching one of international soccer's most anticipated game. Else-where, Parisians and tourists were enjoying this surprisingly mild November evening, sitting on terraces or attending concerts in ven-ues such as the Bataclan where the Eagles of Death Metal were per-forming for more than a thousand fans.

Experts were quick to point out that the horrendous attacks per-petrated between 9:20 p.m. and 12:20 a.m. were expected and that ever since the January attacks, the question had been not *if* such a bloodbath would happen but *when*. Yet the atmosphere since Janu-ary had never been one of impending doom, despite a close call in August when carnage on a high-speed train between Amsterdam and Paris was averted by the courageous reaction of several passen-gers who wrestled the lone shooter before he could go on a ram-page (only two passengers were injured).

Paris represented in many ways the ideal target, the most-visited city in the world, one that resonates with Japanese honeymooners, North American backpackers, European exchange students, and various lovers of art, culture, and fine cuisine. Paris, more than any other European city would achieve maximum publicity for ISIS. Turkey, Tunisia, Nigeria, and Lebanon had been recently targeted in equally horrendous ways, but somehow only the sight of Parisian joie de vivre cut short by the blasts and bullets of suicide terrorists could trigger global angst.[185] The massive media cover-age that followed was evidence than when Paris bleeds, the West-ern world reels.[186]

At 9:20 p.m., a three-man commando made several unsuccessful at-tempts to enter the Stade de France while the game had already been underway for a few minutes. Finally realizing that they could not proceed with their initial plan, which was to kill hundreds in front of a TV audience of millions, the three men detonated their explo-sive belts outside the stadium, killing one passerby and injuring a dozen more people. For spectators and TV viewers, the explosions sounded like fireworks so common at sporting events. The tragedy taking place around the stadium and across the city would only be revealed to those in attendance at the end of the game.[187] Meanwhile, Hollande was evacuated shortly after the explosions took place.

The second commando launched its attack at 9:25 in the heart of Paris – the tenth and eleventh arrondissement – gunning down people in restaurants and terraces. Within a few minutes thirty-nine lay dead and more than thirty were injured. And while two of the armed men escaped, the third detonated his explosive belt within a café.

By 9:40, the third and final act of this macabre plan started at the Bataclan where about 1,500 people were attending a concert. Three men entered into the venue as the band started playing "Kiss the Devil" and went on a killing spree that left ninety dead and many more injured. At 10:15 the Brigade de recherche et d'intervention (BRI) assisted by members of the Recherche assistance intervention dissuasion (RAID) launched an assault, which ended at 12:20 a.m. with the death of the last remaining terrorists.

In the end, 130 people were killed and 351 injured in what became the deadliest terrorist attack in France since World War II and the second-largest in Europe after the Madrid attacks in 2004. Later that evening after the assault ended, Hollande declared that "this is an act of war committed by a terrorist army, Daech" and imposed a state of emergency across France.[188] The president reminded his fellow citizens that now was a time to display unity and stay calm.[189] Another attack planned a few days later at La Défense, a major business district, was foiled, and on 18 November, Abdelhamid Abaaoud, one of the masterminds, was killed during a police operation.

At around 1 a.m., minutes after the the stand-off at the Bataclan and Hollande's declaration, Nicolas Sarkozy, as head of the opposition Les Républicains (formerly the UMP), issued a statement supporting the president: "In this tragic circumstances, the solidarity of all French people is a necessity. With this in mind, I support the decision taken tonight to decree a state of emergency and the closing of the borders."[190]

By the following morning, many world leaders had expressed their sorrow and full support to France. US president Barack Obama noted that the attacks were not only attacks against Paris but against humanity and our universal values. Back in Paris, Prime Minister Manuel Valls on national television underlined once more that France was at war with ISIS and swore to destroy it, using a military response proportionnal to the magnitute of the terrorist attacks (TF1). And though Valls insisted that the upcoming regional elections would be held, across France many candidates and most parties decided to suspend their campaign for a few days.

Though the mainstream opposition seemed to respect the rally in those early hours, some prominent right-wing figures were striking a different cord. Alain Juppé (Les Républicains), a former prime minister and a potential candidate for the 2017 presidential election, considered that the international coalitions' objectives in Syria had to be clarified for they were not effective anymore. He was keen to reappraise the policy of opposing both ISIS and Bashar al-Assad, pointing out that today destroying the former must be the priority (France 2TV).

The FN lost no time criticizing the government. Nicolas Bay, party general secretary, tweeted the following at 10:48 p.m. as the police were storming the Bataclan: "While this [sic] Hollande and this [sic] Valls were combatting the FN, bloodthirsty assassins were preparing their attacks! Shame, shame, shame on both of them."[191] Louis Aliot (FN) using slightly toned-down rhetoric called out Valls through a tweet of his own asking, "Mister Valls, do you see where the danger is? The real one! Irresponsible!"[192] Gilbert Collard, one of two FN members of the National Assembly, lamented an "abandonned France."[193] For her part, Marine Le Pen remained relatively restrained and merely expressed a "cold anger."[194]

Criticisms of the government also came from more mainstream quarters, such as Républicains backbenchers. Nicolas Dhuic suggesting that "money" from Qatar and Saudi Arabia were at the heart of the terrorist problem, and Lionel Luca remarking that France was on its way to becoming "lebanized." Yet the more prominent members of Les Républicains remained cautious and avoided outright criticisms, with Sarkozy saying that France needed to understand why such attacks had occurred and the security policy needed major overhaul, and his former prime minister, François Fillon, stressing that the president had taken the necessary decisions to protect the security of French people and insisting that national unity is a duty.[195] Acknowledging the rather subdued response from Sarkozy and Fillon, Jean-Christophe Cambadélis, PS first secretary, reminded everyone that now was indeed the time for national unity and thanked President Sarkozy and other political leaders for rallying.[196]

For another day at least, the national union was maintained. Jean-Luc Mélenchon (PG) remained committed to the rally as he had done in January, and repeated that "at this time, all quarrels end" and hoped that "our governmental decision-makers have the mean to react as they wish," a strong support for someone who had been very critical of the socialist government.[197] Even Le Pen, despite warning shots from some of her henchmen, declared that she approved of the state of emergency and border closures as decided by the president, but underlined the need for France to recover the control of its borders for good.[198] In her opinion, "France and the French are not secure anymore.[199]

As had been the case in January, the majority of French muslims expressed grief. Anouar Kbibech, president of the Conseil français du culte musulman (the main organization representing French muslims) remarked that unity and national solidarity were needed to cope with the horror of the attacks.[200] On Sunday, less than forty-eight hours after the attacks, Hollande met with all main political leaders (including Le Pen) at the Élysée Palace. During the initial twenty-four hours after the attacks, only the Trotskyist Nouveau Parti Anticapitaliste (NPA, formerly the LCR) announced that it refused the national union.

By the third day, many in the mainstream opposition were ready to distance themselves from the government. Sarkozy, Juppé, and Fillon, the main contenders to represent Les Républicains at the 2017 presidential election, were demanding policy changes regarding Syria, notably a rapprochement with Russia. Sarkozy proposed to expel radical imams and close down Salafist mosques.[201] Bruno Le Maire, another Républicain presidential hopeful, wondered why ten months had been lost since the January attacks and lamented that the true nature of the menace had not been understood.[202]

On Monday 16 November, Hollande addressed the Parliament gathered in a congress at Versailles, both the National Assembly and the Senate, for the first time since he became president. He reaffirmed that France was at war. His proposal to eradicate terrorism while respecting French values seemed to contradict his wish to strip binationals convicted of engaging in terrorist activities of their French citizenship.[203] A quasi-unanimous standing ovation accompanied by the singing of "La Marseillaise" followed the presidential address. This, as pointed out by David Revault d'Allonnes in *Le Monde*, is when Hollande became a hawk, and made it that more difficult for Les Républicains to lambaste the socialists for being the eternal permissive doves that endanger the country's security.[204]

Yet the rally around the flag proved more difficult to maintain than in the aftermath of the January attacks. During question period the next day (Tuesday) in the National Assembly, some Républicains representatives booed Justice Minister Christiane Taubira before her address, prompting Républicains house leader, Christian Jacob to say the session was "not up to standard."[205] By Wednesday, a certain calm had been restored in the lower house. "Now is not the time for polemics," said Alain Marty (Les Républicains), asking why ISIS hadn't been targeted by the French air force sooner.[206] Others, like Edouard Philippe (Les Républicains), warned against falling in the partisan trap.[207]

Prime Minister Valls was keen to avoid a repetition of the post-January attacks period during which socialists openly disagreed on the best strategy and repeatedly called for unity.[208] However some of the new proposed legislation, such as striping binationals of the French citizenship if they are convicted of terrorist acts, remained a bone of contention among the cadres of the PS, including Taubira and Carlos Da Silva, an MP close to Manuel Valls. "Now is not the time to debate amongs ourselves," Da Silva said, "but to take into account the fear felt by French people."[209]

Hollande's pro-security stance left the opposition little leeway; indeed, Juppé and Sarkozy were at odds on the strategy. Juppé underlined the need for unity and acknowledged the Right's responsibility in the reduction of police forces between 2002 and 2012, whereas Sarkozy lamented the waste of time in the fight against terror and refused to admit his part in reducing the manpower necessary to fight terrorism.[210]

Five days after the attacks, Hollande drummed up support during an address to the mayors of France in which he asserted that:

[t]he objectives of the terrorists is to plunge our country in dread and division. We must therefore preserve our unity, which makes us strong. Our social cohesion is the best response and our national union is its expression ... Faced with this

threat, there are no more territorial differences, partisan cleavages do not hold anymore. There are only women and men of duty, reresentatives elected by universal suffrage conscious of their responsibilities.[211]

Six days after the attacks, the National Assembly voted with near unanimity (551 for, 6 against, and 1 abstention) in favour of reinforcing the state of emergency and extending it for another three months. Among those who opposed the government were three members of les Verts and a socialist representing French citizens living abroad.[212]

The rally was less evident this time around than in January. No march was organized across Paris, although numerous people paid their respects to the victims in front of the Bataclan concert hall. As in January, the messages of support were often directed at the victims and their families, as well as to the various French police forces involved in the antiterror operations. Once again, the atrocity and magnitude of the attacks were such that criticism from the opposition was subdued and limited to a few right-wing backbenchers arguably doing what Sarkozy could not afford to be seen and heard doing during a major tragedy. In fact, Hollande made it difficult for the Right to criticize him and his government, especially after displaying a tough stance and adopting what could only be described as the kind of hawkish policies usually associated with right-wing parties. Unable to criticize Hollande, except perhaps for waiting too long to adopt this tough stance, some opposition representatives decided to target Taubira, the justice minister, who many viewed as the embodiment of left-wing laxity. In fact, ever since her appointment in 2012, she had been viewed as the ideal "punching bag" for the Right, in particular for her role in introducing the same-sex marriage law.[213]

When the National Assembly reconvened four days after the attacks, the rally around the flag appeared in peril as various right-wing backbenchers booed and criticized the government. Yet for the most part the mainstream opposition leaders, including Sarkozy, remained supportive. The only rifts were the ones within each of the main parties: within the socialist government where Valls and

Taubira disagreed on the treatment of binationals convicted of terrorist activities, and within Les Républicains where Sarkozy and Juppé were at odds on those same issues (Sarkozy was keen to avoid losing more ground to the FN on the security issue, whereas Juppé tried to remain close to the centre-right electorate).

Le Pen for her part did not need to be too openly critical of the government. Apart from the initial Twitter messages posted by some of her closest advisers on the night of the attacks, she understood that public criticisms in the wake of the most horrific attacks in more than half a century could be politically dangerous. Besides, the unfolding events were in her view confirming her thesis; that the French state was letting too many foreigners and potential terrorists into the country.

CONCLUSION

This chapter validates the magnitude-repetition model and identifies several other key variables, some of which can offset the effects that magnitude and repetition have on the behaviour of political elites. The qualitative analysis contributes to our understanding of the reaction of political elites in seven important ways.

First, several of the cases analyzed in this chapter suggest that the magnitude of an attack does not depend solely on the number of fatalities but also on the number of wounded. To be sure, this only applies to attacks causing a large number of wounded. Yet it reinforces the perception that the number of victims – fatalities or wounded – represents a good proxy for the level of threat on the national security.

Second, the chapter suggests that a caveat must be introduced regarding the effects of the repetition variable. The recurrence of attacks can signal a suboptimal handling of affairs by the government and prompt the opposition to be critical. However, the repetition variable becomes less of an issue with waves of attack, such as the GIA attacks in 1995, as the political elite is more likely to perceive these terrorist acts as a continuous crisis instead of a succession of crises. In other words, under these particular circumstances the opposition is likely to be more patient with the government.

Third, the analysis confirms that in France, at least, the political re-action is determined to some extent by the identity of the target. As hypothesized, attacks against state representatives are more likely to elicit a rally, particularly when the victims are high-ranking officials, as with the assassinations of Besse and Erignac; although the sup-port in these cases might be intended for the republic as a whole rather than the government itself.

Fourth, the qualitative analysis confirms that the perpetrators identities will occasionly influence the reaction of political elites, as when neo-Nazi groups were wrongly accused of setting off a bomb in the vicinity of a synagogue. The socialists were able to criticize the right-wing government for its perceived permissiveness with far-right fanatics who had been responsible for a string of attacks in France and across Europe. The RPR and UDF would reciprocate a few years later, pointing out Mitterrand's leniency with far-left ter-rorists. However, the socialists and the conservatives found it more difficult to criticize one another over Middle Eastern terrorism for which the responsibility was shared. Interestingly, the 1982 wave of attacks suggest that political elites will find it harder to criticize the government if the identity of the culprit is unknown.

Fifth, this chapter further demonstrates that contextual variables are crucial in understanding the behaviour of political elites. Foreign affairs can bring the parties together (e.g., Begin's criticisms in the aftermath of the rue des Rosiers shooting) or on the contrary fuel criticisms (e.g., disagreement over the Chirac-Zéroual meeting). The proximity of electoral contests is also likely to affect the behaviour of parties, such as when Mitterrand accused Giscard of being permissive with terrorists a few months before the presidential election.

Sixth, the case studies indicate that history matters and that po-litical events, whether or not related to terrorism, can influence be-haviour in the wake of terrorist attacks even years after they occur. French political elites, although no strangers to political feuding, have regularly rallied in support of the government throughout the 1990s and onward. The 1980s, however, were a different story. The lingering resentment caused by the election of François Mitterrand in 1981 led many prominent right-wing politicians to question the legitimacy of a socialist president, thereby creating an acrimonious atmosphere not conducive to rallies. Rather than abate, these criticisms became particularly fierce during terrorist crises. The cohabitation period resulted in an unforeseen scenario: the governing right-wing coalition refusing the opposition's support. Behind this rather bizarre attitude was perhaps an attempt to salvage the Right's reputation on national security issues, particularly with an ever-more threatening Le Pen. Years later the Left would make it a point to rally around right-wing governments while reminding everyone that under similar circumstances the Right had failed to support left-wing governments.

Finally, this chapter suggests that the behaviour of radical parties is not as predictable as hypothesized.[214] To a large extent the FN behaved as expected, railing against the government and all other establishment parties. The FN remained a Downsian party in the worst of times, using each terrorist act as an opportunity to formulate policies to win elections. In other words, the Front National never lost sight of its electoral interest and never showed any inclination to favour the national interest except perhaps in the immediate aftermath of the *Charlie Hebdo* attacks and to a lesser extent after the 13 November attacks. The PC, on the other hand, rallied almost every time, whether around left- or right-wing governments. To be fair, the communists were part of several governmental coalitions and unlikely to turn against their own partners. Their strategy might have been motivated by the necessity to appear less radical and more responsible at a time when the party was declining and looking for political allies.

Conclusion

Fear is the foundation of most governments; but it is so sordid and
brutal a passion, and renders men in whose breasts it predominates so
stupid and miserable, that Americans will not be likely to approve of
any political institution which is founded on it.

John Adams, president of the United States 1797–1801
(Wakelyn 2006, 608)

Having reached at long last the closing stages of this inquiry into
the logic of political behaviour in times of terror, I am tempted to
agree with John Adams. Then as now, fear might well be the foundation of most governments, a claim made all the more compelling
in the aftermath of 9/11 as Americans rallied en masse around their
president amid warnings of more terror to come. As a seemingly
endless cycle of terror alerts began, many succumbed to what Adams
called a "sordid and brutal passion" and entered in a frenzy of patriotism. Meanwhile, the political elite in Washington, moved by a
similar combination of fear and devotion to the nation, and in some
cases blatant political opportunism, gave the Bush administration
all the necessary leeway to wage a war that the president assured us
would only end with the demise of terrorism itself. With political
debates on Capitol Hill virtually halted for several weeks, party politics became the first collateral damage of the war on terror.

To be sure, not all terrorist acts impact party politics to the extent
9/11 did. Yet the effect of terrorism on party politics can never be
stressed enough, for terrorism is nothing less than the repudiation
of party politics. Regardless of who the immediate targets are, the
gun sight is always pointed toward the legitimate holders of powers,

which in representative democracies are the parties. Terrorism is about political ascendancy, and from the terrorists' point of view, parties stand in their way, as evidenced in one of the inaugural acts of modern terrorism when Auguste Valliant threw a bomb into the hemicycle of the French National Assembly.

In the end, political parties are at once the prime targets of terrorists and the first line of defence against terrorism through their ability to legislate and govern. Understanding how political parties and their elites behave during terrorist crises is therefore anything but trivial. Following a summary of my research and of the main results, I present a series of substantive and methodological implications. I conclude by suggesting avenues of research and offering a final remark.

WHAT HAVE WE LEARNED?

Chapter 1 presented the paradox that is terrorism: an ancient phenomenon that scholars have only recently begun to study, a common occurrence that we find impossible to define. I remarked that despite the obvious implications of terrorism on party politics and electoral politics, studies on the effects of terrorist activities on parties and elections are scarce.

Chapter 2 introduced the notions of ordinary and extraordinary politics, and underlined the innate tension within each political party between the need to defend particular interests while at the same time remaining mindful of the national interest. I argued that the electoral rationale put forth by Downs (1957) and his successors could not necessarily make sense of party behaviour during extraordinary times; that is, times when the national interest is threatened. Although the Western world is relatively more peaceful now than it was a half-century ago, military and diplomatic crises are still recurring phenomena, making it unlikely for party elites to ignore them and focus solely on electoral objectives. Three case studies presented at the end of the chapter suggest that the national interest matters for parties, and that political elites are likely to rally around the flag when the threat is perceived as imminent.

Chapter 3 began with a discussion of what rallies around the flag are and how they come about in the context of foreign policy crises.

I presented both the "patriotic-reflex" explanation put forth by John Mueller (1973), which centres on the type of events likely to trigger rallies, and the "opinion-leadership" explanation put forth by Richard Brody (1991), which focuses on the control of sensitive information by the government. I argued that Mueller's and Brody's views were particularly relevant to the study of parties' reactions to terrorist acts, and hinted that terrorist crises, much like diplomatic and military crises, were likely to trigger rallies around the flag. I then presented the magnitude-repetition model for analyzing the reaction of parties. I argued that the magnitude of the attacks in terms of fatalities and the repetition of attacks were likely to be the two main explanatory variables, and could either activate the patriotic imperative and trigger a rally, or activate the partisan instinct and lead to criticisms of the government. I then presented a series of hypotheses based on these two variables and a host of secondary variables.

Chapters 4 and 5 presented the results of the statistical and qualitative analysis. What follow are the findings based in large part on the eight hypotheses presented in chapter 3.

Mainstream Opposition Parties Rally around the Flag Following Terrorist Attacks

The overwhelming majority of terrorist acts analyzed in this book triggered rallies. To be more precise, mainstream political parties have not been critical of their government's handling of terrorism and national security–related issues in 84 per cent of the cases included in the dataset – up from 33 per cent during non-terrorist periods. These findings suggest that the patriotic imperative, rather than the partisan interest, determines party behaviour when the national security is threatened. Furthermore, these results suggest that party politics becomes less conflictual in the immediate aftermath of terrorist attacks. However, a couple of caveats must be introduced. First, this finding only applies to the five-day period following the attacks and, thus, any conclusion for the longer term would be premature. Second, results vary from one country to another. Whereas German, British, and American mainstream political elites very rarely criticized their governments in the aftermath of terrorist attacks, French and Spanish political elites were slightly more vindictive.

Mainstream Opposition Parties Are More Likely to Rally
When the Terrorist Act Causes a Larger Number of Casualties

The number of victims (referred in this study as the magnitude) represents a strong predictor of party behaviour. Relatively high numbers of fatalities or wounded underline the gravity of the crisis and the threat on national security, making a rally all the more likely. Attacks of lesser magnitude on the other hand are more likely to be ignored by the political elites.

The Recurrence of Terrorist Attacks Makes a Rally Less Likely

Governments are expected to limit the occurrence of terrorist acts. Failure to do so is an indication that those in charge of governing the country are not handling national security well, and will encourage opposition parties to be critical. However, political elites are likely to be more patient and forgiving when the government faces a series of attacks perpetrated over a relatively short time period by the same group. Such a wave of attacks tends to be perceived as one major crisis rather than a succession of crises, thereby making the threat to national security more obvious.

In General, Political Elites Are Not More Likely to Rally
When Representatives of the State Are Victims of Terrorist Attacks

By and large governments cannot expect opposition parties to be more supportive when an agent of the state is targeted by terrorists. However this remark does not apply to French political elites which, perhaps as a result of the prevailing Jacobin political tradition, are more likely to rally under these circumstances – particularly when high-ranking officials are targeted.

International Terrorism Is More Likely to Trigger a Rally
Than Domestic Terrorism

Terrorist attacks originating from abroad are likely to be perceived as particularly threatening to national security and thus encourage political elites to present a unified front. In other words, international terrorism triggers the same reaction as conventional threats on national security, such as military conflicts. When facing domestic terrorism, opposition parties can criticize the government's handling of affairs without necessarily running the risk of being accused of siding with a foreign foe. To be fair, domestic terrorism is usually associated with longer-lasting terrorist campaigns (e.g., FLNC, IRA, ETA, BR, and RAF) than international terrorism, and therefore tends to give opposition parties more reasons to criticize the government's failure to handle a recurring security problem.

Since the Events of 9/11, Political Elites Are More Likely to Support Their Government after Terrorist Attacks

The multiple attacks of 9/11 had an impact not just on American party politics but also in France, Germany, Spain, and the United Kingdom where political elites are now more likely to rally around the flag than before that fateful September day. A heightened sense of urgency regarding national security and the realization that some terrorist groups operating today do not refrain from large-scale attacks are a probable explanations for why now more than ever terrorism is likely to initiate rallies.

In General, Right-Wing Governments Are Not More Likely to Benefit from Rallies after Terrorist Attacks Than Left-Wing Governments

Despite their reputation for being too soft on terrorism, left-wing parties are not criticized more by opposition parties in the aftermath of terrorist attacks. However, the situation varies from one country to the other (e.g., in Spain the Left has benefited from more rallies than in the other four countries) and overtime (e.g., in France left-wing governments were heavily criticized throughout the 1980s for being too permissive but less in the 1990s and early twenty-first century).

Far-Right Parties Are Almost Always Critical of Their Political Adversaries in the Aftermath of Terrorist Attacks

This finding is based on an analysis of the behaviour of the FN and is thus only valid for France. Not only has the FN been repeatedly critical of the French government – right-wing and left-wing alike – but its criticisms have also been directed at other parties in the opposition, especially the Far Left. In addition, the FN has regularly used the opportunity created by terrorist attacks to advance parts of their electoral program, such as the reinstatement of the death penalty. To a large extent, this was part of a strategy to discredit the main right-wing parties and take ownership of national security issues.

The Far Left Almost Always Supports the Government after Terrorist Attacks

This finding is based on an analysis of the behaviour of the PC and is thus only valid for France. Unlike the far-right, the PC has been in government twice during the period studied. However, even during its years in opposition, the PC was always prompt to support left- and right-wing governments alike, sometimes in the most explicit manner. This unexpected behaviour was, to a large extent, strategic and aimed at finding political allies and differentiating itself from other left-wing parties in a period of electoral decline.

The Presence of a Formal Antiterrorist Pact Increases the Likelihood of a Rally

The period during which the two main Spanish parties formerly agreed to support one another in the fight against Basque terrorism resulted in a noticeably higher percentage of rallies. In retrospect, this antiterrorist pact seemed effective only as long as the conservatives were in power and only as long as terrorism remained linked to ETA. Likewise, the particularly high rallying rate in the United Kingdom suggests that the existing informal agreement that existed between the main parties at Westminster was also likely to favour rallies in the aftermath of Ulster-related terrorist attacks.

Rallying around the Flag Can Be an Electoral Strategy

The last two findings suggest that rallying can be strategic. Obviously it can be a strategy to defeat a terrorist group by projecting an image of unity throughout the political elite. Recent history is replete with instances when the patriotic imperative has led opposition parties to support the government rather than seek electoral objectives. Yet rallying can also be an electoral strategy. Indeed, if terrorism can represent an opportunity for the opposition to rail against the government (instead of becoming a rallying issue, the crisis becomes a disputed one) it can also represent an opportunity to make electoral gains by rallying. In other words, defending the interest of the nation becomes part of the electoral rationale. The French Communist Party (PC) is a case in point as it repeatedly joined rallies, even in support of right-wing governments, in an attempt to halt its electoral decline and project an image of responsibility during critical situations. Finally, the behaviour of the French Socialist Party (PS) throughout much of the period under consideration also seems to indicate a willingness to rally with right-wing governments in order to set an example and promote consensus during critical periods. Rallying after all is first and foremost a collective strategy to overcome a crisis.

To be fair, other variables could influence the behaviour dynamic during terrorist crises. In particular, contextual variables such as foreign policy crises and elections seem to affect behaviour. Diplomatic and military crises tend to favour rallies but have on occasion stirred domestic controversies, thereby ending the rallies. Electoral campaigns, on the other hand, seem unfavourable to rallies. Finally, the case studies suggest that lingering resentments during transition periods, such as the one linked to an electoral defeat, can affect elite behaviour and prevent certain individuals from rallying.

This study contributes to our understanding of party behaviour by demonstrating that party politics is not only about electoral and partisan objectives, but also about the national interest. These results suggest that there is an emergency behaviour and a routine behaviour, and that the former will be activated whenever the country is perceived as being under threat. Yet rallies are fragile and the Downsian rationale always lurks behind the patriotic imperative ready to seize the opportunity created by terrorism.

SUBSTANTIVE IMPLICATIONS

Throughout this book I have tried, to paraphrase Alex Schmid and Albert Jongman, to be a "student of combustion" and to understand how the terrorist fire spreads into politics. I have also tried to contribute to our understanding of party politics during critical times, and see to what extent political elites are likely to promote by their joint endeavours the national interest valued by Edmund Burke rather than defend their own specific and partisan interest.

The first implication is that research on party behaviour, and indeed electoral behaviour in general, would benefit from becoming more context sensitive, rather than relying too much on the *ceteris paribus* expedient. The political context changes constantly at home and abroad. National and international crises matter, whether they are terror-related or not, and should be taken into account by those of us studying the dynamics of party and elite behaviour. In other words, the Downsian party cannot always be taken for granted. The electoral rationale is bounded and cannot account for party behaviour each time. Other rationales such as the *raison d'état* play a role.

If students of party and electoral behaviour should take into account the context in which domestic political actors evolve more often, scholars working on the response to terror should be mindful of how terror impacts party politics. In the end, the response to terrorism is in the hands of these parties and their elites. It is therefore crucial to understand how terrorism affects their behaviour. One could venture to say that high-magnitude terror is likely to facilitate the passage of antiterror bills whereas the high recurrence of terrorist acts will be more likely to impede the passage of laws as it creates dissent within the political elite.

The third implication follows from the previous one. Terrorism is likely to have repercussions not just on the response to terror, but more generally on the functioning of representative democracies. High-magnitude terrorist acts, which considering the current trend are unfortunately increasingly likely, could lead to more domestic political consensus, whereas the repetition of acts of terror could lead to more conflictual exchanges between parties, and crucially between the government and the opposition. This research should add to the ongoing reflection on the effects of terrorism on the quality of democracy. The tragic example set by the Uruguayan elite in the face of the Tupamaros-led terrorist campaign in the early 1970s should serve as a reminder that parties, and the democratic structure they uphold, can crumble just as easily as any mastodon of steel and concrete.

These implications all point toward the necessity to know more about rallies around the flag. To be sure, our knowledge of rallies has greatly benefited from the works of John Mueller (1973) and Richard Brody (1991), to name just two pioneering figures, and this research validates as much the patriotic interpretation as the opinion-leadership explanation. Yet despite the large body of research on rallies, we still know too little on the effects of rallies on the political game.

AVENUES OF RESEARCH

The interplay between terrorism and politics has existed for centuries, and yet studies on the interaction between terrorism, party politics and electoral behaviour only started in earnest in recent years. It is fair to say that much remains to be done. Based on this book, I envisage four avenues of research.

First, the impact of terrorism on countries other than established democracies needs to be addressed. In particular, we need to look at how political elites in authoritarian regimes and newly established democracies react to terrorist attacks. It is doubtful that terrorism affects elite behaviour in autocracies the way it affects elite behaviour in open societies. Obviously under autocratic forms of government the opposition will have far less leeway, if any, than its democratic counterparts, and might actually be the prime instigator of terrorist activities. In some cases, the fear of repression might prompt regime opponents to rally around the flag. Yet the opposition is more likely to view terrorism as an opportunity to reach its political objectives by undermining the existing regime. Evidently, a wide array of regimes fit into the category of autocratic, with some tolerating a limited opposition and others rejecting any form of disagreement. I would suggest that with more repressive regimes, the opposition has little to lose and is therefore more likely to criticize the government during terrorist crises. Of equal interest is the reaction to terrorism in countries undergoing a transition toward democracy. Here again, elites are likely to play politics with terrorism. Those who stand to lose most under the new regime, such as members or supporters of the former regime, might be less inclined to rally around the government when terrorists strike and are therefore likely to impede the transition process.

Second, the impact of terrorism on intraparty dynamics, whether in established or new democracies, needs to be explored further. We need to understand whether terrorism favours consensus within parties or whether it leads to disagreement and even fragmentation of the party system. This book suggests that the reaction within certain parties might not always be homogeneous and might for instance pit doves against hawks. This tension is illustrated in France by the debate on Corsica, which created a rift within the French Left in 2000 and led the minister of the interior, Jean-Pierre Chevènement, to leave the government following a wave of attacks perpetrated by the separatists. Similarly, the British Labour Party split over the decision to send troops to Iraq as part of the war on terror and led Robin Cook to resign from his position as leader of the House of Commons in 2003. Any number of reasons could account for this type of behaviour, but these two examples suggest that the decision to leave a party or quit a position of authority is linked to political ideology.

Third, the question of diffusion and habit-forming needs to be addressed. We know from the findings presented in this thesis that political elites across the five countries studied here were more inclined to rally after the events of 9/11. What this suggests among others is that political elites from different countries who share a similar experience with terrorism adopt a similar reaction. In particular, since 9/11 Western elites might find it more difficult to avoid rallying in the aftermath of an attack perpetrated by Islamic terrorists. We need to examine other terrorist waves (Euroterrorism, nationalist-separatists, etc.) and determine whether a pattern of behaviour emerged there to.

Finally, a comparative analysis of the impact of different types of crises on party politics and elite behaviour needs to be conducted. Domestic politics might be usually associated with peaceful times, but a fair amount of it takes place during and in the aftermath of extraordinary events such as military conflicts, diplomatic crises, terrorist attacks and natural catastrophes. Some groundbreaking work has already been done on crisis and postcrisis politics (see Boin et al. 2005; 2008), but a specific effort must be made toward understanding how these crises affect party politics in the long term. We must ask ourselves whether behaviour during critical times affects the conduct of politics during ordinary times, for instance by rendering it less conflictual. The question of the impact of terrorism on party politics and elite behaviour is of course closely linked to that of the effects of terrorism on voting behaviour and electoral results. In the end, we need to recognize that context matters and that politics during extraordinary times deserves far more scholarly attention.

FINAL REMARKS

As I write these last words I cannot but think of my last glimpse of the World Trade Center while aboard the Staten Island ferry surrounded by commuters enjoying the late afternoon sun on the deck. That was on 10 September 2001. I suspect that for some of them that was their last ever sunset. For the rest of us who made it through at least another day, it was a cruel reminder that the world is never as appeased as it seems. For me, a member of Generation X, born not only on the right side of the twentieth century but on the right side of this otherwise still troubled planet, 11 September was a frightening glance into the everyday horror that had befallen some of my European relatives a mere sixty years before. Buildings crumbling down on thousands of civilians, blank stares and frightened attitudes where before there was laughter and insouciance, and the feeling that this calamity did not belong to this time and place, an anachronism if ever there was one. In the midst of it all, I must admit to have lost some of my bearings. Yes, we were all Americans on that day, and I do not suppose that political affiliations and past debates mattered at all for some time after that. We shared a tragedy and had somehow become similar, no longer diverse.

Appendix on the Treatment of Data

The database is used to conduct quantitative analyses and produce both descriptive and inferential statistics. I then use a qualitative approach to analyze cases that diverge from an ideal-type magnitude-repetition model, that is, cases when the elite responds unexpectedly to the two main variables (magnitude and repetition).

The extent of the rallying phenomenon during terrorist crises (hypothesis 1, page 66), both overall and in each of the five countries under consideration, is measured through univariate descriptive statistics. The other hypotheses (with the exception of hypothesis 7, page 72, on radical parties) are tested using univariate descriptive statistics on the effects of the following variables: magnitude (hypothesis 2, page 68), repetition (hypothesis 3, page 68), target (hypothesis 4, page 69), perpetrators (hypothesis 5, page 70), right-wing/left-wing (hypothesis 6, page 72), and 9/11 (hypothesis 8, page 73).

The hypotheses are then tested jointly using the following logistic regression model to assess the likelihood of witnessing a rally – that of having no criticism toward the government – in the five days following the attacks:

$\text{Log}(p/(1\text{-}p)) = \alpha + \beta_1{}^*First5Attacks + \beta_2{}^*Magnitude + \beta_3{}^*Pact + \beta_4{}^*Crisis + \beta_5{}^*Domestic + \beta_6{}^*Post9/11 + \beta_7{}^*France + \beta_8{}^*UK + \beta_9{}^*Spain$

where p is the probability of having a rally.

Variables used in the model include:

- *First Five Attacks*, which takes value 1 if the attack is one of the first five under the current government, and 0 otherwise;[1]
- *Magnitude*, which takes value 0 if there were two deaths or fewer involved in the attack (but at least six injured) and value 1 if there were three fatalities or more;[2]
- *Pact (Spain)*, which takes value 1 if the attack took place in Spain during the period covered by the Spanish antiterrorist pact (between December 2000 and March 2004), and 0 otherwise;[3]
- *Crisis*, which takes value 1 if the attack happened during a period of diplomatic crisis or military conflict for the country under attack, and 0 otherwise;[4]
- *Domestic*, a variable taking value 1 if the group claiming the attack (or perceived as having perpetrated the attack) is a domestic group, and 0 otherwise. Domestic groups encountered in the dataset are almost exclusively separatist groups; they include the IRA, INLA, RIRA, CIRA (groups which operated mostly in the UK), ETA (operating mostly in Spain), as well as Corsican, Basque, and Breton separatist groups (operating in France); and
- *Post 9/11*, which takes value 1 if the attack took place before 11 September 2001, and 0 if it took place afterwards (12 September 2001, or after).

I use binary controls for the three countries for which sufficient data is available:

- *France* takes value 1 if the attack took place in France and value 0 otherwise;
- *Spain* takes value 1 if the attack took place in Spain and value 0 otherwise; and
- *UK* takes value 1 if the attack took place in the UK and value 0 otherwise.

Notes

INTRODUCTION

1 David W. Moore, "Bush Job Approval Highest in Gallup History," *Gallup*, 24 September 2001, http://www.gallup.com/poll/4924/bush-job-approval-highest-gallup-history.aspx.

2 House Committee on the Judiciary, Administration's Draft Anti-Terrorism Act of 2001, 107th Cong., 1st session, 24 September 2001, 2.

3 House Committee on the Judiciary, Administration's Draft Anti-Terrorism Act of 2001, 107th Cong., 1st session, 24 September 2001, Part II, 1.

4 Senator Feingold (D-WI) voted against whereas Senator Landrieu (D-LA) did not vote. Bill H.R. 3162, US Senate Roll Call Votes 107th Cong., 1st Session, 25 October 2001. In the House, out of the 66 representatives who voted against only 3 were Republicans.

5 By October 2001, Noam Chomsky had already published a pamphlet called *9-11*.

6 Guy Benhamou, "Une véritable déclaration de guerre. L'assassinat de Claude Erignac est l'aboutissement d'une stratégie de la tension," *Libération*, 7 February 1998, 3.

7 Chérif and Saïd Kouachi were responsible for murdering nine contributors, one policeman, and one visitor at the offices of the satirical weekly *Charlie Hebdo*, and another policeman outside the building.

CHAPTER ONE

1 Ewen MacAskill, "Fivefold Increase in Terrorism Fatalities," *The Guardian*, 18 November 2014. http://www.theguardian.com/uk-news

/2014/nov/18/fivefold-increase-terrorism-fatalities-global-index; Geoff
Dyer and Chloe Sovino, "$1 tn Cost of Longest US War Hastens Re-
treat from Military Intervention," *Financial Times*, 14 December 2014,
http://www.ft.com/cms/s/2/14beoeoc-8255-11e4-ace7-00144feabdco
.html#slideo.

2 John Roth, Douglas Greenburg, and Serena Wille, "Appendix A: The
Financing of the 9/11 Plot," *Monograph on Terrorist Financing*, Staff
Report to the National Commission on Terrorist Attacks upon the
United States, n.d., http://www.9-11commission.gov/staff_statements
/911_TerrFin_Monograph.pdf.

3 Hrair Dekmejian distinguishes state-sponsored terrorism with domestic targets (i.e., enforcement terrorism) from state-sponsored terrorism with transnational targets, which he defines as "the projection
of coercive force overtly or covertly across territorial boundaries in
order to annex territory, establish friendly regimes, subvert unfriendly
regimes, assassinate or capture enemy leaders, or destroy terrorist
bases and cells" (2007, 14).

4 According to David Rapoport (1984), the Thuggee (in the Indian
subcontinent) might have been the most murderous terrorist group
of all time, killing about half a million people over the course of
four centuries, still a few million short of the most brutal political
regimes.

5 Rudolf Rummel (1994, 15) estimates that more than 169 million
people have been killed by their own governments from 1900 to
1987.

6 The expression "years of lead" refers to the 1981 German movie *Die
bleierne Zeit* directed by Margarethe von Trotta that tells the story of
the Ensslin sisters, one of whom decides to join the Rote Armee
Fraktion. The expression *bleierne Zeit* originally came from a
Friedrich Hölderlin poem entitled *Der Gang aufs Land*. Trotta used
the expression as a metaphor to describe the circumstances in
which the Ensslin sisters grew up in the 1950s, a defeated Germany
living under a "lead sky." The expression was then translated into
other languages (*anni di piombo* in Italy where the movie was
awarded the Golden Lion at the Venice Film Festival) and came to
describe the use of bullets by left-wing and right-wing terrorists in
the seventies.

7 Fred Halliday makes this point in *Islam and the Myth of Confrontation: Religion and Politics in the Middle East*, remarking that

an organization such as *al-qa'ida* uses traditional Islamic language, thereby giving the impression of a conflict with timeless cultural roots. Its origins, however, are to be found in the modern history of the Middle East and West Asia more generally, where it grew as a consequence of recent political and military events. Bin Laden and his followers draw on a variety of traditions within political Islam to justify their actions but their selections of influences reflect contemporary political concerns and convenience rather than any generic loyalty to a religion. Their goal is equally modern and rooted in a contemporary political context, that of challenging the Western presence in the Middle East, and also the rulers of Saudi Arabia and other countries who are regarded as linked to the West in the post-Cold War epoch. (2003, X)

8 See Dingley (2006, 451–65).

9 In the case of the Omagh attack, the police were warned a few minutes before the explosion. The warning (intentionally or unintentionally) gave contradicting information as to exactly which part of the Omagh shopping street was targeted. Tragically, the police evacuated the wrong part.

10 See the remarkable documentary by Sam Green and Bill Siegel, *The Weather Underground* (2002).

11 MacAskill, "Fivefold Increase in Terrorism Fatalities."

12 "Chapter 1 – Dying to Lose: Explaining the Decline in Global Terrorism," *The Human Security Brief,* http://www.hsrgroup.org/docs /Publications/HSB2007/2007HumanSecurityBrief-FullText.pdf.

13 Ibid., 9.

14 Ibid., 1.

15 According to the Syrian Center for Policy Research. Anne Barnard, "Death Toll from War in Syria Now 470,000, Group Finds," *New York Times*, 11 February 2016, http://www.nytimes.com/2016/02/12/world /middleeast/death-toll-from-war-in-syria-now-470000-group-finds .html?_r=0.

16 The majority of attacks in 2013 were in France, Spain, and the United Kingdom. Europol, *2013 EU Terrorism Situation and Trend Report* (The

Hague: Europol, 2013) https://www.europol.europa.eu/content/te-sat-2013-eu-terrorism-situation-and-trend-report; Europol, *2015 European Union Terrorism Situation and Trend Report* (The Hague: Europol, 2015) https://www.europol.europa.eu/content/european-union-terrorism-situation-and-trend-report-2015.

17 Europol, *2015 European Union Terrorism Situation and Trend Report.*

18 Marc Kaufman, "A Mars Mission for Budget Travelers," *National Geographic*, 23 April 2014, http://news.nationalgeographic.com/news/2014/04/140422-mars-mission-manned-cost-science-space/.

19 An axiom that has not been lost on certain international media outlets. The BBC World Service, for example, avoids using the word *terrorist* "without attribution" as it can be "a barrier rather than an aid to understanding." "Editorial Guidelines," *BBC*, http://www.bbc.co.uk/editorialguidelines/guidance/terrorism-language/guidance-full.

20 Some twenty-five years before, Laqueur had even abandoned the idea of defining terrorism (Laqueur 1977).

21 Rather than agreeing on what should be included in a definition, Jean-Marc Sorel suggests to focus on what is not worth incorporating in a definition. In his view, "it does not seem useful to specify the type of political aim, the means used or to qualify the nature of the perpetrators (by country, group, individual); they are already qualified by their objective, which is to spread terror" (Sorel 2003, 371).

22 See Michael J. Kelly's account of the hostage crisis at the Turkish embassy in Ottawa in 1985 (in Rosenthal et al. 1989).

23 *The Guardian* reported that more than thirty Egyptian military officers were onboard, including two brigadier-generals. Michael Ellison, "Search for Air Crash Survivors Abandoned," *The Guardian*, 2 November 1999, http://www.theguardian.com/world/1999/nov/02/egyptaircrash.usa1.

24 This being said, more radical elites and their constituencies might have a different view

CHAPTER TWO

1 A view taken by Russell Dalton, David Farrell, and Ian McAllister, *Political Parties and Democratic Linkage: How Parties Organize Democracy* (New York: Oxford University Press, 2011).

2 See also Allison and Zelikow 1999.

3 Putnam's article spurred a larger study involving contributions by several scholars that led to the publication of Evans, Jacobson, and Putnam 1993.

4 For a review of the literature on the interaction between the domestic and international levels, see Peter Gourevitch, "Domestic Politics and International Relations," in *Handbook of International Relations* ed. Walter Carlsnaes, Thomas Risse, and Beth A. Simmons (London: SAGE, 2002), 309.

5 According to the Correlates of War project. Other datasets have a different threshold. For instance, the Uppsala dataset on armed conflict has a much lower threshold.

6 Korea (1950–53), Vietnam (1965–75), and the First Gulf War (1991). This account is based on the list of interstate wars published by the Correlates of War project. This list does not include the Iraq War (2003–11), which resulted in more than 1,000 battle-deaths, nor does it include the current military operation in Afghanistan. As of 2016, 3,517 coalition soldiers have died in Afghanistan according to iCasualties.org (http://www.icasualties.org/oef/). The Falkland War (1982) caused 910 battle-deaths and is therefore not included. The Indochina War (1945–54) and the Algerian War (1954–62), both of which caused tens of thousands of battle-deaths, are considered extra-state wars by the Correlates of War.

7 Michael Brecher (2008), in his study of 391 international crises (non-intrawar crises) from the end of World War I to the end of 2002, classified 7.7 per cent of these crises as *high-severity* (the 1948–49 Berlin Blockade and 1962 Cuban Missile Crisis), 35.8 per cent as *medium-severity* (the 1993–94 North Korean nuclear crisis), and 56.5 per cent as *low-severity* crises (the 1991 Ecuador–Peru border dispute).

8 Initially, institutions were brought into the equation to explain the legislators' behaviour in the US Congress.

9 Rational choice theorists contend that occasionly the rules are altered by external shocks.

10 Evans, Jacobson, and Putnam (1993) being one of them.

11 General elections in Britain were suspended during World War II. There were, in fact, no such elections between 1935 and 1945.

12 The isolationists were not the only ones to oppose US meddling in

European affairs. Noninterventionists and pacifists joined the opposition, although for the different reasons.

13 According to a Gallup poll taken in May 1940, two-thirds of interviewees preferred a candidate willing to assist England and France in any way possible, as long as the army and navy would not be sent into battle (Divine 1974, 8).

14 *Newsweek*, 8 November 1948, 21.

15 The Democrats were blamed for their failure to obtain secure access rights to Berlin at the Potsdam conference (Divine 1974, 224).

16 To be sure, other factors played a role in Truman's victory. Harold Gullan (1998) suggests that internal conflicts within the Republican Party as well as Dewey's excessive cautiousness worked in Truman's favour. Gullan also points out that the Democrats outspent the Republicans throughout the campaign. Yet the Democratic Party was divided (Lemelin 2001). Henry Wallace, who had been Roosevelt's vice-president for four years and was secretary of commerce under Truman, decided to run for president on a third-party ticket. In addition, thirty-five Democratic delegates from Mississippi and Alabama left the party to support Strom Thurmond's presidential bid.

17 Was Kennedy influenced by domestic politics? Clearly the subject was raised during meetings and Kennedy was keeping a close watch on the opinion polls (Paterson and Brophy 1986; McKeown 2000). McGeorge Bundy later acknowledged that congressional pressure did influence the president (McKeown 2000, 79).

18 The Monroe Doctrine issued on 2 December 1823, stated that European powers were no longer allowed to meddle in the affairs of American countries, thereby making Latin America Washington's exclusive sphere of influence.

CHAPTER THREE

1 Walmart sold 88,000 US flags on 12 September 2001, up from 6,400 flags sold on the same day a year before. Mary Beth Sheridan and Lena H. Sun, "Assault on U.S. Fuels Flag Sales, Blood Donations, Enlistments," *Washington Post*, 13 September 2001, B01.

2 "State of the Union Address: The Text of George Bush's Speech," *The Guardian*, 21 September 2001, http://www.theguardian.com/world /2001/sep/21/september11.usa13.

3 Although there are rallies in support of other types of communities, in this context we only consider rallies around the flag in support of the state in terms of its symbols or representatives.

4 Marc J. Hetherington and Michael Nelson, for instance, describe a rally effect as "the sudden and substantial increase in public approval of the president that occurs in response to certain kinds of dramatic international events involving the United States" (2003, 37). Cindy Kam and Jennifer Ramos state that "rally events refer to a dramatic upsurge in presidential approval, triggered by an international crisis" (2008, 620).

5 Here I present a conceptual definition. In the methodology chapter, I will present an operational definition better suited to data gathering.

6 Phil Scraton (ed.) presents a patchwork of dissenting voices on the events of 9/11 and their aftermath in *Beyond September 11: An Anthology of Dissent* (London: Pluto, 2002).

7 Munich stands out for the sheer audacity of the act, which insured an instant and by-the-minute international coverage of the hostage crisis. However, already in the 1940s and 1950s, actions by groups such as Irgun, the Stern Gang, and the FLN had drawn worldwide attention through similar strategies.

8 According to a poll conducted by IPSOS following France's triumph in the 1998 World Cup, President Jacques Chirac gained fifteen points of popularity overnight – from 53 per cent to 68 per cent of respondents approving his action. Whether this constitutes a full-fledged rally is doubtful. Despite joining in the celebration the opposing elite certainly did not rally. "Record de popularité pour Chirac et Jospin," *Les Échos*, 10 July 1998, http://www.lesechos.fr/10/07/1998/LesEchos/17685-137-ECH_records-de-popularite-pour-chirac-et-jospin.htm.

9 Psychological theories provide some insights into people's behaviour during trying times and suggest, for instance, that members of a group are likely to be more cohesive when facing a common threat (Huddy 2003), especially a terrorist threat (Landau et al. 2004). Landau et al. suggest that "heightened concerns about mortality should intensify the appeal of charismatic leaders" (2004, 1136).

10 Brody considers remaining silent a sign of support.

11 Despite opposing Mueller's "event-response" theory, Berinsky acknowledges that some cataclysmic events such as 9/11 and the attack on Pearl Harbor can directly influence public opinion.

12 Others have distanced themselves from Brody's and Mueller's inter-
pretations, stressing the importance of individual-level dynamics.
For instance, Sigelman and Johnston's study of public opinion dur-
ing the Iran hostage crisis indicates that support of President Jimmy
Carter was enhanced "if one holds a favorable personal image of the
President, if one's own policy preferences are congruent with the
President's actions, and if one belongs to the President's party"
(1981, 303).

13 Hymans suggests that the large number of rallies taking place in the
United States during the past sixty years is because it is a superpower
and that its citizens have come to expect success whenever the American might is tested.

14 Lydia Saad, "Iraq War Triggers Major Rally Effect," *Gallop*, 25 March
2003, http://www.gallup.com/poll/8074/Iraq-war-triggers-major-rally-
effect.aspx.

15 US presidents tend to follow the public, particularly during election
periods, but they become less responsive outside this period (Nacos
et al. 2000, 231–4).

16 Norris et al. quote two journalists who reported the following two
days after the 2003 invasion of Iraq: "Some reporters investigating
claims against Iraq said they felt no compunction to poke holes in
the administration's case because they did not find it to be so off
base. Many reported being in the same position as the administration: confident that Mr. Hussein is hiding weapons of mass destruction but unable to definitively prove it." Jim Rutenberg and Robin
Toner, "Critics Say Coverage Helped Lead to War," *New York Times*, 22
March 2003, http://www.nytimes.com/2003/03/22/us/nation-war-
media-critics-iraq-war-say-lack-scrutiny-helped-administration-
press.html.

17 The realist take on the national interest has been criticized by liberal
thinkers for whom the concept is changing because it depends on
which societal actors are prevalent at any one time, and on their capacity to impose their view of the national interest at the state level
(Smouts et al. 2003, 283). The constructivists, for their part, even suggest that the national interest is defined by norms and values shared
by states on the international scene rather than by elites in each state
(Smouts et al. 2003, 283–4; see also Finnemore 1996).

18 Of course paradoxically the military junta that took over the power did so to "protect" the nation from the Tupamaros.

19 My translation of "le terrorisme a (ré)insufflé à la question sécuritaire une dimension territoriale."

20 This hypothesis implies that each new government or each government starting a new mandate will be given a clean sheet and will not necessarily be held responsible for the homeland security failures of the previous government.

21 For a long time, political dissent was a criminal offence in the United States in times of war. The 1918 Sedition Act outlawed "conspiracy to publish disloyal material intended to obstruct the war and cause contempt for the government of the United States" (Stone 2004, 139).

22 Party ideologies affect the conduct of the state (Hibbs 1977; Schmidt 1996; Alesina et al. 1997; Boix 1998). However, the "parties-do-matter" hypothesis is concerned above all with the influence of parties on public policy with regard to socio-economic issues (Schmidt 1996 for a good review; see also Downs 1957; Sartori 1976; Budge and Robertson 1987; Blais, Blake, and Dion 1993). Parties from the Right are more likely to support market-oriented policies, whereas parties from the Left are more likely to favour state intervention. Similarly, social-democratic parties tend to spend more on foreign aid (Thérien and Noël 2000). As for foreign policy, Schuster and Maier (2006, 233) remark that in Western Europe "the party affiliation of a government seems to be a good indicator of how a country behaved during the Iraq crisis." For instance, out of the six EU members that joined the US-led coalition, five were governed by centre-right parties (see also Noël and Thérien 2008).

23 Petrocik (1996) reports similar differences on national defence, with 68 per cent trusting the Republicans and 17 per cent trusting the Democrats. Interestingly, the GOP is not necessarily doing a better job and is certainly not always tough against terrorists. President Reagan, for instance, pulled out US troops from Lebanon after the 1983 attacks that killed several hundred marines (Nacos 2007, 188). He also negotiated with Iran the liberation of hostages held by Hezbollah in exchange for secret arms shipment (Nacos 2007, 188). Nacos suggests that the Democrats are perhaps still paying for President

Jimmy Carter's mishandling of the hostage crisis in Tehran (Nacos 2007, 188).

24 Lydia Saad, "Americans Still Prefer Republicans for Combating Terrorism," *Gallup* 11 September 2009, http://www.gallup.com/poll /122921/americans-prefer-republicans-combating-terrorism.aspx.

25 Frank Newport, "Republicans Expand Edge as Better Party against Terrorism," *Gallup*, 11 September 2014, http://www.gallup.com /poll/175727/republicans-expand-edge-better-party-against-terrorism .aspx. A similar trend is observed elsewhere in the world: In Israel, Likud has a better reputation on security issues than Labor (Berrebi and Klor 2006). The same holds in the United Kingdom where the Tories enjoyed the same reputation (Budge and Farlie 1983), although under Tony Blair the Labour Party became more hawkish (Oborne 2008); likewise in France where Jacques Chirac (right-wing) was seen as the best candidate to deal with terrorism during the 2002 presidential campaign (Mayer and Tiberj 2004).

26 Reputation is not enough to convince voters. Eric Bélanger and Bonnie Meguid (2005) suggest that issue ownership affects the vote only when voters consider the issue relevant. For instance, Nadeau, Blais, Gidengil, and Nevitte (2001) point out that more Canadians voted for the Liberal party when it was perceived as more competent on issues such as job creation and national unity.

27 We can still expect inertia to influence behaviour. Downs argues that parties are obliged by electoral competition to have consistent policy positions over time (1957, 103–9). This being said, electoral competition can drive parties to make certain types of promises while making sure that they remain consistent (Downs 1957, 103–9). Leaders who do not follow the policies advocated by their supporters run the risk of losing support. Warwick (1992) shows that this happens where economic policies are concerned. At the same time, Downs suggests that parties in a two-party system will converge toward the centre to maximize votes, a process that should favour issue-trespassing.

28 This hypothesis clearly rests on the assumption that issue-trespassing takes place with regards to terrorism and national security.

29 Jean-Marie Colombani, chief editor of *Le Monde,* famously declared on the newspaper's front page, "Nous sommes tous Américains!"

CHAPTER FOUR

1 Edward T. Imparato, *General MacArthur Speeches and Reports 1908–1964* (Paducah, KY: Turner, 2000), 206.

2 See their rankings at www.freedomhouse.org in terms of political rights and civil liberties.

3 With the exception of the qualitative analysis that will cover the period from 1980 to 2015.

4 In 2004, the TKB launched online as a free and open-source database providing data and related information on close to 30,000 terrorist incidents across the world since 1968. Unfortunately, this remarkable research tool was discontinued on 31 March 2008, after the US Department of Homeland Security, which oversaw its funding, decided that the money would be better spent elsewhere.

5 In the aftermath of a terrorist attack, national security is often so prevalent that other issues are temporarily disregarded.

6 In that case, the newspaper reports the act but the elite does not react publicly to it.

7 The tenth edition of the *Oxford Dictionary* offers the following definition of *rally*: "bring or come together for concerted action."

8 Similarly Cunningham (1991, 245), in his book on British government policy in Ulster, defines bipartisanship (a phenomenon akin to a rally) as "the tendency of the party in opposition to support or, slightly differently, not to oppose the policy of the government towards Ireland."

9 The reaction might evolve afterward in light of new information, but what we are looking at in this study is how elites behave in the heat of the moment. A number of studies have looked beyond the initial stages of crises and more at the duration of rallies: Brody (1991), Callaghan and Virtanen (1993), Lian and Oneal (1993), Kam and Ramos (2008) to name a few. Kam and Ramos (2008) suggest that at first patriotism and national in-group identification triggers and maintains support for the president, but that eventually partisan identities will give rise to criticism of the president.

10 The decision to use a dichotomous variable (i.e., support or no support) rather than a gradation in support (i.e., strong support, mild support, weak support, no support; or strong criticisms, mild criticisms, etc.) resulted from a lack of detailed information on the

reaction of political elites. In order to create such a scale, I would need access to the reactions of many more frontbenchers and backbenchers. An ideal system would be one where the reaction of each member of Parliament, member of government, and other prominent politicians would be coded. An instance of strong support would be one where 95 per cent of respondents support the government over a certain period of time. Ideally such a gradation system would give more weight to prominent figures such as ministers and less to backbenchers.

11 Finally, the qualitative analysis is based on a larger pool of newspapers and magazines: *Le Monde, Libération, Le Figaro, Les Échos, L'Humanité, Le Parisien, Le Journal du dimanche, L'Express, Le Point,* and *Le Nouvel Observateur.*

12 This difference is significant at the 5 per cent level.

13 The UK is dealing with a number of reported attacks similar to that of France, but most of them occur in Ulster rather than in London or Manchester. Additionally, unlike what takes place in France, the British political elite has usually relied on a bipartisan approach to tackle Ulster-related terrorism.

14 Left and Right have been in power eight years each in France, Spain, Germany and the United States. In the United Kingdom, the Left has been in power slightly longer (nine years) than the Right (seven years).

15 The 9/11 effect is based on observations between 1998 and 10 September 2001 for the first part (to avoid confounding due to the higher proportion of international attacks in the database prior to 1998), and 11 September 2001 and 2006 for the second part.

16 The PSOE was in power until 1996 when the PP took over. The PSOE returned to power in 2004.

17 The PS was in power until 1993 when the right-wing UDF and RPR took over. In 1997, a left-wing coalition led by the PS was elected and remained in power until 2002. The right-wing UMP (previously RPR) governed until 2012.

18 The French case is covered extensively in the next chapter.

19 The CDU/CSU (right-wing) and its coalition partner – FDP (centre-right) – were in power from 1982 to 1998. The SPD (left-wing) and its coalition partner – Grüne (ecologist) – governed from 1998 to 2005. After the 2005 election a grand coalition (CDU-SPD) took over.

20 See Cunningham (2001). The Conservative Party was in power until 1997 whereupon the Labour Party took over.

21 Since the TKB database was incomplete with regards to domestic acts taking place prior to 1998, I chose to compare the period 1998–2001 to post-2001. The United States had a Republican administration until 1992 when the Democrats took over. The Republicans returned to power in 2000.

CHAPTER FIVE

1 I am not equating resistance to terrorism but merely pointing out that the experience of occupation could affect the way certain terrorist groups are perceived by the French political elite.

2 Obviously, many other types of terrorism have existed or still exist in France: reactionary terrorism most notably from the Organisation de l'armée secrète (OAS) during the later stages of the conflict in Algeria; but also ecoterrorism or cyberterrorism.

3 Of course the idea of more autonomy, let alone full-fledged independence, has always been anathema in a centralized country like France.

4 Autonomists remained opposed to using violence.

5 On 16 April 1981, shortly after the arrival of French president Valéry Giscard d'Estaing at Ajaccio airport, an explosion killed one and injured eight people. In 1983, the secretary general of the department of Haute-Corse was shot dead by the FLNC.

6 The separatist movement is also represented by political parties and associations, some of which act as legal representatives of the terrorist groups. From 2004 to 2007, the Unione Naziunale grouped several parties, among them the Corsica Nazione (independantists) and the Partitu di a Nazione Corsa (autonomists), and had eight seats in the Assembly of Corsisa.

7 See Pizam and Smith (2000) for the impact of terrorism on tourism.

8 During this period, the right-wing Chirac shared the executive power with the left-wing Jospin, a period known as cohabitation. The plan was eventually ratified by the National Assembly following some heated debates. However, the Conseil Constitutionnel declared the transfer of legislative power unconstitutional.

9 In February 2007, Philippe Bidart was freed.

10 Martine Valo and Vincent Durupt, "Attentat de Quévert : les enquêteurs estiment avoir démantelé l'ARB," *Le Monde*, 9 May 2000, 7.

11 This was a worldwide groupuscular phenomenon with revolutionary chapters in the United States (the Weathermen and the Symbionese Liberation Army), in Japan (the Japanese Red Army), in Belgium (les Cellules Communistes Combattantes), etc. In Italy this brand of terrorism was responsible for 12,690 incidents between 1969 and 1980, killing 362 people and injuring another 4,524 (Townshend 2002).

12 The bombing of the Bologna train station, known as the *Strage di Bologna* (Bologna Massacre), killed 86 people on 2 August 1980. On 26 September 1980, an explosion killed 13 people at the Munich Oktoberfest.

13 On 23 October 1983, a suicide bombing, likely organized by Hezbollah, killed 58 soldiers stationed in Beirut. Hours later 241 US soldiers died nearby following a similar attack.

14 The tally would have been far worse had the GIA activists been able to carry out their initial plan, which was either to crash the plane against the Eiffel Tower or blow it up over Paris.

15 In 2000, an attack against the Strasbourg Christmas Market by terrorists close to al Qaeda was foiled at the last minute. It should be noted that al Qaeda had developed ties with Algerian jihadists and GIA members in the 1990s.

16 Jean-Pierre Chevènement, unwilling to see France participate in Operation Desert Storm, resigned as minister of defence shortly before the start of the military operation. It should be noted, however, that Mitterrand spared no efforts in trying to achieve a diplomatic breakthrough during the crisis.

17 DGSE are a branch of the French secret service in charge of gathering intelligence outside French borders.

18 One person was killed by the explosion.

19 Minister of Defense Charles Hernu resigned in the aftermath of the crisis.

20 The PS and their left-wing allies won a majority of seats in the National Assembly in the 1997 legislative elections. The Jospin government lasted from 1997 to 2002. The president remained the Gaullist Jacques Chirac.

21 A second cohabitation took place between 1993 and 1995. This time the right-wing government was led by Édouard Balladur (RPR).

22 The abductions were linked to the French support to Iraq in its war against Iran.

23 The UDF was split into two political parties following the 2007 presidential elections: Modem and Nouveau Centre.

24 Two AD activists, Nathalie Menignon and Jean-Marc Rouillan, were arrested in November 1980 only to be freed a few months later after Mitterrand's victory over Giscard in the presidential election.

25 A proportional representation system was used for the 1986 election in place of the traditional two-round majority system. This change accounts for the FN's performance.

26 Yet whatever the strategy used, Shaun Gregory (2003) remarks that both left-wing and right-wing governments succeeded in eradicating the jihadist menace by defeating the GIA and preventing further attacks.

27 See page 174, note 6 for the origin of the expression.

28 Abu Nidal's last known *fait d'armes* took place on 17 January 1980, when a Palestinian activist was gunned down – an act which Nidal never officially claimed.

29 The UDF regained some momentum when it finished first in the European elections of 10 June 1979.

30 France was one of the few Western countries that did not boycott the summer Olympic Games in Moscow in 1980. On a more personal note, in October 1979 a French newspaper accused Giscard of receiving diamonds as a "present" from Jean-Bédel Bokassa, dictator of the Central African Republic.

31 Alain de Rothschild, president of the Consistoire Central Israélite de France and the Conseil Représentatif des Institutions Juives de France, spoke of "the passivity of public authorities and the indifference of those governing us" ("la passivité des pouvoirs publics et l'indifférence de nos gouvernants"). This translation as well as the others in the text or in footnotes are mine. *Le Monde*, 5 October 1980, news release, n.p.

32 Philippe Boucher, author of the editorial, spoke of "letting madness grow on our land, and horror bloom" ("laisser sur son sol croître la folie, s'épanouir l'horreur"). *Le Monde*, 5 October 1980, n.p.

33 *Le Monde*, 5 October 1980, news release, n.p.

34 Ibid.

35 *Le Monde*, 7 October 1980, news release, n.p.

36 Ibid.

37 Other far-right groups simply declared their indignation without hinting at any communist-led conspiracy.

38 *Le Monde*, 7 October 1980, news release, n.p.

39 "While some scream at the resurgence of the Nazi scare, one forgets the political crimes committed by the KGB, the preparations to invade Poland and the never-ending scandals involving French politicians, notably President Giscard and head of the French Communist Party Georges Marchais" ("Pendant qu'on crie à la résurgence de la bau-druche nazie, on passe sous sience [*sic*] les crimes politiques du K.G.B., les préparatifs d'invasion de la Pologne ou encore les scandales permanents de la vie politique française, notamment l'affaire des diamants de Giscard et les nouveaux rebondissements de l'affaire Marchais." *Le Monde*, 7 October 1980, news release, n.p.

40 Although Le Pen had already made a name for himself, as a member of the Poujadist movement in the 1960s, the FN was still "groupuscular" and had not yet gained a noticeable electoral support.

41 Through this attack, Syria was trying to force France to abandon its pro-Iraq policy.

42 Other attacks of lesser magnitude had taken place between the rue Marbeuf explosion and the rue des Rosiers shooting: an explosion on 20 July on place Saint-Michel (fifteen wounded), and three attacks by AD at the beginning of August.

43 There were 1.6 million unemployed in March 1981 and more than 2 million in March 1983 (Becker 2003, 193).

44 According to polls carried out by SOFRES.

45 The Left lost more than a hundred seats in the departmental assemblies as well as the presidency of eight *conseil généraux* (Becker 2003, 194). Each department has a *conseil généraux*, the equivalent of a departmental government.

46 *Le Monde*, 31 March 1982, news release, n.p. Carlos had asked the government to release his close friend, Magdalena Kopp.

47 *Le Monde*, 2 April 1982, news release, n.p. Yet Bonnet did express concern at some of the appointments made by the socialist government within the police forces.

48 *Le Monde*, 23 April 1982, news release, n.p.

49 "On était en droit d'attendre des actes, on n'a eu que de nouvelles victimes" *Le Monde*, 23 April 1982, news release, n.p.

50 *Le Monde*, 24 April 1982, news release, n.p.

51 *Le Monde*, 27 April 1982, news release, n.p.

52 "Security must be willed, and this will is more and more lacking in the minds of those governing us. I called upon the President of the Republic to finally realize what the security of our fellow citizens requires" ("La sécurité procède d'une volonté et celle-ci est de plus en plus absente de l'esprit de nos gouvernants. J'en ai appelé au président de la République pour qu'il prenne enfin conscience des exigences de la sécurité de nos concitoyens.") *Le Monde*, 29 April 1982, news release, n.p.

53 "Je le dis avec solennité et une certaine brutalité, nous avons à demander à ces dirigeants de partir. C'est notre rôle d'opposants. Qu'ils s'en aillent, ce sont des incapables." *Le Monde*, 29 April 1982, news release, n.p.

54 *Le Monde*, 30 April 1982, news release, n.p.

55 "Moisissure d'une certaine société parisienne et d'objecteurs de conscience," *Le Monde*, 3 May 1982, news release, n.p.

56 "Je plains les hommes de droite qui, par souci d'exploitation politique n'ont pas hésité à faire des déclarations intolérables et abjectes contre le gouvernement de la République ... La vérité est claire. Vous êtes animés par une véritable rage de détruire. Seule la revanche électorale, la reconquête du pouvoir vous intéressent." *Le Monde*, 28 April 1982, news release, n.p.

57 "Je ne considère pas que nous soyons véritablement dans une situation d'alternance. En se proclamant dès le jour de son accession à l'Élysée, président socialiste, François Mitterrand a commis une lourde faute et limité sa capacité à être reconnu comme président de tous les Français. En s'engageant dans une politique de bouleversement généralisé et ne correspondant pas vraiment au sentiment d'une large majorité de Français, le gouvernement n'a pas respecté cette continuité du pouvoir par laquelle se définit l'alternance." *Le Monde*, 2 May 1982, news release, n.p.

58 Japanese terrorist Furyukata Muraya and Palestinian terrorist Abu Daoud. *Le Monde*, 2 May 1982, news release, n.p.

59 *Le Monde*, 11 August 1982, news release, n.p.

60 "Nous ne pouvons pas accepter que la France, fût-elle socialiste ...

soit accusée en tant que France de sentiments antisémites ... Désigner
le président de la République, un homme qui a été légitimement élu
par une majorité des Français – même si nous pensons qu'il s'agissait
là d'une de ces aberrations à laquelle l'histoire condamne, hélas, de
temps en temps tous les peuples – comme l'instigateur, voire le com-
plice, du massacre de la rue des Rosiers, c'est là une accusation igno-
ble que rien ne peut excuser à nos yeux." *Le Figaro*, 11 August 1982,
news release, n.p.

61 "Il y a eu des morts et des blessés très graves. Il serait scandaleux d'es-
    sayer d'exploiter politiquement cet attentat." *Le Monde*, 12 August
    1982, news release, n.p.

62 *Le Monde*, 12 August 1982, news release, n.p. Other recent attacks in-
    cluded the assassinations of Israeli diplomat Yacov Barsimantov and
    of the PLO deputy director in Paris.

63 *Le Monde*, 19 September 1982, news release, n.p.

64 Ibid.

65 *Le Monde*, 19 September 1982, news release, n.p. As Mayor of Paris,
    Chirac asked for the immediate hiring of 3,000 more police
    personnel.

66 Ibid.

67 *Le Monde*, 1 and 24 April 1982, news release, n.p.

68 *Le Monde*, 11 August 1982, news release, n.p.

69 "Le processus de libanisation de la France s'accroît à une allure verti-
    gineuse ... Les limites de notre patience sont atteintes" ("The process
    of Lebanisation of France grows at a dizzying pace ... Our patience
    has reached its limit"). *Le Monde*, 19 September 1982, news release,
    n.p.

70 *Le Monde*, 14 August 1982, news release, n.p.

71 The *rentrée politique* describes the time, traditionally in early Septem-
    ber, when politicians return from their summer break and Parlia-
    ment reconvenes.

72 FARL, a Palestinian organization created in 1979, was based in
    Lebanon. Its objectives were twofold: creating a Palestinian state, and
    ousting French, American, and Israeli forces from Lebanon.

73 Upon receiving news of the latest attack, newly appointed minister of
    the interior Charles Pasqua said that his government would "terrorize
    the terrorists." *Le Monde*, 22 March 1986, news release, n.p. By Septem-
    ber 1986, eight French nationals were held hostage in Lebanon.

74 "Face à ce terrorisme odieux et lâche, la communauté nationale doit se souder et l'ensemble des forces politiques affirmer leur determination face au défi qui est lancé à la France" ("Faced with this odious and cowardly terrorism, the national community must come together and all political forces must assert their resolve to overcome this challenge"). *Le Monde*, 10 September 1986, news release, n.p.

75 "J'approuve tout à fait l'attitude [du premier ministre]. L'attitude de toute la population, de toutes les formations politiques, doit être de soutenir l'action de nos responsables. Pour ma part, c'est ce que je ferai." *Le Monde*, 10 September 1986, news release, n.p.

76 "Nous n'allons pas chipoter le gouvernement sur les limites de cantons, alors que des bombes explosent; les gens ne comprendraient pas qu'on embête le gouvernement avec cela." *Le Monde*, 12 September 1986, news release, n.p.

77 RPR secretary general Jacques Toubon said, "Les socialistes, soit par idéologie, soit par faiblesse, avaient été complaisants à l'égard d'organisations étrangères qui portent une responsabilité dans les attentats terroristes" ("The socialists, either because of ideology or because of weakness, were permissive with foreign organizations bearing a responsibility in these terrorits acts"). Minister of Justice Albin Chalandon lamented that France had become a sanctuary for terrorists. Some within the majority believed that the socialist government had agreed to the liberation of Georges Ibrahim Abdallah in exchange for the release of Gilles Peyroles (a diplomat taken hostage in Beirut), but eventually rescinded their offer when they realized that Abdallah was a much bigger fish than anticipated. *Le Monde*, 11 September 1986, news release, n.p.

78 The PS executive bureau stated, "L'heure n'est pas à la vindicte politicienne. Les difficultés que rencontre aujourd'hui la droite au pouvoir pour assurer la sécurité devraient l'inciter à plus de cohérence et de décence. Les propos de MM. Pasqua, Toubon, Peyrefitte et Chalandon sont non seulement injustifiés, mais indignes. Ils mettent en cause la cohésion de la nation au moment ou la communauté nationale doit manifester sa solidarité" ("This is not the time for political accusations. The difficulties encountered by the right-wing government to ensure national security should encourage it to be more coherent and decent. The declarations of Pasqua, Toubon, Peyrefitte, and Chalandon are not only unjustified but also disgraceful. They jeopardize the unity of the nation at a time when the national community must

demonstrate its solidarity"). To be fair, Roland Dumas, former minister of foreign affairs, blamed the RPR for the recent attack. *Le Monde*, 12 September 1986, news release, n.p.

79 "La lutte contre le terrorisme est l'affaire de la nation tout entière" ("The fight against terrorism concerns the entire nation"). *Le Monde*, 16 September 1986, news release, n.p.

80 "Le Parti socialiste a toujours souligné que la question du terrorisme ne devait pas être le prétexte d'une polémique intérieure … Il ne faut pas diviser la communauté nationale au moment où elle doit manifester sa solidarité face à des agressions qui visent à faire pression sur la France. Les citoyens attendent du gouvernement qu'il fasse preuve d'esprit de responsabilité et de fermeté dans l'action tout en respectant l'État de droit." *Le Monde*, 16 September 1986, news release, n.p.

81 *Le Monde*, 16 September 1986, news release, n.p.

82 The following day, the French military attaché was gunned down in Beirut.

83 *Le Monde*, 19 September1986, news release, n.p.

84 Ibid.

85 "Circumstances require that all of the nation's representatives contribute to the ongoing struggle" ("Les circonstances exigent que tous les représentants de la nation apportent leur contribution à la lutte qui est engagée"). *Le Monde*, 20 September 1986, news release, n.p.

86 Ibid.

87 "We did not come here for political considerations, but to help bring together the national community" ("Nous ne sommes pas venu pour nous prêter à une quelconque récupération politique, mais pour contribuer à souder la communauté nationale"). *Le Monde*, 21–22 September 1986 and *Le Monde* 23 September 1986, news release, n.p.

88 *Le Journal du dimanche*, 21 September 1986, news release, n.p. Source: IFOP.

89 Chirac cancelled an official visit to Canada whereas Mitterrand maintained his visit to Indonesia.

90 Both the president, as head of state, and the prime ministrer, as head of the government, are in charge of the executive branch; however the prime minister is appointed by the president and is subordinate to him or her. In times of cohabitation, the prime minister has far more leeway, particularly in terms of domestic policies. The president traditionally retains the upper hand over foreign policy and defence.

91 "C'est le premier ministre qui se pose aujourd'hui en garant de l'unité nationale, celui autour duquel se cristallisent l'unité natio-nale, la solidarité du pays, de la classe politique et des gouverne-ments étrangers ... [Chirac] apparaît aujourd'hui, dans le couple exécutif, comme celui qui exerce la réalité et la totalité du pouvoir." *Le Monde*, 18 September 1986, news release, n.p.

92 *Le Monde*, 25 September 1986, news release, n.p.

93 *Le Monde*, 10 September 1986, news release, n.p.

94 *Le Monde*, 16 September 1986, news release, n.p.

95 "Far from terrorizing the imperialism, these attacks terrorize the population held hostage" ("Loin de terroriser l'impérialisme, ces attentats terrorisent la population prise en otage"). *Le Monde*, 16 September 1986, news release, n.p.

96 "Le Front national ne pourra jamais adhérer à un consensus fondé sur des rodomontades et une série de petites mesures prises à la sauvette ... Nous n'avons pas confiance dans M. Chirac pour mettre en œuvre une politique efficace de lutte contre le terrorisme. Seule la constitution d'un gouvernement de salut public, incluant le Front national, et s'appuyant ainsi sur une véritable majorité, pourrait prendre les mesures concrètes qu'impose la guerre qui nous a été déclarée" – Jean-Pierre Stirbois, secretary general of the FN). *Le Monde*, 24 September 1986, news release, n.p.

97 "This act of war demands more than the traditional teary homilies to which politicians from the gang of four are accustomed" ("[C'est une] action de guerre qui ne saurait se satisfaire des homélies lar-moyantes habituelles aux politiciens de la bande des quatre"). *Le Monde*, 22 March 1986, news release, n.p.

98 *Le Monde*, 16 September 1986, news release, n.p.

99 *Le Monde*, 10 September 1986, news release, n.p.

100 *Le Monde*, 25 September 1986, news release, n.p. Source: SOFRES (8–9 September).

101 The socialist government released many AD members and offered sanctuary to former Brigate Rosse activists.

102 The press argued that AD, which had not been in the spotlight for some time, had waited for the CSPPA to be finished with its own at-tacks.

103 *Le Monde*, 18 November 1986, news release, n.p.

104 *Le Monde*, 19 November 1986, news release, n.p.

105 *Le Monde*, 21 November 1986, news release, n.p.

106 "The cohabitation between Mr Mitterrand and Mr Chirac has now entered a phase of daily competition" ("La cohabitation entre M. Mitterrand et M. Chirac est entrée dans une phase de concurrence quotidienne," *Le Monde*, 21 November 1986, news release, n.p.

107 "The blood of a CEO in a gutter does not solve issues of class struggle" ("Le sang d'un PDG dans un caniveau ne règle pas les problèmes de la lutte des classes"). *Le Monde*, 18 November 1986, news release, n.p.

108 *Le Monde*, 19 November 1986, news release, n.p.

109 Ibid.

110 From July to November 1995, ten attacks linked to the same group were carried out in France.

111 In the second round of the presidential election, Chirac defeated Lionel Jospin (PS).

112 Minister of the Interior Jean-Louis Debré's over-emotional handling of the situation outside the Saint-Michel subway station projected an image of a frail government clearly overtaken by the events.

113 *Le Monde*, 19 August 1995, news release, n.p.

114 "[The socialists] intend to display the highest sense of responsibility and support the government in whatever it will do to fight terrorism effectively" ("[Les socialistes] entendent témoigner du plus grand sens des responsabilités et soutiennent le gouvernement dans tout ce qu'il entreprendra pour lutter efficacement contre le terrorisme"). *Le Monde*, 19 August 1995, news release, n.p.

115 "Today we are responsible and united. I hope that our adversaries will remember this when we return to power" ("Aujourd'hui, nous sommes responsables et solidaires. J'espère que nos adversaires sauront s'en souvenir quand nous serons à nouveau au gouvernement"), *Le Monde*, 22 August 1995, news release, n.p. The 1982 wave of attacks is analyzed in case study two.

116 He spoke of "a duty to oppose, to renew, to propose" – i.e. "a devoir d'opposition, de renouvellement, de propositions." *Le Monde*, 22 August 1995, news release, n.p.

117 *Le Monde*, 19 August 1995, news release, n.p.

118 "[D]es conflits qui lui sont fondamentalement étrangers." *Le Monde*, 22 August 1995, news release, n.p.

119 Accorrding to *Le Monde*, the investigating officers were convinced

that this act was part of a series of attacks planned and perpetrated by the same group, likely linked to the GIA. *Le Monde*, 21 August 1995, news release, n.p.

120 *L'Humanité*, 5 June 1995, news release, n.p.

121 Two more terrorist acts were foiled, with no casualties.

122 Jospin regretted the meeting and explained that, in view of the current terrorist crisis, France should not be seen as a contradicting actor. *Libération*, 18 October 1995, news release, n.p.

123 "I am sure that I speak for everyone in the National Assembly when I solemnly denounce this vile methods that nothing could ever explain" ("Je suis sûr de me faire l'interprète de la représentation nationale unanime pour dénoncer solennellement des méthodes ignobles qu'aucune cause ni aucune passion ne saurait expliquer"). *Le Monde*, 19 October 1995, news release, n.p.

124 "J'en appelle à la solidarité de tous. Je veux remercier les responsables de toutes les formations politiques qui, depuis le début de cette crise, ont fait preuve, dans leurs réactions, d'un esprit de responsabilité … Il est dans la vie d'une nation des circonstances où les citoyens rassemblés doivent faire face tous ensemble aux défis qui pourraient mettre en jeu les intérêts supérieurs du pays." *Libération*, 18 October 1995, news release, n.p.

125 "Je voudrais, M. le Premier ministre, tirant les leçons de l'expérience que nous avons nous-mêmes connue, sachant par ailleurs les divergences qui peuvent nous opposer, vous dire que dans ces moment-là, nous souhaitons, au-delà de toute divergence, faire prévaloir la solidarité nationale dans la lutte contre des violences inadmissibles." *Libération*, 18 October 1995, news release, n.p.

126 *Le Parisien*, 18 October 1995, news release, n.p.

127 "We have expressed a few days ago our doubts. Today, following this attack, we do not want to say anything that could in any way sustain a process that could be dangerous for our community" ("Nous avons exprimé, il y a quelques jours, nos doutes. Aujourd'hui, face à cet attentat, nous ne voulons rien dire qui puisse alimenter en quoi que ce soit un processus qui serait dangereux pour notre communauté"). *Libération*, 18 October 1995, news release, n.p.

128 "During these times, our support of the government and of the President of the Republic is the only one that counts" ("En ces moments, seule compte notre union derrière vous et derrière le

président de la République"). *Le Monde*, 19 October 1995, news release, n.p.

129 *Libération*, 18 October 1995, news release, n.p.

130 *Le Monde*, 19 October 1995, news release, n.p.

131 Ibid.

132 *Le Monde*, 20 October 1995, news release, n.p.

133 Ibid.

134 This was one of four alleged exigencies. *Le Monde*, 20 October 1995, news release, n.p.

135 *Le Monde*, 20 October 1995, news release, n.p.

136 "[What] started with a blunder ... has ended with an affront. This is the example of what should not be done" ("[Ce qui a] commencé par une maladresse ... s'est terminée par un camouflet. C'est l'exemple de ce qu'il ne faut pas faire"). *Le Monde*, 24 Octobre 1995, news release, n.p.

137 *Les Echos*, 18 October 1995, news release, n.p.

138 *Le Monde*, 20 October 1995, news release, n.p.

139 *Libération*, 18 October 1995, news release, n.p.

140 *Le Monde*, 19 October 19, 1995, news release, n.p.

141 *Le Monde*, 24 Octobre 24, 1995, news release, n.p.

142 In fact, the decision to side with the Algerian government to snatch the electoral victory out of the FIS jaw was taken by François Mitterrand (PS) in the early 1990s.

143 Throughout the campaign for the 1995 presidential election, Jacques Chirac had built momentum by promising to address, once elected, what he called "la fracture sociale," namely the increasing social gap between what former prime minister Jean-Pierre Raffarin would later refer to as "la France d'en haut" and "la France d'en bas," "upper France" and "lower France."

144 "Nous avons toujours soutenu les actions des pouvoirs publics qui visaient à lutter contre ce fléau, et nous avons récusé toute exploitation politicienne. Il en sera de même aujourd'hui." *Le Monde*, 4 December 1996, news release, n.p.

145 "Our only conviction as a force of progress is to carry on bringing the population together and pushing back terrorism" ("Notre seule attitude en tant que force de progrès c'est de continuer à souder la population et à repousser les actes terroristes"). *Libération*, 4 December 1996, news release, n.p.

146 "The moment has come for French people to express their solidarity and to demonstrate their capacity to rally around the President of the Republic, who today is in charge of the security and unity of France" ("C'est le moment pour les Français de marquer leur solidarité et de faire preuve de la même entente et de la même capacité de se réunir derrière le président de la République, qui est en charge aujourd'hui de la sécurité et de l'unité de la France" – F. Bayrou. "We salute the swiftness and determination with which the President of the Republic addressed our fellow citizens, and we ask them under these circumstances to rally around him" ("Nous saluons la rapidité et la détermination avec laquelle le président de la République s'est adressé à nos compatriotes et nous les appelons, dans ces circonstances, à se rassembler autour de lui") – J.-F. Mancel, *Le Monde*, 5 December 1996, news release, n.p.

147 *Les Echos*, 4 December 1996, news release, n.p.

148 "Again innocents have paid with their lives the inconsequence and weakness of a useless government. Jacques Chirac's pathetic declaration is ridiculous in view of the ongoing series of criminal acts taking place on our territory ... None of those behind these recent terrorist attacks have been found and punished. France does not need tough words but tough acts" ("Une nouvelle fois, des citoyens innocents ont payé de leur vies l'inconséquence et la faiblesse d'un gouvernement incapable. Les propos lénifiants d'un Jacques Chirac accablé sont dérisoires au regard des actes criminels qui se multiplient sur notre territoire ... Aucun commanditaire des attentats terroristes de ces dernières années n'a réellement été trouvé et châtié. La France n'a pas besoin de fermeté dans les mots mais dans les actes"). *Le Monde*, 5 December 1996, news release, n.p.

149 Other attacks that caused many wounded did not have similar outcomes, suggesting that fatalities are still central to the concept of magnitude. The number of wounded at Port-Royal was off the charts. The database indicates that attacks occurring in Spain and resulting in high numbers of wounded triggered rallies as well: 53 wounded (no deaths) on 20 July 1996; 60 wounded (no deaths) on 6 November 2001; 42 wounded (no deaths) on 9 February 2005. The ETA was blamed for all three attacks.

150 This is why acts of terrorism that claimed no lives and injured five people or fewer were left out of the dataset, as preliminary survey

indicated that acts causing such a low number of casualties (and no fatalities) were most often ignored by the media.

151 Both far-right leaders Jean-Marie Le Pen (FN) and Bruno Mégret (MNR) condemned the act. Mégret, president of the MNR – of which Maxime Brunerie, the shooter, was a member – wrote to Chirac expressing his "vive emotion" ("profound emotion") and his sympathy, telling the president he was shocked by the risk this terrorist act brought upon Chirac and the institution he represents. *Le Monde*, 17 July 2002, news release, n.p. François Holland expressed the socialists' solidarity with Chirac, and declared that by targeting the president the would-be assassin had targeted the Republic. *Libération*, 16 July 2002, news release, n.p. Similar concerns and expressions of sympathy were voiced by other socialist leaders, including the mayor of Paris and the president of the socialist group in the National Assembly.

152 From 1986 to 1988 and 1993 to 1995 François Mitterrand (PS) cohabited with Jacques Chirac (RPR) and Édouard Balladur (RPR), respectively.

153 "The assassination of a representative of the state in Corsica is a barbarous act of extreme gravity and without precedent in our history" ("L'assassinat du représentant de l'État en Corse est un acte barbare d'une extrême gravité et sans précédent dans notre histoire"). *Le Monde*, 8 February 1998, news release, n.p.

154 "By striking the representative of the state, this despicable act affects the entire nation" ("Cet acte inqualifiable et abject, en frappant le représentant de l'État atteint la nation toute entière"). *Le Monde*, 8 February 1998, news release, n.p. "We will need the state to be completely united" ("Nous aurons besoin de l'unité absolue de l'État"). *Le Monde*, 13 February 1998, news release, n.p.

155 "C'est à la République qu'on a voulu porter un coup. Ce crime odieux appelle la réprobation la plus totale de l'ensemble de la communauté nationale" ("The Republic has been targeted. This odious crime calls for the absolute disapproval by the entire national community"). *Le Monde*, 8 February 1998, news release, n.p.

156 *Le Figaro*, 7 February 1998, news release, n.p.

157 "The assassination of a prefect is an act of such symbolic value that it must bring us all together" ("L'assassinat d'un préfet est un acte

d'une portée symbolique si lourde qu'elle doit tous nous réunir").
Le Monde, 10 February 1998, news release, n.p.

158 "C'est la France unanime, c'est la France debout, par-delà les différences, par-delà les clivages politiques, que nous représentons ici … La France est une et indivisible." *Le Monde*, 11 February 1998, news release, n.p.

159 *Le Monde*, 12 February 1998, news release, n.p.

160 *Le Monde*, 10 February 1998, news release, n.p.

161 *Le Monde*, 8 February 1998, news release, n.p.

162 *Le Figaro*, 8 February 1998, news release, n.p.

163 In 1986, the opposition (PS) was by and large supporting the government when the country was hit by a wave of attacks (see page 123).

164 This governmental alliance lasted from 1997 to 2002 and included five parties: Parti Socialiste, Parti Communiste, Parti Radical de Gauche, les Verts, and Le Mouvement des Citoyens.

165 *Le Monde*, 13 February 1998, news release, n.p.

166 "Charlie Hebdo: Le pays doit se dresser d'un seul bloc pour la liberté," *Libération*, 7 January 2015, http://www.liberation.fr/societe /2015/01/07/reactions-politiques-apres-l-attaque-de-charlie-hebdo _1175395.

167 Ibid.

168 The Mouvement Démocrate (MoDem) was created in 2007 on the remnants of the centre-right UDF.

169 "Il y a un seul devoir, faire l'union nationale." "Attentat contre Charlie Hebdo : la classe politique appelle à l'unité nationale," *Le Monde*, 7 January 2015, http://www.lemonde.fr/attaque-contre-charlie-hebdo/article/2015/01/07/attaque-contre-charlie-hebdo-choc-et-horreur-absolue-dans-la-classe-politique_4550685 _4550668.html.

170 "Les criminels espèrent nous intimider; non, ils renforcent notre courage! Ils espèrent nous diviser; ils renforcent notre unité! … Aux criminels terroristes, opposons notre unité nationale, notre sang-froid, notre détermination implacable." Alexandre Boudet, "Unité nationale dans la classe politique qui met (provisoirement) de côté les questions qui fâchent," *Le Huffington Post*, 7 January 2015, http://www.huffingtonpost.fr/2015/01/07/unite-nationale-classe-politique-met-cote-questions-fachent_n_6429848.html.

171 *Libération*, 8 January 2015, news release, n.p.

172 "Il faut qu'il y ait une union nationale et une solidarité. Ce n'est plus le moment de se critiquer les uns et les autres. Soyons tous unis les uns avec les autres pour lutter contre ces terroristes." "Les réactions politiques après l'attentat à Charlie Hebdo," *Sud-Ouest*, 7 January 2015, http://www.sudouest.fr/2015/01/07/les-reactions-politiques-apres-l-attentat-a-charlie-hebdo-1788547-5209.php.

173 "Il y aura un avant et un après 7 janvier. C'est une situation qui, à l'échelle de la France, est équivalente à celle du 11-Septembre 2001 pour les Etats-Unis." *Le Monde*, 9 January 2015, news release, n.p.

174 "La direction nationale du PCF appellent à ce que partout dans le pays s'exprime l'unité nationale de toutes les forces républicaines face à la barbarie. L'heure est aujourd'hui à rassembler autour des valeurs républicaines le maximum de forces, de citoyennes et de citoyens. Par millions, exprimons partout dans le pays notre détermination à faire vivre les valeurs de Liberté, d'Egalité et de Fraternité. Les militants communistes, les élus communistes et républicains, seront de toutes les initiatives qui, dans les prochains jours, permettront le rassemblement de la nation dans un esprit de grande confiance en notre peuple réuni sur l'essentiel, sans distinction des pensées philosophiques et politiques, de convictions religieuses. Nous appelons à refuser les amalgames et les stigmatisations, à rejeter fermement les appels à la haine et aux racismes." "Charlie Hebdo: Les réactions syndicales et politiques," *L'Humanité*, 7 January 2015, http://www.humanite.fr/charlie-hebdo-les-reactions-syndicales-et-politiques-562050.

175 "Il s'agit de faire la démonstration que nous sommes capables de nous serrer les coudes, de faire peuple ensemble, et que rien ne nous divisera." Pierre-Alain Furbury, "Charlie Hebdo: Hollande appelle à 'l'unité nationale' face à la 'barbarie,'" *Les Échos*, 7 January 2015, http://www.lesechos.fr/07/01/2015/lesechos.fr/0204062547657 _charlie-hebdo—hollande-appelle-a—l-unite-nationale—face-a-la—barbarie-.htm.

176 "Un climat particulier, malsain, existe aujourd'hui dans notre société: beaucoup de confusions, d'amalgames." "'Charlie Hebdo': Le pays doit se dresser d'un seul bloc pour la liberté," *Libération*, 7 January 2015, http://www.liberation.fr/societe/2015/01/07/reactions-

politiques-apres-l-attaque-de-charlie-hebdo_1175395. Cosse was re-
ferring to the debate around the publication of books by polemist
Eric Zemmour about the French decline, and by novelist Michel
Houellebecq about the election in France of a Muslim president.

177 "Douleur et colère. Je pense aux victimes et à leurs familles.
Pourquoi Vigipirate n'était il pas au niveau maximum? Le gouvernement doit s'expliquer ... Je demande le contrôle de nos frontières et
la suspension de Schengen. Assez de la libre circulation des armes
de guerre! ... Unité nationale mais aussi réflexion collective et débat
sur les moyens de renforcer la sécurité." – Nicolas Dupont-Aignan
@dupontaignan "Attentat à Charlie Hebdo: première voix discor-
dante à l'union nationale, Nicolas Dupont-Aignan estime que 'le
gouvernement doit s'expliquer,'" *Europe 1*, 7 January 2015.
http://lelab.europe1.fr/Attentat-a-Charlie-Hebdo-premiere-voix-
discordante-a-l-union-nationale-Nicolas-Dupont-Aignan-estime-que-
le-gouvernement-doit-s-expliquer-20054.

178 "La nation est unie pour dire que nous, Français de toutes origines,
nous n'accepterons pas que soit attenté à nos vies et à nos libertés."
Abel Mestre, "Marine Le Pen: 'La peur est là,'" *Le Monde*, 7 January
2015, http://www.lemonde.fr/politique/article/2015/01/07/marine-
le-pen-la-peur-est-la_4551041_823448.html.

179 "[L'unité nationale] ça ne veut rien dire, ce sont des mots. On a de la
solidarité, de la compassion pour les familles. Pour le reste, le devoir du
président et du gouvernement, c'est de protéger ses concitoyens contre
une menace qui est déterminée. Jusqu'à présent, ils ont voulu relativis-
er la menace en toutes circonstances. Nous sommes quand même le
principal pays qui fournit des troupes aux jihadistes et à l'État islamique ... Cet épisode criminel va relancer le débat sur la présence de
l'islamisme dans nos banlieues et sur l'ensemble du territoire français."
"Les réactions politiques après l'attentat à Charlie Hebdo," *Sud-Ouest*, 7
January 2015, http://www.sudouest.fr/2015/01/07/les-reactions-
politiques-apres-l-attentat-a-charlie-hebdo-1788547-5209.php.

180 "C'est le sens même de l'union sacrée. A partir du moment où l'on
est exclu de cette démarche, ce n'est plus une union sacrée mais une
manoeuvre politicienne minable. De la basse politique. C'est pitoy-
able." "Marine Le Pen veut tirer profit de sa mise à l'écart," *Le Monde*,
9 January 2015.

181   "Dans ces conditions, l'UMP ne devrait pas accepter de participer à cette petite manifestation politicienne sectaire." *Le Monde*, 9 January 2015, news release, n.p.

182   "L'unité nationale est le bouclier qui protège notre société de la division." "'La Marseillaise' entonnée par l'Assemblée nationale, une première depuis 1918," *Libération*.

183   *Libération*, 13 January 2015, news release, n.p.

184   "Je ne demande pas à être intégrée à l'union nationale. L'union nationale, ce n'est pas un chantage où on peut venir à condition de la fermer. Je n'entends pas me soumettre à ce chantage. Il y a un dévoiement total du concept. Ils en assumeront les conséquences auprès des électeurs." "Pour Marine Le Pen, l'exclusion du FN de la marche républicaine est 'une manœuvre politicienne'," *Le Monde*.

185   An ISIS attack in the south part of Beirut killed forty-three the day before the Paris attacks.

186   ISIS claimed responsibility for the attacks calling France the "capital of prostitution and obscenity." In their statement the group explained that "eight brothers, wrapped in explosive belts and armed with machine rifles, targeted sites that were accurately chosen in the heart of the capital of France, including the Stade de France during the match between the Crusader German and French teams, where the fool of France, François Hollande, was present." Rukmini Callimachi, "ISIS Claims Responsibility, Calling Paris Attacks 'First of the Storm'," *New York Times*, 14 November 2015. http://www.nytimes.com/2015/11/15/world/europe/isis-claims-responsibility-for-paris-attacks-calling-them-miracles.html?_r=0.

187   TF1, the French TV network broadcasting the game, decided to proceed with the live coverage and only informed its commentators in the last minute of play of the extent of the tragedy unfolding around the stadium and across the city (a decision likely imposed by the government in order to avoid chaos in this packed stadium).

188   "C'est un acte de guerre commis par une armée terroriste, Daech." On the use of the word *war*, French philosopher Pascal Bruckner prefers the expression *war in peace* or *war in times of peace*. Vincent Tremolet de Villiers, "Pascal Bruckner: 'La repentance permanente nous désarme face à la barbarie'," *Le Figaro*, 22 January 2016, http://www.lefigaro.fr/vox/monde/2016/01/22/31002-20160122

ARTFIG00256-pascal-bruckner-notre-attitude-d-auto-accusation-nous-desarme-face-a-la-barbarie.php.

189 "Mais nous devons également faire preuve d'unité et de sang-froid." "François Hollande: 'C'est une épreuve terrible qui, une nouvelle fois, nous assaille," *Le Monde*, 15 November 2015. http://www.lemonde .fr/journalelectronique/donnees/protege/20151115/html/1221869 .html.

190 "Dans ces circonstances tragiques, la solidarité de tous les Français s'impose. C'est dans cet esprit que je soutiens la décision prise ce soir de décréter l'état d'urgence et la fermeture des frontières." Geoffroy Clavel, "Fusillades et explosions à Paris: les réactions des politiques à chaud," *Le Monde*, 16 November 2015, http://www .huffingtonpost.fr/2015/11/13/fusillades-explosions-paris-politiques-chaud_n_8559426.html. The law on the state of emergency was put in place in 1955 during the war in Algeria and has been used only three time before (1958 and 1961 in relation to events in Algeria, and during the 2005 riots in the Paris suburbs).

191 "Pendant que ce Hollande et ce Valls combattaient le FN, des assassins sanguinaires préparaient leurs attentats! Honte, honte honte à deux!" Nicholas Bay, Twitter post, @nicolasbayfn, 13 November 2015, 22:48 (This tweet has since been deleted.) Clavel, "Fusillades et explosions à Paris."

192 "Monsieur Valls, vous voyez où est le danger? Le vrai! Irresponsable!" Louis Aliot, Twitter post, @louis_aliot, 13 November 2015, 16:59. Clavel, "Fusillades et explosions à Paris."

193 "Fusillade en plein Paris, pauvre, pauvre France abandonnée!" Gilbert Collard, Twitter post, @GilbertCollard, 13 November 2015, 16:35. Clavel, "Fusillades et explosions à Paris."

194 "Une colère froide nous serre le cœur." Marine Le Pen Twitter post, @MLP_officiel, 13 November 2015, 4:03 p.m., https://twitter.com /mlp_officiel/status/665319168913358849.

195 "Nous devons comprendre les raisons qui expliquent que de telles attaques soient possibles et en tirer immédiatement toutes les conséquences. Notre politique extérieure doit intégrer le fait que nous sommes en guerre. Notre politique de sécurité également. ... Nous avons besoin d'inflexions majeures pour que la sécurité des Français soit pleinement assurée" – Nicolas Sarkozy. "Attentats à Paris: l'essentiel

des réactions politiques," *Europe 1*, 16 November 2015, http://www.europe1.fr/politique/attentats-les-reactions-politiques-2620441. "La guerre est parmi nous. L'heure est à la résistance et au combat contre le fanatisme djihadiste. Tous ensemble nous devons agir avec solidarité pour les victimes et confiance à l'égard de nos forces de sécurité. Le président de la République a pris les décisions nécessaires à la sécurité des Français. L'état d'urgence est décrété et l'unité nationale est maintenant notre devoir." François Fillon, "La guerre est parmi nous," *Le blog de François Fillon*,14 November 2015, http://www.blog-fillon.com/2015/11/la-guerre-est-parmi-nous.html.

196 "La France pleure ses morts, c'est le temps du recueillement. Notre peine est immense. François Hollande a réagi rapidement et avec fermeté. Nous soutenons les mesures d'exception décidées, elles en appellent d'autres. J'en appelle à la concorde nationale, je remercie le président Nicolas Sarkozy et tous les responsables politiques d'apporter leur concours à cette union." "Attentats de Paris: Cambadélis appelle les dirigeants politiques à la 'concorde nationale'," *Bfmtv*, 16 November 2015, http://www.bfmtv.com/politique/attentats-de-paris-cambadelis-appelle-les-dirigeants-politiques-a-la-concorde-nationale-930139.html.

197 "À cette heure, toute querelle s'interrompt. … Je forme le vœu que nul ne s'abandonne à la vindicte et conserve sa capacité de discernement. Je forme le vœu que nos responsables gouvernementaux aient tous les moyens d'agir comme ils le souhaitent." Jean-Luc Mélenchon's Facebook page, 13 November 2015, https://www.facebook.com/JLMelenchon/posts/10153766091078750.

198 "Le président de la République a annoncé l'état d'urgence et le contrôle temporaire aux frontières, c'est bien. Mais quoi qu'en dise l'Union européenne, il est indispensable que la France retrouve la maîtrise de ses frontières nationales définitivement." "Attentats à Paris: Valls jure de 'détruire' l'EI, Sarkozy veut davantage de mesures de sécurité," *Francetvinfo*, 15 November 2015, http://www.francetvinfo.fr/faits-divers/terrorisme/attaques-du-13-novembre-a-paris/attentats-a-paris-valls-jure-de-detruire-l-ei-sarkozy-veut-davantage-de-mesures-de-securite_1176483.html.

199 "La France et les Français ne sont plus en sécurité." "Attentats à Paris: Valls jure de 'détruire' l'EI, Sarkozy veut davantage de mesures de sécurité," *Francetvinfo*.

200 "Devant l'horreur du terrorisme aveugle, unité et solidarité de la nation. Prions pour que la France puisse faire face à cette terrible épreuve." Agence France-Presse, "Hollande promet un 'combat impitoyable' contre le terrorisme," *La* Presse, 13 November 2015, http://www.lapresse.ca/le-soleil/actualites/monde/201511/13/01-4920594-hollande-promet-un-combat-impitoyable-contre-le-terrorisme.php.

201 *Les Échos*, 16 November 2015, news release, n.p.

202 Ibid.

203 Hollande also proposed to modify the constitution in order to institute a "state of crisis" and not merely a "state of emergency." He announced the recruitment of 5,000 police officers and gendarmes, and guaranteed that the number of soldiers would not be reduced.

204 *Le Monde*, 18 November 2015, news release, n.p.

205 "La séance n'était pas au niveau." *Les Échos*, 19 November 2015, news release, n.p.

206 "L'heure n'est pas à la polémique." *Les Échos*, 19 November 2015, news release, n.p.

207 "Un député Les Républicains invite l'Assemblée à 'ne pas sombrer dans les invectives et les provocations,'" *Francetvinfo*, 13 November 2015, http://www.francetvinfo.fr/faits-divers/terrorisme/attaques-du-13-novembre-a-paris/video-un-depute-les-republicains-invite-toute-l-assemblee-a-ne-pas-sombrer-invectives-et-provocations_1181517.html.

208 "[N]e pas tomber dans le piège de l'énervement … et du réflexe partisan." "Question au gouvernement No. 3351 de M. Edouard Philippe," French National Assembly, 19 November 2015, http://questions.assemblee-nationale.fr/q14/14-3351QG.htm.

209 "Le moment n'est pas de débattre entre nous, mais de répondre à la peur générale des Français." *Le Monde*, 19 November 2015, news release, n.p.

210 *Les Échos*, 19 November 2015, news release, n.p.

211 "Le dessein des terroristes est de plonger notre pays dans l'effroi et la division. Nous devons donc veiller à préserver l'unité qui fait notre force. Notre cohésion sociale est la meilleure réponse et notre union nationale en est l'expression … Nous devons veiller à préserver l'unité qui est notre force … Face à la menace, il n'y a plus de différences de territoires, il n'y a plus de clivages partisans qui tiennent,

a-t-il dit. Il n'y a plus que des femmes et des hommes de devoir, des élus du suffrage universel conscients de leurs responsabilités." "Discours du président de la République au rassemblement des Maires de France," Elysee de France, http://www.elysee.fr/declarations/article/discours-du-president-de-la-republique-au-rassemblement-des-maires-de-france/; and "L'union nationale, privilège présidentiel," *Le Monde*, 19 November 2015, http://www.lemonde.fr/idees/article/2015/11/19/l-union-nationale-privilege-presidentiel_4813806_3232.html.

212 *Le Monde*, 21 November 2015, news release, n.p.

213 Taubira eventually resigned on 27 January 2016 because of major disagreements with the government's terror policy, a plan to strip people convicted of terrorism of their French citizenship.

214 Hypothesis 7 suggested that radical parties would not rally around the flag following acts of terror; rather, they would be outspoken in their criticism toward the government.

APPENDIX ON THE TREATMENT OF DATA

1 Since the original RAND dataset for the period 1990–97 does not include all the domestic acts (only those related to international terrorism are included), I created an alternative repetition variable that accounts for other domestic acts over the period 1990–98. These data, which are only added for the repetition variable, were imported from the Global Terrorism Database. Two international acts that occurred in Germany did not appear in the TKB and were thus added. Of course, the definition used by GTB is more inclusive than the one used by TKB, but broadly compatible.

2 The database does not take into consideration acts of terror that have caused no fatalities and fewer than six injuries. A preliminary survey of these low-magnitude incidents in the newspapers used to determine the reaction indicates that they simply do not register on the media radar and do not elicit any reaction from the political elite. Including these acts would have brought no valuable information and would have lengthened considerably the data-gathering process.

3 The conservative PP governed during the period covered by the pact. In December 2000, the two main political parties (the conservative PP in government since 1995, and the socialist PSOE) signed an an-

titerrorist pact agreeing to support one another in the fight against terror. "El pacto de Estado por la libertades y contra el terrorismo" was announced on 9 December 2000, and signed four days later. *El País*, 9 December 2000, and 13 December 2000, news release, n.p.

4 Crises include the First Gulf War (Operation Desert Storm), the NATO operation in Afghanistan, and the invasion of Iraq in 2003.

Bibliography

Abadie, Alberto. 2006. "Poverty, Political Freedom, and the Roots of Terrorism." *The American Economic Review* 96, no. 2: 50–6.

Abadie, Alberto, and Javier Gardeazabal. 2003. "The Economic Costs of Conflict: A Case Study of the Basque Country." *American Economic Review* 93, no. 1: 113–32.

Aldrich, John. 1995. *Why Parties?: The Origin and Transformation of Political Parties in America.* Chicago: University of Chicago Press.

Aldrich, John, and Richard Niemi. 1990. "The Sixth American Party System: The 1960s Realignment and the Candidate-Centered Parties." *Duke University Working Paper in American Politics* 107.

Alesina, Alberto, Nouriel Roubini, and Gerald Cohen. 1997. *Political Cycle and the Macroeconomy.* Cambridge, MA: MIT Press.

Allison, Graham. 2004. *Nuclear Terrorism: The Ultimate Preventable Catastrophe.* New York: Times Books.

– 1969. "Conceptual Models and the Cuban Missile Crisis." *American Political Science Review* 63, no. 3: 689–718.

Allison, Graham, and Philip Zelikow. 1999. *Essence of Decision: Explaining the Cuban Missile Crisis.* New York: Longman.

Arnold, Ron. 1997. *Ecoterror: The Violent Agenda to Save Nature.* Bellevue, WA: Free Enterprise Press.

Aust, Stefan. 1970. *Der Baader Meinhof Komplex.* Munich: Goldmann, 1998.

Axelrod, Robert. 1970. *Conflict of Interest.* Chicago: Markham.

Baird-Windle, Patricia, and Eleanor Bader, eds. 2001. *Targets of Hatred: Anti-Abortion Terrorism.* New York: Palgrave Macmillan.

Baker, William, and John Oneal. 2001. "Patriotism or Opinion Leadership? The Nature and Origins of the 'Rally 'Round the Flag' Effect." *The Journal of Conflict Resolution* 45, no. 5: 661–87.

Bali, Valentina. 2007. "Terror and Elections: Lessons from Spain." *Electoral Studies* 26, no. 3: 669–87.

Barker, Jonathan. 2002. *The No-Nonsense Guide to Global Terrorism*. Norton and Company.

Baum, Matthew. 2002. "The Constituent Foundations of the Rally-Round-the-Flag Phenomenon." *International Studies Quarterly* 46: 263–98.

Baum, Matthew, and Tim Groeling. 2004. "Crossing the Water's Edge: Elite Rhetoric, Media Coverage and the Rally-around-the-Flag Phenomenon, 1979–2003." Presentation, American Political Science Association, Chicago, IL, 2–5 September.

Becker, Jean-Jacques. 2003. *Histoire politique de la France depuis 1945*. Paris: Armand Colin.

Bélanger, Éric, and Bonnie Meguid. 2005. "Issue Salience, Issue Ownership and Issue-Based Vote Choice: Evidence from Canada." Presentation, Canadian Political Science Association, London, ON. 2–4 June.

Bell, J. Bowyer. 1993. *The Irish Troubles: A Generation of Violence, 1967–1992*. New York: St. Martin's.

– 1978. *A Time of Terror*. New York: Basic Books.

– 1975. *Transnational Terror*. Washington, DC: American Enterprise Institute.

– 1970. *The Secret Army: A History of the IRA*. Cambridge, MA: MIT Press.

Bergen, Peter and Paul Cruickshank. 2007. "The Iraq Effect: War Has Increased Terrorism Sevenfold Worldwide." *Mother Jones*. 1 March. http://www.motherjones.com/politics/2007/03/iraq-101-iraq-effect-war-iraq-and-its-impact-war-terrorism-pg-1.

Berinsky, Adam. 2007. "Assuming the Costs of War: Events, Elites, and American Public Support for Military Conflict." *Journal of Politics* 69, no. 4: 975–97.

Berkowitz, B.J. 1972. *Superviolence: The Civil Threat of Mass Destruction Weapons*. Santa Barbara, CA: ADCON Corporation.

Berrebi, Claude. 2007. "Evidence about the Link between Education, Poverty and Terrorism among Palestinians." *Peace Economics, Peace Science and Public Policy* 13, no. 1.

Berrebi, Claude and Esteban Klor. 2008. "Are Voters Sensitive to Terrorism?

Direct Evidence from the Israeli Electorate." *American Political Science Review* 102: 279–301.

– 2006. "On Terrorism and Electoral Outcome: Theory and Evidence from the Israeli-Palestinian Conflict." *Journal of Conflict Resolution* 50, no. 6: 899–925.

Bishop, P., and E. Mallie. 1987. *The Provisional IRA*. London: Heinemann.

Bjørgo, Tore. 2005. *Root Causes of Terrorism: Myths, Reality and Ways Forward*. Abington, UK: Routledge.

– 1995. *Terror from the Extreme Right*. London: Frank Cass.

Blais, André, Donald Blake, and Stéphane Dion. 1993. "Do Parties Make a Difference? Parties and the Size of Government in Liberal Democracies." *American Journal of Political Science* 37, no. 1: 40–62.

Bloom, Mia. 2005. *Dying to Kill: The Allure of Suicide Terror*. New York: Columbia University Press.

Boettcher, William, and Michael Cobb. 2006. "Echoes of Vietnam? Casualty Framing and Public Perceptions of Success and Failure in Iraq." *The Journal of Conflict Resolution* 50, no. 6: 831–54.

Boin, Arjen, Allan McConnell, and Paul 't Hart. 2008. *Governing after Crisis: The Politics of Investigation, Accountability and Learning*. Cambridge: Cambridge University Press.

Boin, Arjen, Paul 't Hart, Eric Stern, and Bengt Sundelius. 2005. *The Politics of Crisis Management: Public Leadership under Pressure*. Cambridge: Cambridge University Press.

Boix, Carles. 1998. *Political Parties, Growth and Equality*. Cambridge: Cambridge University Press.

Brecher, Michael. 2008. *International Political Earthquakes*. Ann Arbor: University of Michigan Press.

Broder, David. 1972. *The Party's Over: The Failure of Politics in America*. New York: Harper and Row.

Brody, Richard. 2002. "The American People and President Bush." *The Forum* 1, no. 1: 1–8.

– 1991. *Assessing the President: The Media, Elite Opinion, and Public Support*. Stanford, CA: Stanford University Press.

Brody, Richard and Catherine Shapiro. 1989. "Policy Failure and Public Support: The Iran-Contra Affair and Public Assessment of President Reagan." *Political Behavior* 11, no. 4: 353–69.

Brown, Michael, Sean Lynn-Jones, and Steven Miller, eds. 1996. *Debating the Democratic Peace*. Cambridge, MA: MIT Press.

Budge, Ian, and Dennis Farlie. 1983. *Explaining and Predicting Elections.* London: Allen and Unwin.

Budge, Ian, and Richard Hofferbert. 1990. "Mandates and Policy Outputs: U.S. Party Platforms and Federal Expenditures." *American Political Science Review* 84, no. 1: 111–31.

Budge, Ian, and Michael Laver. 1986. "Office Seeking and Policy Pursuit in Coalition Theory." *Legislative Studies Quarterly* 11, no. 4: 485–506.

Budge, Ian, and David Robertson. 1987. "Do Parties Differ and How? Comparative Discriminant and Factor Analyses." In *Ideology, Strategy and Party Change. Spatial Analyses of Post-War Election Programmes in 19 Democracies*, edited by Ian Budge, David Robertson, and Derek Hearl, 387–416. Cambridge: Cambridge University Press.

Burke, Jason. 2003. *Al-Qa'eda: Casting a Shadow of Terror.* London: I.B. Taurus.

Callaghan, Karen and Simo Virtanen. 1993. "Revised Models of the 'Rally Phenomenon': The Case of the Carter Presidency." *Journal of Politics* 55, no. 3: 756–64.

Campbell, James. 2005. "Why Bush Won the Presidential Election of 2004: Incumbency, Ideology, Terrorism, and Turnout." *Political Science Quarterly* 120, no. 2: 219–41.

Carlsnaes, Walter, Thomas Risse-Kappen, and Beth Simmons, eds. 2002. *Handbook of International Relations.* London: SAGE.

Cassese, Antonio. 1989. *Terrorism, Politics and Law: The Achille Lauro Affair.* Princeton, NJ: Princeton University Press.

Chaliand, Gérard, and Arnaud Blin. 2007. *The History of Terrorism.* University of California Press.

Chari, Raj. 2004. "The 2004 Spanish Election: Terrorism as a Catalyst for Change?" *West European Politics* 27, no. 5: 954–63.

Charters, David, ed. 1994. *The Deadly Sin of Terrorism: Its Effect on Democracy and Civil Liberty in Six Countries.* Westport, CT: Greenwood Press.

Chen, Andrew, and Thomas Siems. 2004. "The Effects of Terrorism on Global Capital Markets." *European Journal of Political Economy* 20, no. 2: 463–78.

Chomsky, Noam. 2001. *9-11.* New York: Open Media/Seven Stories Press.

Clark, Robert. 1984. *The Basque Insurgents: ETA, 1952–1980.* Madison: University of Wisconsin Press.

Clarke, Thurston. 1981. *By Blood and Fire: The Attack on the King David Hotel.* New York: Putnam.

Colomer, Josep. 2004. "The General Election in Spain, March 2004." *Electoral Studies* 24, no. 1: 149–56.

Crank, John, and Patricia Gregor.2005. *Counter-Terrorism after 9/11: Justice, Security and Ethics Reconsidered*. Newark, NJ: Lexisnexis/Matthew Bender.

Crenshaw, Martha, ed. 1995. *Terrorism in Context*. University Park: Penn State Press.

– 1989. *Terrorism and International Cooperation*. New York: Institute for East-West Security Studies.

– 1981. "The Causes of Terrorism." *Comparative Politics* 13, no. 4: 379–99.

– 1978. *Revolutionary Terrorism: the FLN in Algeria, 1954–1962*. Stanford, CA: Hoover Institution Press.

Crotty, William. 2001. *The State of Democracy in America*. Washington, DC: Georgetown University Press.

Crotty, William, Donald Freeman, and Douglas Gatlin, eds. 1966. *Political Parties and Political Behavior*. Boston: Allyn and Bacon.

Crozier, Michel, Samuel Huntington, and Joji Watanuki. 1975. *The Crisis of Democracy*. New York: New York University Press.

Cunningham, Michael. 1991. *British Government Policy in Northern Ireland 1969–89*. Manchester: Manchester University Press.

Dalton, Russell, and Martin Wattenberg, eds. 2002. *Parties without Partisans: Political Change in Advanced Industrial Democracies*. Oxford: Oxford University Press.

Damore, David. 2004. "The Dynamics of Issue Ownership in Presidential Campaigns." *Political Research Quarterly* 57, no. 3: 391–7.

Dartnell, Michael. 1995. *Action Directe: Ultra-Left Terrorism in France, 1979–1987*. London: Frank Cass.

David, Charles-Philippe, and Benoît Gagnon, eds. 2007. *Repenser le terrorisme: concepts, acteurs et réponses*. Quebec City: Les Presses de l'Université Laval.

Davis, Richard. 2005. *Politics Online. Blogs, Chatrooms, and Discussion Groups in American Democracy*. Milton Park, UK: Routledge.

– 1999. *The Web of Politics. The Internet's Impact on the American Political System*. Oxford: Oxford University Press.

Dekmejian, Hrair. 2007. *Spectrum of Terror*. Washington, DC: CQ Press.

Della Porta, Donatella, and Dieter Rucht. 1995. "Left-Libertarian Movements in Context: A Comparison of Italy and West Germany, 1965–1990." In *The Politics of Social Protest: Comparative Perspectives on States and Social Movements*, edited by Craig Jenkins and Bert Klandermans, Minneapolis: University of Minnesota Press.

Dingley, James. 2001. "The Bombing of Omagh, 15 August 1998: The Bombers, Their Tactics, Strategy, and Purpose Behind the Incident." *Studies in Conflict and Terrorism* 24, no. 6: 451–65.

Divine, Robert. 1974. *Foreign Policy and US Presidential Elections, 1940–1948*. Nfew York: New Viewpoints.

Dougherty, James, and Robert Pfaltzgraff. 1981. *Contending Theories of International Relations: A Comprehensive Survey*. New York: Harper and Row.

Douglass, William, and Joseba Zulaika. 1990. "On the Interpretation of Terrorist Violence: ETA and the Basque Political Process." *Comparative Studies in Society and History* 32, no. 2: 238–57.

Downs, Anthony. 1957. *An Economic Theory of Democracy*. New York: Harper and Row.

Drake, Richard. 1995. *The Aldo Moro Murder Case*. Cambridge, MA: Harvard University Press.

Eldersveld, Samuel. 1966. "Social Conflict, Political Parties and Democracy." In *Political Parties and Political Behavior*, edited by William Crotty, Donald Freeman, and Douglas Gatlin. Boston: Allyn and Bacon.

Eley, Geoff. 2002. *Forging Democracy: The History of the Left in Europe, 1850–2000*. Oxford: Oxford University Press.

Elias, Norbert. 2000. *The Civilizing Process*. Oxford: Wiley-Blackwell. First published in 1939.

Enders, Walter, and Todd Sandler. 2006. *The Political Economy of Terrorism*. Cambridge: Cambridge University Press.

Entman, Robert. 2006. *Projections of Power: Framing News, Public Opinion, and U.S. Foreign Policy*. Chicago: University of Chicago Press.

Esposito, John. *Unholy War: Terror in the Name of Islam*. Oxford: Oxford University Press, 2002.

Etzioni, Amitai. 2007. *Security First: For a Muscular, Moral Foreign Policy*. New Haven, CT: Yale University Press.

Eubank, William, and Leonard Weinberg. 2001. "Terrorism and Democracy: Perpetrators and Victims." *Terrorism and Political Violence* 13, no. 1: 155–64.

– 1994. "Does Democracy Encourage Terrorism?" *Terrorism and Political Violence* 6, no. 4: 417–35.

Evans, Peter, Harold Jacobson, and Robert Putnam, eds. 1993. *Double-*

Edged Diplomacy: International Bargaining and Domestic Politics. Berkeley: University of California Press.

Eyerman, Joe. 1998. "Terrorism and Democratic States: Soft Targets or Accessible Systems." *International Interactions* 24, no. 2: 151–70.

Ferracuti, F. 1983. "Psychiatric Aspects of Italian Left-Wing and Right-Wing Terrorism." Presentation, VII World Congress of Psychiatry, Vienna, Austria.

Finnemore, Martha. 1996. *National Interests in International Society*. Ithaca, NY: Cornell University Press.

Fiorina, Morris. 1995. "Rational Choice and the New (?) Institutionalism." *Polity* 9: 107–15.

Fournier, Louis. 1984. FLQ, *histoire d'un mouvement clandestin*. Montreal: Michel Brûlé.

Frears, John. 1991. *Parties and Voters in France*. London: Hurst.

Fuchs, Dieter, and Hans-Dieter Klingemann. 1990. "The Left-Right Schema." In *Continuities in Political Action*, edited by M.K. Jennings, Jan W. van Deth, S.H. Barnes, Dieter Fuchs, F.J. Heunks, and Ronald Inglehart, 203–34. Berlin: Walter de Gruyter.

Gambetta, Diego. 2006. *Making Sense of Suicide Missions*. Oxford: Oxford University Press.

Ganor, Boaz. 1998. "Defining Terrorism: Is One Man's Terrorist Another Man's Freedom Fighter?" *The Institute for Counter-Terrorism*. Online. https://www.ict.org.il/Article/1123/Defining-Terrorism-Is-One-Mans-Terrorist-Another-Mans-Freedom-Fighter www.ict.org.il/Article/define.htm. Accessed on 6 February 2006.

Garfinkel, Michelle. 2004. "Global Threats and the Domestic Struggle for Power." *European Journal of Political Economy* 20, no. 2: 495–508.

Garrison, Arthur. 2004. "Defining Terrorism: Philosophy of the Bomb, Propaganda by the Deed and Change Through Fear and Violence." *Criminal Justice Studies* 17, no. 3: 259–79.

Gartner, Scott Sigmund. 2008. "The Multiple Effects of Casualties on Public Support for War: An Experimental Approach." *American Political Science Review* 102, no. 1: 95–106.

Gartner, Scott Sigmund, and Gary Segura. 1998. "War, Casualties and Public Opinion." *The Journal of Conflict Resolution* 42, no. 3: 278–300.

Gartner, Scott Sigmund, Gary Segura, and Bethany Barratt. 2004. "Casualties, Positions and Senate Elections in the Vietnam War." *Political Research Quarterly* 53, no. 3: 467–77.

Gaubatz, Kurt. 1999. *Elections and War: The Electoral Incentive in the Democratic Politics of War and Peace*. Stanford, CA: Stanford University Press.

Gelpi, Christopher, Peter Feaver, and Jason Reifler. 2006. "Success Matters: Casualty Sensitivity and the War in Iraq." *International Security* 30: 7–46.

George, Alexander, and Andrew Bennett. 2005. *Case Studies and Theory Development in the Social Sciences*. Cambridge, MA: MIT Press.

Giovagnoli, Agostino. 2005. *Il caso Moro: una tragedia repubblicana*. Bologna, Italy: Il mulino.

Gleditsch, Nils, Peter Wallensteen, Mikael Eriksson, Margareta Sollenberg, and Havard Strand. 2002. "Armed Conflict 1946–2001: A New Dataset." *Journal of Peace Research* 39, no. 5: 615–37.

Gourevitch, Peter. 1978. "The Second Image Reversed: The International Sources of Domestic Politics." *International Organization* 32, no. 4: 881–912.

Gregory, Shaun. 2003. "France and the War on Terrorism." *Terrorism and Political Violence* 15, no. 1: 124–47.

Guelke, Adrian, and Jim Smyth. 1992. "The Ballot Bomb: Terrorism and the Electoral Process in Northern Ireland." *Terrorism and Political Violence* 4, no. 2: 103–24.

Guidère, Mathieu, and Nicole Morgan. 2007. *Le Manuel de recrutement d'Al-Qaïda*. Paris: Seuil.

Guilmartin, Eugenia. 2004. "Terrorist Attacks and Presidential Approval from 1949–2002." Presentation, American Political Science Association, Chicago, IL. 2–5 September.

Gullan, Harold. 1998. *The Upset That Wasn't: Harry S. Truman and the Crucial Election of 1948*. Chicago: Ivan R. Dee.

Gunaratna, Rohan. *Inside Al Qaeda: Global Network of Terror*. New York: Berkley Book, 2002.

Hall, Peter, and Rosemary Taylor. 1996. "Political Science and the Three New Institutionalism." *Political Studies* 44: 936–57.

Halliday, Fred. 2003. *Islam and the Myth of Confrontation: Religion and Politics in the Middle East*. London: I.B. Tauris.

Hamon, Alain, and Jean-Charles Marchand. 1986. *Action directe: du terrorisme français à l'euroterrorisme*. Paris: Seuil.

Haubrich, Dirk. 2006. "Modern Politics in an Age of Global Terrorism: New Challenges for Domestic Public Policy." *Political Studies* 54: 399–423.

Heller, Joseph. 1995. *The Stern Gang: Ideology, Politics, and Terror, 1940–1949*. London: Routledge.

Hermann, Charles F. 1996. "International Crisis as a Situational Variable." In *Classics of International Relations*, edited by John Vasquez, 191–9. Upper Saddle River, NJ: Prentice Hall.

Hess, Henner, Martin Moerings, Dieter Pass, Sebastian Scheerer, and Heinz Steinert. 1988. *Angriff auf das Herz des Staates*. Frankfurt, Ger.: Suhrkamp.

Hetherington, Marc, and Michael Nelson. 2003. "Anatomy of a Rally Effect: George W. Bush and the War on Terrorism." *PS: Political Science and Politics* 36, no. 1: 37–44.

Hewitt, C. 1984. *Effectiveness of Anti-Terrorist Policies*. Lanham, MD: University Press of America.

Hibbs, Douglas. 1977. "Political Parties and Macroeconomic Policy." *American Political Science Review* 71, no. 4: 1467–87.

Hills, Alice. 2002. "Responding to Catastrophic Terrorism." *Studies in Conflict & Terrorism* 25, no. 4: 245–61.

Hoffman, Bruce. 2006. *Inside Terrorism*. New York: Columbia University Press.

– 1984. "Right-Wing Terrorism in Europe." *Conflict* 5, no 3.

Holian, David. 2004. "He's Stealing My Issues! Clinton's Crime Rhetoric and the Dynamics of Issue Ownership." *Political Behavior* 26, no. 2: 95–124.

Holmes, Jennifer S. and Sheila Amin Gutiérrez de Piñeres.2002. "Sources of Fujimori's Popularity: Neo-liberal Reform or Ending Terrorism." *Terrorism and Political Violence* 14, no. 4: 93–112.

Holmes, Stephen. 2007. *The Matador's Cape: America's Reckless Response to Terror*. Cambridge: Cambridge University Press.

Howard, Lawrence, ed. 1992. *Terrorism: Roots, Impact, Responses*. Westport, CT: Praeger.

Howard, Russell, and Reid Sawyer. 2004. *Defeating Terrorism: Shaping the New Security Environment*. New York: McGraw-Hill/Dushkin.

Huckshorn, Robert. 1984. *Political Parties in America*. Monterey, CA: Brooks/Cole.

Huddy, Leonie. 2003. "Group Membership, Ingroup Loyalty, and Political Cohesion." In *Oxford Handbook of Political Psychology*, edited by David Sears, Leonie Huddy, and Robert Jervis, 511–58. New York: Oxford University Press.

Huntington, Samuel. 1981. *American Politics: The Promise of Disharmony*. Cambridge, MA: Harvard University Press.

Hymans, Jacques. 2005. "Why Rally? Re-examining the Theoretical Bases for the Rally Round the Flag Effect." Presentation, American Political Science Association, Washington, DC, 1–4 September.

Indridason, Indridi. 2008. "Does Terrorism Influence Domestic Politics? Coalition Formation and Terrorist Incidents." *Journal of Peace Research* 45, no. 2: 241–59.

Iyengar, Shanto, and Donald Kinder. 1987. *News That Matters*. Chicago: University of Chicago Press.

Jacobson, Gary. 2003. "Terror, Terrain, and Turnout: Explaining the 2002 Midterm Elections." *Political Science Quarterly* 118, no. 1: 1–22.

Jasper, J., and D. Nelkin. 1992. *The Animal Rights Crusade: The Growth of a Moral Protest*. New York: Free Press.

Jenkins, Brian. 2001a. "Terrorism and Beyond: A 21st-Century Perspective." *Studies in Conflict and Terrorism* 24: 321–27.

– 2001b. "The Organization Men: Anatomy of a Terrorist Attack." In *How Did This Happen? Terrorism and the New War* edited by James Hoge and Gideon Rose, 1–14. Oxford: Public Affairs.

– 1975. *International Terrorism*. Los Angeles: Crescent.

– 1975. *Will Terrorists Go Nuclear?* Santa Monica, CA: RAND Corporation.

Jenkins, Philip. 2003. *Images of Terror: What We Can and Can't Know about Terrorism*. New York: Aldine de Gruyter.

Johnson, Paul. 1993. "The Seven Deadly Sins of Terrorism." In *Terrorism and Political Violence: Limits and Possibilities of Legal Control*, edited by Henry H. Han, 189–95. New York: Oceana.

Juergensmeyer, Mark. 2002. "Terror as Deadly Theater." *Oklahoma City Memorial Institute for the Prevention of Terrorism*. www.terrorisminfo .mipt.org. Accessed 7 October 2008.

– 1992. *Violence and the Sacred in the Modern World*. London: Routledge.

Kam, Cindy, David Greenwald, and Jennifer Ramos. 2004. "Who Leaves the Rally? Explaining Declines in Presidential Approval Following Round the Flag Events." Presentation, American Political Science Association, Chicago, IL. 2–5 September.

Kam, Cindy, and Jennifer Ramos. 2008. "Joining and Leaving the Rally: Understanding the Surge and Decline in Presidential Approval Following 9/11." *Public Opinion Quarterly* 72, no. 4: 619–50.

Karol, David, and Edward Miguel. 2007. "The Electoral Cost of War: Iraq Casualties and the 2004 U.S. Presidential Election." *Journal of Politics* 69, no. 3: 633–48.

Karpin, Michael, and Ina Friedman. 1998. *Murder in the Name of God: The Plot to Kill Yitzhak Rabin.* New York: Metropolitan Books.

Kassimeris, George. 2008. *Playing Politics with Terrorism, A User's Guide.* New York: Columbia University Press.

Katz, Richard, and William Crotty, eds. 2006. *Handbook of Party Politics.* London: SAGE.

Keene, Karlyn. 1980. "Rally 'Round the President." *Public Opinion* 3, no. 1: 28–9.

Kegley, Charles. 1990. *International Terrorism: Characteristics, Causes, Controls.* Basingstoke, UK: Palgrave Macmillan.

Kelly, Michael J. 1989. "The Seizure of the Turkish Embassy in Ottawa: Managing Terrorism and the Media." In *Coping with Crises – The Management of Disasters, Riots and Terrorism,* edited by Uriel Rosenthal, Michael T. Charles, and Paul 't Hart, Springfield, IL: Charles C. Thomas.

Keman, Hans. 1982. "Securing the Safety of the Nation-State." In *The Impact of Parties: Politics and Policies in Democratic Capitalist States,* edited by Francis G. Catles, 177–221. London: SAGE.

Keohane, Robert, and Helen Milner, eds. 1996. *Internationalization and Domestic Politics.* Cambridge: Cambridge University Press.

Kepel, G. 1993. *Muslim Extremism in Egypt.* Berkeley: University of California Press.

Kern, Montague, Patricia Levering, and Ralph Levering. 1983. *The Kennedy Crisis: The Press, the Presidency, and Foreign Policy.* Chapel Hill: University of North Carolina Press.

Kernell, S. 1975. *Presidential Popularity and Electoral Preferences: A Model of Short Term Political Change.* Berkeley: University of California Press.

Key, V.O. 1964. *Politics, Parties, and Pressure Groups.* New York: Crowell.

Khelladi, A. 1992. *Algérie: Les Islamistes face au pouvoir.* Algeria: Alfa.

Knapp, Andrew, and Vincent Wright. 2006. *The Government and Politics of France.* London: Routledge.

Kohli, Atul, Peter Evans, Peter Katzenstein, Adam Przeworski, Susanne Hoeber Rudolph, James Scott, and Theda Skocpol. 1995. "The Role of Theory in Comparative Politics: A Symposium." *World Politics* 48, no. 1: 1–49.

Kramer, Martin. 1990. "The Moral Logic of Hizballah." In *Origins of Terrorism: Psychologies, Ideologies, Theologies, States of Mind*, edited by Walter Reich, 131–57. Cambridge: Cambridge University Press.

Kraushaar, Wolfgang, ed. 2006. *Die RAF und der linke Terrorismus*. Hamburg: HIS Verlages.

Kronenwetter, Michael. 2004. *Terrorism: A Guide to Events and Documents*. Westport, CT: Greenwood Press.

Krueger, Alan. 2007. *What Makes a Terrorist: Economics and the Roots of Terrorism*. Princeton, NJ: Princeton University Press.

Krueger, Alan, and Jitka Maleckova. 2003. "Education, Poverty and Terrorism: Is There a Causal Connection?" *Journal of Economic Perspectives* 17, no. 4: 119–44.

Kydd, Andrew, and Barbara F. Walter. 2002. "Sabotaging the Peace: The Politics of Extremist Violence." *International Organization* 56, no. 2: 263–96.

Lafree, Gary, and Laura Dugan. 2007. "Introducing the Global Terrorism Database." *Terrorism and Political Violence* 19: 181–204.

Lai, Brian, and Ruth Melkonian-Hoover. 2005. "Democratic Progress and Regress: The Effect of Parties on the Transitions of States to and Away from Democracy." *Political Research Quarterly* 58, no. 4: 551–64.

Landau, Mark, Sheldon Solomon, Jeff Greenberg, Florette Cohen, Tom Pyszczynski, Jamie Arndt, Claude Miller, Daniel Ogilvie, and Alison Cook. 2004. "Deliver Us from Evil: The Effects of Mortality Salience and Reminders of 9/11 on Support for President George W. Bush." *Personality and Social Psychology Bulletin* 30, no. 9: 1136–50.

Laqueur, Walter. 2004. *No End to War: Terrorism in the Twenty-First Century*. New York: Continuum.

– 1999a. *The Age of Terrorism*. New Brunswick, NJ: Transaction.

– 1999b. *The New Terrorism: Fanaticism and the Arms of Mass Destruction*. Oxford: Oxford University Press.

– 1977. *Terrorism*. Boston: Little, Brown and Company.

Lee, Jong R. 1977. "Rallying 'Round the Flag: Foreign Policy Events and Presidential Popularity." *Presidential Studies Quarterly* 7: 252–6.

Lee, Martha. 1995. *Earth First! Environmental Apocalypse*. Syracuse, NY: Syracuse University Press.

Leiser, Burton. 1977. "Terrorism, Guerrilla Warfare, and International Morality." *Stanford Journal of International Studies* 12: 39–65.

Lemelin, Bernard. 2001. "The U.S. Presidential Election of 1948: The

Causes of Truman's 'Astonishing' Victory." *Revue française d'études américaines* 87, no. 1: 38–61.

Leroux, Manon. 2002. *Les silences d'octobre*. Montreal: VLB.

Li, Quan. 2005. "Does Democracy Promote or Reduce Transnational Terrorist Incidents?" *Journal of Conflict Resolution* 49, no. 2: 278–97.

Lian, Bradley, and John Oneal. 1993. "Presidents, the Use of Military Force, and Public Opinion." *Journal of Conflict Resolution* 37, no. 2: 277–300.

Lifton, Robert. 2000. "Destroying the World to Save It." In *Voices of Trauma: Treating Psychological Trauma across Cultures*, edited by Boris Drozdek and John Wilson, 59–86. New York: Springer.

Lijphart, Arend. 1984. *Democracies: Patterns of Majoritarian and Consensus Government in Twenty-One Countries*. New Haven, CT: Yale University Press.

– 1969. "Consociational Democracy." *World Politics* 21, no. 2: 207–25.

– 1968. "Typologies of Democratic Systems." *Comparative Political Studies* 1, no. 1: 3–44.

Lipset, Seymour, and Stein Rokkan. 1967. *Party Systems and Voter Alignments: Cross-National Perspectives*. New York: Free Press.

Lodge, Juliet, and Avi Shlaim. 1979. "The U.S. and the Berlin Blockade, 1948–1949." In *Studies in Crisis Behavior*, edited by Michael Brecher, 51–80. New Brunswick, NJ: Transaction.

MacKuen, Michael. 1983. "Political Drama, Economic Conditions, and the Dynamics of Presidential Popularity." *American Journal of Political Science* 27: 165–92.

Mair, Peter. 2013. *Ruling the Void. The Hollowing Out of Western Democracy*. New York: Verso.

Marty, Martin, and Scott Appleby, eds. 1995. *Fundamentalism Comprehended*. Chicago: University of Chicago Press.

Mathews, John. 1919. "Political Parties and the War." *American Political Science Review* 13, no. 2: 213–28.

Mayer, Nonna, and Vincent Tiberj. 2004. "Do Issues Matter? Law and Order in the 2002 French Presidential Election." In *The French Voter: Before and After the 2002 Elections*, edited by Michael Lewis-Beck, 33–46. New York: Palgrave MacMillan.

McCauley, C., and M. Segal. 1987. "Social Psychology of Terrorist Groups." In *Group Processes and Intergroup Relations: Review of Personality and Social Psychology*, edited by C. Hendrick, 231–56. Newbury Park, CA: SAGE.

McKeown, Timothy J. 2000. "The Cuban Missile Crisis and Politics as Usual." *Journal of Politics* 62: 70–87.

Meade, Robert. 1990. *Red Brigades: The Story of Italian Terrorism.* New York: Macmillan.

Merari, Ariel. 1990. "The Readiness to Kill and Die: Suicide Terrorism in the Middle East." In *Origins of Terrorism*, edited by Walter Reich, 192–207. Cambridge: Cambridge University Press.

Milner, Henry. 2002. *Civic Literacy: How Informed Citizens Make Democracy Work.* Lebanon, NH: University Press of New England.

Montalvo, José. 2006. "Voting after the Bombing: Can Terrorist Attacks Change the Outcome of Democratic Elections?" UPF Department of Economics Working Paper.

Moravcsik, Andrew. 1997. "Taking Preferences Seriously: A Liberal Theory of International Politics." *International Organization* 51, no. 4: 513–53.

Morgenthau, Hans. 1996. "Another 'Great Debate': The National Interest of the United States." In *Classics of International Relations*, edited by John Vasquez, 147–9. Upper Saddle River, NJ: Prentice Hall.

Moruzzi, Jean-François, and Emmanuel Boulaert. 1988. *Iparretarrak: Séparatisme et terrorisme en pays basque français.* Paris: Plon.

Mueller, John. 2008. "The Atomic Terrorist: Assessing the Likelihood." Presentation, Program on International Security Policy, University of Chicago, 15 January.

– 2007. "Reactions and Overreactions to Terrorism: The Atomic Obsession." Presentation, American Political Science Association, Chicago, IL. 30 August–2 September.

– 2006. "Is There Still a Terrorist Threat?: The Myth of the Omnipresent Enemy." *Foreign Affairs* 85, no. 5.

– 2005. "Terrorism and the Dynamics of Threat Exaggeration." Presentation, American Political Science Association, Washington, DC, 1–4 September.

– 1973. *War, Presidents and Public Opinion.* New York: John Wiley and Sons.

Müller, Harald, and Thomas Risse-Kapen. 1993. "From the Outside In and from the Inside Out: International Relations, Domestic Politics and Foreign Policy." In *The Limits of State Autonomy: Societal Groups and Foreign Policy Formulation*, edited by David Skidmore and Valerie Hudson, 25–48. Boulder, CO: Westview Press.

Nacos, Brigitte. 2007. *Mass-Mediated Terrorism: The Central Role of the Media in Terrorism and Counterterrorism*. Lanham, MD: Rowman and Littlefield.

– 2000. "Accomplice or Witness? The Media's Role in Terrorism." *Current History*, April.

Nacos, Brigitte, Robert Shapiro, and Pierangelo Isernia, eds. 2000. *Decision-making in a Glass House: Mass Media, Public Opinion, and American and European Foreign Policy in the 21st Century*. Lanham, MD: Rowman and Littlefield.

Nadeau, Richard, André Blais, Elisabeth Gidengil, and Neil Nevitte. 2001. "Perceptions of Party Competence in the 1997 Election." In *Party Politics in Canada*, edited by Hugh G. Thorburn and Alan Whitehorn, 413–30. Toronto: Prentice Hall.

Nesser, Petter. 2008. "Chronology of Jihadism in Western Europe 1994–2007: Planned, Prepared, and Executed Terrorist Attacks." *Studies in Conflict & Terrorism* 31, no. 10: 924–46.

Noël, Alain, and Jean-Philippe Thérien. 2008. *Left and Right in Global Politics*. Cambridge: Cambridge University Press.

Norris, Pippa, Montague Kern, and Marion Just. 2003. *Framing Terrorism: The News Media, the Government, and the Public*. London: Routledge.

Oates, Sarah, and Monica Postelnicu. 2005. "Citizen or Comrade? Terrorist Threat in Election Campaigns in Russia and the U.S." Presentation, American Political Science Association, Washington, DC, 1–4 September.

Oborne, Peter. 2008. "The Use and Abuse of Terror: The Construction of a False Narrative on the Domestic Terror Threat." In *Playing Politics with Terrorism: A User's Guide*, edited by George Kassimeris. New York: Columbia University Press.

Olmeda, José. 2008. "A Reversal of Fortune: Blame Games and Framing Contests after the 3/11 Terrorist Attacks in Madrid." In *Governing After Crisis: The Politics of Investigation, Accountability and Learning*, edited by Arjen Boin, Allan McConnell, and Paul 't Hart, 62–84. Cambridge: Cambridge University Press.

Oneal, John, and Anna Lillian Bryan. 1995. "The Rally 'Round the Flag Effect in U.S. Foreign Policy Crises, 1950–1985." *Political Behavior* 17, no. 4: 379–401.

Oots, K.L. 1986. *A Political Organization Approach to Transnational Terrorism*. Santa Barbara, CA: Greenwood Press.

Ostrom, C.W., and D. Simon. 1985. "Promise and Performance: A Dynamic Model of Presidential Popularity." *American Political Science Review* 79: 334–58.

Pape, Robert. 2005. *Dying to Win: The Strategic Logic of Suicide Terrorism.* New York: Random House.

– 2003. "The Strategic Logic of Suicide Terrorism." *American Political Science Review* 97, no. 3: 343–61.

Parker, Tom. 2007. "Fighting an Antaean Enemy: How Democratic States Unintentionally Sustain the Terrorist Movements They Oppose." *Terrorism and Political Violence* 19, no. 2: 155–79.

Paterson, Thomas, and William Brophy. 1986. "October Missiles and November Elections: The Cuban Missile Crisis and American Politics, 1962." *Journal of American History* 73, no. 1: 87–119.

Paust, Jordan. 1977. "Response to Terrorism: A Prologue to Decision Concerning Private Measures of Sanction." *Stanford Journal of International Studies* 12.

Pedhazur, Ami. 2006. *Root Causes of Suicide Terrorism: The Globalization of Martyrdom.* London: Routledge.

Petrocik, John. 1996. "Issue Ownership in Presidential Elections, with a 1980 Case Study." *American Journal of Political Science* 40, no. 3: 825–50.

Pinker, Steven. 2011. *The Better Angels of Our Nature: Why Violence Has Declined.* New York: Viking.

Pizam, A., and G. Smith. 2000. "Tourism and Terrorism: A Quantitative Analysis of Major Terrorist Acts and Their Impact on Tourism Destinations." *Tourism Economics* 6, no. 2: 123–38.

Polsby, Nelson. 1964. *Congress and the Presidency.* Englewood Cliffs, NJ: Prentice Hall.

Post, Jerrold. 2007. *The Mind of the Terrorist.* New York: Palgrave Macmillan.

– 2005. "When Hatred Is Bred in the Bone: Psycho-cultural Foundations of Contemporary Terrorism." *Political Psychology* 26, no. 4: 615–36.

– 1987. "Rewarding Fire with Fire: Effects of Retaliation on Terrorist Group Dynamics." *Studies in Conflict & Terrorism* 10, no. 1: 23–35.

– 1984. "Notes on a Psychodynamic Theory of Terrorist Behavior." *Studies in Conflict & Terrorism* 7, no. 2: 241–56.

Putnam, Robert. 1988. "Diplomacy and Domestic Politics: The Logic of Two-Level Games." *International Organization* 42, no. 3: 427–60.

Rabert, Bernhard. 1995. *Links und Rechtsterrorismus in der Bundesrepublik Deutschland von 1970 bis heute.* Bonn, Ger.: Bernard and Graefe.

Ramsay, Kristopher. 2004. "Politics at the Water's Edge: Crisis Bargaining and Electoral Competition." *Journal of Conflict Resolution* 48, no. 4: 459–86.

Ranstorp, Magnus. 2007. *Mapping Terrorism Research.* London: Routledge.

Rapoport, David. 2004. "The Four Waves of Modern Terrorism." In *Attacking Terrorism: Elements of a Grand Strategy*, edited by Audrey Cronin and James Ludes, 46–73. Washington, DC: Georgetown University Press.

– 1984. "Fear and Trembling: Terrorism in Three Religious Traditions." *American Political Science Review* 78, no. 3: 668–72.

– 1971. *Assassination and Terrorism.* Toronto: CBD.

Rapoport, David, and Leonard Weinberg. 2001. *The Democratic Experience and Political Violence.* London: Routledge.

Regens, James, Ronald Gaddie, and Brad Lockerbie. 1995. "The Electoral Consequences of Voting to Declare War." *Journal of Conflict Resolution* 39, no. 1: 168–82.

Reich, Walter. 1990. *Origins of Terrorism: Psychologies, Ideologies, Theologies, States of Mind.* Cambridge: Cambridge University Press.

Reid, Edna. 1997. "Evolution of a Body of Knowledge: An Analysis of Terrorism Research." *Information Processing and Management* 33, no. 1.

Reiter, Dan, and Allan Stam. 2002. *Democracies at War.* Princeton, NJ: Princeton University Press.

Rice, Condoleezza. 2000. "Promoting the National Interest." *Foreign Affairs* 79, no. 1: 45–62.

Riker, W. 1962. *The Theory of Political Coalitions.* New Haven, CT: Yale University Press.

Risse-Kappen, Thomas. 1991. "Public Opinion, Domestic Structure, and Foreign Policy in Liberal Democracies." *World Politics* 43: 479–512.

Roberts, Brad, ed. 1997. *Terrorism with Chemical and Biological Terrorism: Calibrating Risks and Responses.* Alexandria, VA: Chemical and Biological Arms Control Institute.

Robertson, D. 1976. "Surrogates for Party Identification in the Rational Choice Framework." In *Party Identification and Beyond: Representations of Voting and Party Competition*, edited by Ian Budge, Ivor Crewe, and Dennis Farlie, 365–82. London: John Wiley and Sons.

Rosenthal, Uriel, Michael T. Charles, and Paul 't Hart. 1989. *Coping with Crises – The Management of Disasters, Riots and Terrorism*. Springfield, IL: Charles C. Thomas.

Rubenstein, Richard. 1987. *Alchemists of Revolution – Terrorism in the Modern World*. New York: Basic Books.

Rummel, Rudolf. 1994. *Death by Government: Genocide and Mass Murder Since 1900*. New Brunswick, NJ: Transaction.

Russett, Bruce. 1990. *Controlling the Sword: The Democratic Governance of National Security*. Cambridge, MA: Harvard University Press.

Sageman, Marc. 2008. *Leaderless Jihad: Terror Networks in the Twenty-First Century*. Philadelphia: University of Pennsylvania Press.

– 2004. *Understanding Terror Networks*. Philadelphia: University of Pennsylvania Press.

Samaan, Jean-Loup. 2007. *Les métamorphoses du Hezbollah*. Paris: Karthala.

Sanchez, Alejandro. 2008. "Corsica: France's Petite Security Problem." *Studies in Conflict and Terrorism* 31: 655–64.

Sartori, Giovanni. 1976. *Party and Party Systems*. Cambridge: Cambridge University Press.

Schattschneider, E.E. 1942. *Party Government: American Government in Action*. New York: Farrar and Rinehart.

Schlesinger, Joseph. 1991. *Political Parties and the Winning of Office*. Ann Arbor: University of Michigan Press.

Schmid, Alex. 2011. *The Routledge Handbook of Terrorism Research*. New York: Routledge.

– 2004. "Frameworks for Conceptualising Terrorism." *Terrorism and Political Violence* 16, no. 2: 197–221.

Schmid, Alex, and Ronald Crelinsten, eds. 1993. *Western Responses to Terrorism*. London: Routledge.

Schmid, Alex, and Janny de Graaf. 1982. *Violence as Communication: Insurgent Terrorism and the Western News Media*. Beverly Hills, CA: SAGE.

Schmid, Alex, and Albert Jongman. 1988. *Political Terrorism: A New Guide to Actors, Authors, Concepts, Databases, Theories and Litterature*. New Brunswick, NJ: Transaction.

Schmidt, Manfred. 1996. "When Parties Matter: A Review of the Possibilities and Limits of Partisan Influence on Public Policy." *European Journal of Political Research* 30: 155–83.

Schultz, Kenneth. 1998. "Domestic Opposition and Signalling in International Crises." *American Political Science Review* 92, no. 4: 829–44.

Schuster, Jürgen and Herbert Maier. 2006. "The Rift: Explaining Europe's Divergent Iraq Policies in the Run-Up of the American-Led War on Iraq." *Foreign Policy Analysis* 2, no. 3: 223–44.

Scraton, Phil. 2002. *Beyond September 11: An Anthology of Dissent*. London: Pluto.

Shermer, Michael. 2011. *The Believing Brain*. New York: Times Books.

Sigelman, Lee, and Pamela Johnston. 1981. "The Dynamics of Presidential Support During International Conflict Situations: The Iranian Hostage Crisis." *Political Behavior* 3, no. 4: 303–18.

Silke, Andrew. ed. 2004. *Research on Terrorism. Trends, Achievements and Failures*. London: Frank Cass.

– ed. 2003. *Terrorists, Victims and Society: Psychological Perspectives on Terrorism and its Consequences*. Chichester, UK: John Wiley and Sons.

– 2002. "The Devil You Know: Continuing Problems with Research on Terrorism." *Terrorism and Political Violence* 13, no. 4: 1–14.

Sloan, Stephen. 2005. "Terrorism and the Media: The Need to Place the Threat in Context." In *Terrorism: Cross Analysis*, edited by Quentin Michel. Brussels: P.I.E.-Peter Lang.

Smith, Adam. 2006. *No Party Now*. Oxford: Oxford University Press.

Smith, Michael. 1995. *Fighting for Ireland?: The Military Strategy of the Irish Republican Movement*. London: Routledge.

Smouts, Marie-Claude, Dario Battistella, and Pascal Vennesson. 2003. *Dictionnaire des relations internationales*. Paris: Dalloz.

Sommier, Isabelle. 2000. "Repentir et dissociation: la fin des années de plomb en Italie?" *Cultures et Conflits* 40, no. 4: 43–61.

Sorel, Jean-Marc. 2003. "Some Questions about the Definition of Terrorism and the Fight against Its Financing." *European Journal of International Law* 14, no. 2: 365–78.

Sprinzak, Ehud. 1998. "Extremism and Violence in Israel: The Crisis of Messianic Politics." *Annals of the American Academy of Political and Social Science* 555: 114–26.

Steinmo, Sven. 2001. "The New Institutionalism." In *The Encyclopedia of Democratic Thought*, edited by Barry Clarck and Joe Foweraker. London: Routledge.

Sterling, Claire. 1981. *The Terror Network*. New York: Holt, Rinehart and Winston.

Stohl, Michael, 1988. *The Politics of Terrorism*. New York: Marcel Dekker.

Stone, Geoffrey. 2004. *Perilous Times: Free Speech in Wartime from the Sedition Act of 1798 to the War on Terrorism*. New York: Norton.

Strøm, Kaare. 1990. "A Behavioral Theory of Competitive Political Parties." *American Journal of Political Science* 34, no. 2: 565–98.

Strøm, Kaare, and Wolfgang Müller. 1999. "Political Parties and Hard Choices." In *Policy, Office or Votes?: How Political Parties in Western Europe Make Hard Decisions*, edited by Wolfgang Müller and Kaare Strøm, 1–35. Cambridge: Cambridge University Press.

Sullivan, John. 1988. *ETA and Basque Nationalism*. London: Taylor and Francis.

Taheri, A. 1987. *Holy Terror: The Inside Story of Islamic Terrorism*. London: Hutchinson.

Talmon, Jacob L. 1952. *The Rise of Totalitarian Democracy*. Boston: Beacon Press.

Taylor, Lily Ross. 1949. *Party Politics in the Age of Caesar*. Berkeley: University of California Press.

Taylor, Peter. 1997. *Behind the Mask: The IRA and Sinn Féin*. New York: TV Books.

Tetley, William. 2007. *The October Crisis, 1970: An Insider's View*. Montreal: McGill-Queen's University Press.

Thérien, Jean-Philippe, and Alain Noël. 2000. "Political Parties and Foreign Aid." *American Political Science Review* 94, no. 1: 151–62.

Thornton, Thomas B. 1964. "Terror as a Weapon of Political Agitation." In *Internal War*, edited by Harry Eckstein, 71–91. New York: Free Press.

Tilly, Charles. 2004. "Terror, Terrorism, Terrorists." *Sociological Theory* 22, no. 1: 5–13.

Townshend, Charles. 2002. *Terrorism: A Very Short Introduction*. Oxford: Oxford University Press.

Tucker, Jonathan. 2000. *Toxic Terror: Assessing Terrorist Use of Chemical and Biological Weapons*. Cambridge, MA: MIT Press.

Van Biezen, Ingrid. 2005. "Terrorism and Democratic Legitimacy: Conflicting Interpretations of the Spanish Elections." *Mediterranean Politics* 10, no. 1: 99–108.

Vasquez, John, ed. 1996. *Classics of International Relations*. Upper Saddle River, NJ: Prentice Hall.

Vidino, Lorenzo and Steven Emerson. 2006. *Al Qaeda in Europe: The New Battleground of International Jihad*. Amherst, NY: Prometheus Books.

Wakelyn, Jon L., ed. 2006. *America's Founding Charters*, Westport, CT: Greenwood Press.

Waltz, Kenneth. 1967. "Electoral Punishment and Foreign Policy Crisis." In *Domestic Sources of Foreign Policy*, edited by James Rosenau. New York: Free Press.

– 1959. *Man, the State and War*. New York: Columbia University Press.

Walzer, Michael. 2002. "Five Questions about Terrorism." *Dissent* 49, no. 1: 5–16.

Walzer, Michael, and Jean-Marc Flükiger. 2006. "A Discussion with Michael Walzer." April. http://www.terrorisme.net/pdf/2006 _Walzer.pdf. Accessed 15 February 2007.

Wardlaw, Grant. 1994. "The Democratic Framework." In *The Deadly Sin of Terrorism: Its Effect on Democracy and Civil Liberty in Six Countries*, edited by David Charters, 5–11. Westport, CT: Greenwood Press.

Warwick, Paul. 1992. "Ideological Diversity and Government Survival in Western European Parliamentary Democracies." *Comparative Political Studies* 25, no. 3: 332–61.

Wattenberg, Martin. 1990. *The Decline of American Political Parties*. Cambridge, MA: Harvard University Press.

Weinberg, Leonard. 1986. "The Violent Life: An Analysis of Left- and Right-Wing Terrorism in Italy." In *Political Violence and Terror*, edited by Peter Merkl, 145–67. Berkeley: University of California Press.

– 1979. "Patterns of Neo-Fascist Violence in Italian Politics." *Terrorism* 2, no. 3: 231–59.

Weinberg, Leonard, and William Eubank. 2008. "A Nested Game: Playing Politics with Terrorism in the United States." In *Playing Politics with Terrorism: A User's Guide*, edited by George Kassimeris, 157–75. New York: Columbia University Press.

– 1998. "Terrorism and Democracy: What Recent Events Disclose." *Terrorism and Political Violence* 10, no. 1: 108–18.

– 1987. *Rise and Fall of Italian Terrorism*. Boulder, CO: Westview.

Weinberg, Leonard, and Ami Pedahzur. 2003. *Political Parties and Terrorist Groups*. London: Routledge.

Weinberg, Leonard, Ami Pedahzur, and Sivan Hirsch-Hoeffler. 2004. "The Challenges of Conceptualizing Terrorism." *Terrorism and Political Violence* 16, no. 4: 777–94.

Weingast, Barry. 2002. "Self-Enforcing Constitutions." Working Paper, Hoover Institution, Stanford University.

White, John. 2006. "What is a Political Party?" In *Handbook of Party Politics*, edited by Richard Katz and William Crotty. London: SAGE.

Wieviorka, Michel, and David Gordon White. 2004. *The Making of Terrorism*. Chicago: University of Chicago Press.

Wilkinson, Paul. 2001. *Terrorism versus Democracy: The Liberal State Response*. London: Taylor and Francis.

– 1977. *Terrorism and the Liberal State*. Hoboken, NJ: John Wiley and Sons.

– 1974. *Political Terrorism*. Hoboken, NJ: John Wiley and Sons.

Wolf, J.B. 1989. *Antiterrorist Initiatives*. New York: Plenum Press.

Wright, Ronald. 2004. *A Short History of Progress*. New York: Carrol and Graph.

Zaki, Chebab. 2007. *Inside Hamas: The Untold Story of Militants, Martyrs and Spies*. London: I.B. Tauris.

Zaller, John. 1992. *The Nature and Origins of Mass Opinion*. Cambridge: Cambridge University Press.

Index